MACCHI C.202 FOLGORE

MACCHI C.202 FOLGORE

ITALY'S BEST FIGHTER OF THE SECOND WORLD WAR

DAVIDE F. JABES,
ALESSANDRO ROMANELLO
AND NICCOLÒ TOGNARINI

FONTHILL

To Stefano Sappino and Ivano Tognarini.

They both left us too soon.

Fonthill Media Language Policy

Fonthill Media publishes in the international English language market. One language edition is published worldwide. As there are minor differences in spelling and presentation, especially with regard to American English and British English, a policy is necessary to define which form of English to use. The Fonthill Policy is to use the form of English native to the author. Davide F. Jabes, Alessandro Romanello, and Niccolò Tognarini were born and educated in Italy; therefore British English has been adopted in this publication.

Fonthill Media Limited
Fonthill Media LLC
www.fonthillmedia.com
office@fonthillmedia.com

First published in the United Kingdom and the United States of America 2021

British Library Cataloguing in Publication Data:
A catalogue record for this book is available from the British Library

ISBN 978-1-78155-830-0

Typeset in 10.5pt on 13pt Sabon
Printed and bound in England

Acknowledgements

There are many people and institutions that have contributed to the making of this volume and that have facilitated us during the period of document research and the writing of the book: to all of them, we owe a great debt of gratitude.

Among these in Rome, we are pleased to mention Carlo Fiorentino, Simona Greco, and Daniela Loyola of the *Archivio Centrale dello Stato*; Luigi Borzise, Massimiliano Barlattani, Giancarlo Montinaro, Emiliano Bianchi, Mauro Bianco, Marco Di Cocco, Pasquale Rubertone, Gaetano Pasqua, Monica Bovino, Marcello Neve, Benedetta Desideri, Maria Grazia Bella, and Andrea Rossi of the *Ufficio Storico dell'Aeronautica*; and Renato Bottiglia of the *Troupe Azzurra*.

In Milan, we thank Marco Vitale, Vincenzo Ficco, and Claudio Camponagra of the Historical Archives of the Politecnico di Milano, and Barbara Buzio of the Leonardo Archive (AerMacchi).

We would also like to thank Professor Fabio De Ninno of the University of Siena for his valuable bibliographical advice; Michael and Michèle Glencross for revising the text; Sergio Casella and Edoardo Baldracco of Fotosciamanna for the work done on some of the illustrations in this book; Raffaele D'Aniello of the Ares Bookshop; Vincenzo Bagnoli; Fabio Cubo; Paolo Sappino; Davide Piacenza; Silvia Rossetti; Fabrizio Proietti; Giampiero Galeotti, Giovanni Carta; and Franco and Emilia Borza. We also wish to thank Jay Slater, Joshua Greenland, and Alan Sutton of Fonthill. Then there are the people who have endured the absences and fatigue of their children, relatives, partners, and husbands: Marisa Tucci and Giuseppe Jabes; Rie Ichinomiya, Irene Sawako, Alessio Massimo Akira; Giovanna Balestreri; and Gabriella Tognarini and Cristina Riva. Our debt to all of them is great, whereas the responsibility for what we have written is ours alone.

Contents

List of Abbrevations

AA	Antiaerea/o	Anti-Aircraft
ACS	Archivio Centrale dello Stato	Italian State Archive
AM	Aeronautica Militare	Italian Air Force
ANR	Aeronautica Nazionale Repubblicana	Fascist Puppet State Air Force 1943–45
AOI	Africa Orientale Italiana	Italian East Africa
A/S	Aerosiluranti	Torpedo bomber
AUSAM	Archivio dell'Ufficio Storico dell'Aeronautica Militare	Air Force Archive
CAI	Corpo Aereo Italiano	Italian Air Corps against Britain
CSIR	Corpo di Spedizione Italiano in Russia	Italian Expeditionary Corps in Russia
CSM	Capo di Stato Maggiore	Chief of Staff
CSMG	Capo di Stato Maggiore Generale	Chief of Defence Staff
CT	Caccia terrestre	Land fighter
DAT	Difesa Aerea Territoriale	Home Air Defence
DBor DB	Daimler-Benz	-
De.Te.	Dezimeter Telegraphie or Dezimetertechnik	German Radar
DL	Decreto Legge	Decree

FIAT	Fabbrica italiana automobili Torino	-
FFAA	Forze Armate	Military Forces
HMS	Nave di Sua Maestà Britannica	His/Her Majesty's Ship
HP	Cavalli Vapore	Horsepower
K	Nodi	Knots
MC; MC2, or M.C.	Macchi Castoldi	-
RA or R.A.	Regia Aeronautica	Italian Royal Air Force
RA	Alfa Romeo	-
RAF	Aeronautica Britannica	Royal Air Force
RSI	Repubblica Sociale Italiana	Italian Social Republic 1943–45
Superaereo	Stato maggiore della Regia Aeronautica (mobilitato)	Royal Air Force Command (in wartime)

Introduction

This volume deals with a monoplane fighter, the Macchi C.202, the first truly competitive fighter (despite being inadequately armed compared to the Allied fighters, and equipped with a German-designed Daimler-Benz 601A twelve-cylinder engine) deployed by the *Regia Aeronautica* from September 1941. The volume is made up of three distinct parts. The first recounts the history and the evolution of the Italian aviation industry and its protagonists from after the First World War up until the country entered the Second World War. During this period, the Fascist regime came to consider the *Aeronautica* its natural 'modern' force, reinforced in this conviction by the way the myths about aviation and technology appealed to the masses. Despite its various achievements, the *Regia Aeronautica*, established in 1923, was unable to adopt a modern industrial culture and it faced the challenges of the Second World War lagging behind in the fields of organisation, technology, and military strategy.

These pages will help the reader understand the reasons for the serious delay in the deployment of a modern in-line engine fighter by the Italian air force.

The second part consists of a detailed technical description of the work of engineer Mario Castoldi of the AerMacchi firm, based in Varese, the designer of the M.C.202 and of the M.C.200 and 205.

The third part is devoted to the use of the M.C.202 in the operational theatres of the Second World War and to the pilots who flew the aircraft, as well as details on the doctrines, the eye-witness accounts, and the memoirs of Italian, German, and Allied pilots.

Last but not least, we should underline another aspect, too: Italian publications on aircraft, and the literature on the subject of the M.C.202 especially, despite being relatively substantial and including various noteworthy titles, basically do not offer scholarly references (notes, mention of sources, etc.). This volume represents the first systematic study of an Italian fighter deployed during the Second World War, and it seeks to encourage further studies in this field.

The introductory chapter was written by Alessandro Romanello; the chapters on the Schneider Trophy, on the engineer Castoldi, and on the Macchi 200 are by Davide F. Jabes; and the chapter on the Macchi 202 is by Niccolò Tognarini.

1

Historical Context

The Post-War Climate, the Advent of Fascism, and the Birth of the *Regia Aeronautica* (1919–26)

At the end of the First World War, which had cost the country the lives of about 650,000 combatants, Italy was one of the victors; however, the combination of the territorial claims that the Treaty of Versailles had not met and the very high human, social, and economic costs of the victory put the country in a difficult, tense, and complex situation that would lead to the fascist dictatorship.

On the one hand, industrial and manual workers, impoverished and radicalised by the experience of war, were pressing for a definitive solution to social problems, just when the spectre of the Russian Revolution was haunting the whole of Western Europe; on the other hand, the middle classes and the dissatisfied veterans of the conflict boosted the D'Annunzian and nationalist myth of the 'mutilated victory' and claimed the right to power in post-war Italy.

The former socialist leader Benito Mussolini understood more than anyone else the political situation in Italy, and it was no coincidence that as early as 1917 he began to talk of *trincerocrazia*—that is, of power to the war veterans—in the columns of his newspaper *Il Popolo d'Italia*.

Alongside Mussolini—and initially far more influential and prestigious than he—the poet Gabriele D'Annunzio, already well-known in Europe for his poems and novels in a decadent and Nietzschean mould, became the champion and spokesman of the most aggressive form of Italian nationalism and distinguished himself by some extraordinary feats of aviation (the Bakar raid and the flight over Vienna on 9 August 1918) that boosted the morale of most of the nation after the shock of the Caporetto rout. It is to D'Annunzio that we owe much of the mythology of aviation that had already fascinated the Futurists and *avant-garde* poets before the war: the themes of flying, of the heroism of aviators, of chivalric duels between the 'aces' also attracted the masses and contributed to their ideological mobilisation while the technical modernity of the aircraft was invested with heroic and superhuman qualities.

These themes would prove to be fundamental, as we shall see, after the rise to power of Mussolini, but, in the depressing climate of demobilisation, they seemed to have lost their gloss and central importance. In fact, during the conflict, the Italian aeronautical industry had developed its potential, attaining by the end of 1918 a daily production of '30 aeroplanes, 60 engines and 200 propellers'.[1] In the immediate post-war period, there was instead a drastic demobilisation and a series of transfers of competence in the field of aeronautics from one ministry to another, factors that certainly caused dissatisfaction both in military and industrial quarters but which also led, as we shall see later, to the strengthening of the link between the production companies and the military placing the orders and the relationship between the two.[2, 3]

It was in this climate of dissatisfaction and tension that, after a two-year civil war between fascists and left-wing worker and peasant organisations, the March on Rome (28 October 1922) took place, followed by the formation of the first Mussolini government (30 October 1922). This is not the place for an examination of fascism, its history, and objectives. Suffice to say, however, that the 'fascist revolution', as Mussolini liked to call it, only happened because of an alliance between the traditional Italian centres of power (the court, the army, the big industrialists, the agrarians of the Po Valley, and the large landowners of the south). This was made possible by Mussolini's dictatorship and the mobilisation of the masses specific to it, only to the extent that any form of real social and political protest from below would have been suppressed with the utmost force; it was in this narrow space, in the management of the 'nationalised' masses that the 'revolutionary' element of fascism, defined not by coincidence as a 'mass reactionary regime' by Palmiro Togliatti, was able to develop.

In the fascist constellation, therefore, enthusiastic support for modernity and technical miracles was accompanied by a firm alliance with the traditional classes; hence also the extraordinary tactical mobility of Mussolini, which enabled him to remain in power for over twenty years, gaining for himself, as we shall see later, an ever-increasing power—above all in foreign policy—but always supported by the aforementioned alliance with the Italian establishment, to which he could never dictate his own conditions. Having come to power also thanks to the broad backing of the senior ranks of the Italian army since the interventionist campaign of 1914–15, Mussolini certainly needed the support of the army and the military caste. In fact, also at the request of King Vittorio Emanuele III, we find among the members of his first government Armando Diaz (minister of war) and Admiral Paolo Thaon di Revel (minister of the navy).

During the First World War, both the army and the navy each had a perfectly respectable air force (about 1,000 aircraft and about 600 seaplanes).[4] In 1923, a few months after coming to power, Mussolini decided to create an independent air force, first by establishing a *Commissariato per l'Aeronautica* (24 January 1923), presided over by Mussolini himself, then by creating the *Regia Aeronautica* (28 March 1923), which brought together 'all the military air forces of the kingdom and colonies' under the aegis of the Commissariat for Aeronautics, which included the general command of the air force and general intendancy of the air force.[5] The first commander-in-chief was *Colonnello* Moizo, and then, from October 1923, *Generale* Pier Ruggero Piccio.[6]

It was a political decision of great import: once the military hierarchy had been reassured, the creation of a new armed force made it possible to reinforce the 'modern' and 'revolutionary' image of fascism and to ensure for Mussolini a new and relatively autonomous sphere of power in the circles of the armed forces. In addition, early fascism was nourished by D'Annunzianism and futurism and all this enabled Mussolini (who had taken flying lessons in 1920–21) not only to appreciate the modernity of the aerial weapon but also to exploit its popularity among the masses for propaganda purposes.

It is no coincidence that the fascist regime can be considered an extraordinarily original case of the political and ideological use of aeronautics, also linked to Mussolini's cult of personality. Diaz and Thaon di Revel did not object, aware as they were of their own power within the world of fascist political intrigue. It was only over time, particularly in the Second World War, that it came to be understood that the abolition of naval aviation had been a serious mistake.[7, 8]

The crisis that followed the murder of Matteotti (10 June 1924), the Socialist opposition deputy assassinated by a fascist squad for having courageously denounced in parliament the fascist fraud in the political elections of April 1924, initially put Mussolini in great difficulty. Aldo Finzi, the deputy head of the Commissariat for Aeronautics, who was involved in the crime, was forced by Mussolini to resign and was replaced by General Alberto Bonzani, a close associate of Armando Diaz.[9]

It was not only the growth of the newly formed air force that was at risk in those months of 1924 but also the fascist regime itself. Once again, abetted by the weakness and acquiescence of the king and of the parliamentary opposition and thanks to the solidarity with fascism of the Italian army and establishment, Mussolini could demonstrate his tactical talent and his flair for power relations, challenging parliament to formally accuse him of Matteotti's killing (speech of 3 January 1925) and finally ushering in the dictatorship with the promulgation of 'very fascist laws' (1925–26). This transformed the liberal order of the Kingdom of Italy into a totalitarian, single-party fascist regime.

Now firmly in power, Mussolini could relaunch his plans for the air force: it is no coincidence that on 30 August 1925, the Air Force Commissariat was replaced by the new Ministry of the Air Force, headed by the *Duce* in person with Bonzani as undersecretary. The air force was thus starting to become the most fascist of the armed forces. In 1926, it had about 260 fighter planes, 190 bombers, 240 reconnaissance planes for the army, and 230 seaplanes for a total of 920 aircraft, of which only about a third dated from after the First World War.[10] The annual spending on the Air Force in those years amounted to about 700 million lire (about a quarter of the army budget and half that of the navy).[11]

Under Bonzani's management, the air force scored some notable successes, such as the Rome–Melbourne–Tokyo–Rome flight of Francesco De Pinedo (1925) and the victory in the Schneider Trophy for seaplanes on 12–13 November 1926. Despite these results, on 6 November 1926, Bonzani was replaced by the young Italo Balbo, a former member of the *Arditi* special forces in the First World War, the fearsome leader of the agrarian fascism of Ferrara and *quadrumviro* of the March on Rome. The fascistisation and modernisation of the air force proceeded at one and the same pace. Instead of one of Diaz's men, Mussolini, now firmly in power, installed one of the leaders of the Paduan squads: it turned out to be a shrewd choice.

Italo Balbo and the *Regia Aeronautica* (1926–33)

Few figures among the protagonists of the 'fascist revolution' can compete with Italo Balbo for charm, energy, and ability. It can be safely said that Mussolini, as we shall see later, even feared him and envied his popularity.

Initially Republican and Mazzinian in orientation, Balbo was an interventionist and a volunteer in the First World War and then head of the Ferrara and Po Valley squads, a sort of modern and ruthless soldier of fortune. After being forced, in November 1924, to resign as commander of the Voluntary Militia for National Security due to his involvement in the murder of the anti-fascist priest Don Giovanni Minzoni in Argenta, he was appointed undersecretary for the National Economy in October 1925, once the crisis caused by the Matteotti murder was over. In November 1926, Balbo became undersecretary of the air force (he would become its minister, taking over from Mussolini, in September 1929) and undertook a far-reaching transformation of the air force under Mussolini's watchful and initially benevolent eye. Giorgio Rochat has written: 'Balbo can be considered the father of the Italian air force, to the development of which he devoted all his energy and the power of his position; he was a good pilot ... a meticulous organizer and brilliant propagandist'.[12]

Mussolini, knowing Balbo's energetic and indomitable nature, decided to entrust him with considerable responsibility under his strict supervision, thus harnessing his strength and channelling it towards goals that furthered the popularity of the regime. Balbo was thus left free to act as long as Mussolini considered his efforts to be useful and controllable. In 1927, Balbo summarised the tasks that awaited him: 'First of all, we need a sporting air force, then a disciplined one and thus a militarily effective one'.[13] By the expression 'sporting air force', Balbo did not mean only an air force that aimed for records or spectacular feats, but one which also, as we shall see, played a leading role in his conception of the armed forces, but there was also another objective: to make the air force into a modern, cohesive, dynamic, and proud body.

The air force mentality had to be different from the 'traditionalist' one of the army and the navy and be imbued with the revolutionary 'modernity' of fascism. In this way, he collaborated in Mussolini's balance of power by managing his relations with the armed forces: the army and the navy were counterbalanced by an air force imbued with modernity and its power of attraction.

It was also through the speed records and spectacular feats that Balbo was able to translate these propaganda goals into reality. A chapter of this volume, to which I refer the reader, is devoted to Italy's participation in the Schneider Trophy during the Balbo years.[14] The technical experiments carried out on the engines (in particular) of the aeroplanes that took part in that competition did not, for reasons that are still unclear, have any immediate application in the aeronautical industry, causing a technological lag that was especially felt during the Second World War, as we will see later.[15]

But Balbo's popularity, also internationally, is linked above all to his celebrated seaplane cruises: in 1928 in the western Mediterranean and the year after in the eastern Mediterranean up to Odessa; in December 1930 to January 1931, the transatlantic flight to Brazil; and, lastly, from 1 July to 12 August 1933, the anniversary air cruise that celebrated the ten years of the *Regia Aeronautica*, which involved twenty-five Savoia-Marchetti S.55 seaplanes flying from Orbetello to Chicago and New York and back. These were meticulously planned events that involved a serious amount of organisation and coordination, and no longer a series of individual 'solos' such as those of the aces of the First World War, and which at the same time were transformed into formidable propaganda successes and images, which we will return to later. America waxed enthusiastic about Balbo's achievements and his prestige seemed for a moment to overshadow even Mussolini's.

Turning now to the second point of Balbo's programme ('a disciplined Air Force'), we can say that he bestowed discipline and *esprit de corps* on the force, also increasing its numbers—the Bonzani order of 1925, for example, planned for 2,340 officials; Balbo, in 1931, reached 3,060.[16] Moreover, he brought together the various offices of the air force in the new Palace of the Ministry of the Air Force, the first building in Italy made entirely of reinforced concrete, the work of the architect Roberto Marino, inaugurated on 28 October 1931, deliberately to coincide with the celebrations for the ninth anniversary of the March on Rome.

The internal organisation of the ministry, the management of recruitment, and of staff careers were subject to careful regulation, which is why at the end of the Balbo era, the air force had achieved the same compactness and bureaucratic and managerial autonomy as the other armed forces.[17] On the other hand, Balbo constantly complained about the insufficient budget granted to him by the state. In comparison with the Bonzani years, he obtained only a limited increase in funding (about 750 million lire a year), for two main reasons: Italy could not have a budget comparable to that of richer and more modern countries, such as France; secondly, Mussolini was aiming for the 'reasoned' growth of the air force, one which would not create discontent in the senior ranks of the army and navy, whose support was indispensable.[18] He still saw the air force as a weapon whose maximum utility lay in the propaganda successes he could obtain for the regime with his extraordinary transoceanic feats, which exalted the dynamism and the technical level reached by fascist Italy.

However, Balbo also set himself the goal of creating a 'militarily effective' air force. In this regard, three types of problems had to be faced: the characteristics of the aircraft produced in the years in which he was head of the air force, the doctrine of the use of the same, and the overall deployment of the air force, which set its objectives in concert with the other armed forces. Since this volume is devoted to a famous fighter plane, I will restrict myself to examining the situation of fighter aircraft.[19]

Around 1928, the decision was taken to equip all the squadrons with the Fiat CR.20 biplane, which despite not having an *avant-garde* design, possessed excellent flying and acrobatic capabilities. In 1932, the Fiat CR.30 was introduced, and shortly thereafter, in 1935, the CR.32, another biplane, one of the best fighters of its time, later used in the Spanish Civil War in support of Franco.[20] So, although the fighter met with some success, General Francesco De Pinedo, deputy head of the General Staff of the Air Force and acting as head of staff and a well-known opponent of Balbo, was not at all satisfied with the overall level of preparation of the air force, to the point of sending a 'personal memorandum' to Mussolini on 22 August 1929 on the gravity of the situation and Balbo's responsibilities. Here are some significant extracts:

> ... when last November I took up my current post ... there was not even any notion of the use of aviation in war, and there was no study on the military characteristics that needed to be found in war planes. This area was within my remit; and so I was able very quickly to prepare three documents ... but ... theory must be put into practice, which is the responsibility of the administrative authority, that is of the ministry.... Meanwhile, there are still none of the types of plane needed for the immediate future, because the best intellectual and industrial energies of aeronautical technology have been employed in the preparations for the Schneider cup...[21]

De Pinedo added to the charge in his 'Considerations on the situation of aeronautical material' included in the 'Personal Memorandum' sent to Mussolini, in which he outlined its overall and very serious backwardness, except for a very few aircraft, inviting the dictator to take all appropriate measures to adapt aeronautics to the rising standards of foreign aeronautical industries.[22] De Pinedo wrote: '... the machines that it is possible to obtain at present from the national industry have military qualities that are decidedly shoddy'.[23] To obtain an effective air force in terms of war would therefore require at least four years of serious experimentation and special funding of 'at least 700 or 800 million'.[24] During this period, any possibility of war should be excluded.

The conclusions of the 'Considerations' deserve to be reported in full, since De Pinedo seems to sense the essence of what was to happen a little more than ten years later, at the outbreak of the Second World War:

> ... if instead the general political situation should make it necessary to keep the country ready for war at all times, it would be necessary to resort to exceptional measures, of which the extremes would consist in

> the rapid sourcing from abroad of a good number of the best fighters and bombers that could be found, meanwhile proceeding simultaneously with the utmost speed to get ready other national planes that could then replace the former; also in this case, it would take one or two years from the beginning of this operation for our forces to become sufficiently effective. The decision about the course of action to be followed in this regard obviously belongs to the authorities responsible for national policy.... When the need to achieve for the air force a level of effectiveness adequate for war is taken into consideration, depending on the choice of prototypes *the problems of the preparation of the national industry for mass production for war must be addressed* [author's italics] as well as those of the creation of reserves needed to keep the front-line force at war until increased production can make up for consumption.[25]

On 29 August 1929, Francesco De Pinedo resigned and shortly thereafter was sent to Buenos Aires as an air *attaché* at the Italian Embassy. His place was taken by Giuseppe Valle. Balbo had prevailed in this crisis at the top of the air force.

There are those who, like Claudio G. Segrè, find that De Pinedo's report was affected by his animosity towards Balbo.[26] Others, like Giorgio Rochat, underline De Pinedo's lack of political realism and his politics of greatness, especially in the context of European political relations, which were relatively stable until 1933.[27] I believe instead, along with Fortunato Minniti, that De Pinedo, although lacking in political realism (the extraordinary funding he requested from Mussolini was beyond the objective possibilities of Italy), paid the price for his intellectual rigour and his unquestionable competence.[28] It is no coincidence that the same Segrè admits:

> ... the Macchi series [of seaplanes] won the Schneider cup and established speed records ... that have never been equalled. However, the Macchi, especially their engines, were never transformed into models for mass production. Balbo, by extension, established a tradition that, in 1940, left the Air Force unprepared to face the Second World War.[29]

The air force, as Balbo and Mussolini wanted it, was therefore above all a 'tool of prestige, a machine for records, cruises and very successful long-distance flights'.[30] Hence the 'fall' of De Pinedo as well as the absence of a clear doctrine for the use of the force, despite all the statements by Balbo in favour of Giulio Douhet and his doctrine, which envisaged, as is well-known, the use of mass bombing of civilian targets to terrorise and weaken enemy morale.[31] In fact, Balbo's aviation was Douhetian 'only in the ambitions and in the rejection of an inter-arm collaboration, but it never gave priority to bombing as demanded by Douhet'.[32]

Conversely, it is not even possible to state that Balbo sided with Amedeo Mecozzi's theory, which envisaged the use of aeronautics in combination with the army and the navy.[33] The organisation of the air force desired by Balbo in 1931 in fact reinforced 'both the isolation of the air force and the separation between the three armed forces', effectively reducing the roles of the auxiliary aviation, drastically reduced in number, to mere reconnaissance.[34, 35] If all this contributed to making the air force more compact, at the same time it did not foster the interarm cooperation necessary in the event of war but decidedly lacking in Italy, especially during the Second World War.

So although Balbo had managed to obtain a 'sporting' and 'disciplined' air force, he did not have time to turn it into a 'militarily effective' force. After the great cruise in the United States in the summer of 1933, Balbo was named air marshal, but on 16 October of the same year, Mussolini invited him to resign as minister of the air force, informing him that he would be appointed governor general of Libya.[36] The news was made public the following 6 November. Again, Mussolini took on the position of minister of the air force, concentrating in his own person the three military ministries, perhaps already in anticipation of the war against Ethiopia, and Giuseppe Valle became chief of staff.

How do we explain Balbo's 'fall' and his 'promotion' to governor of Libya? The 'changing of the guard'—that is to say the periodic rotating of top officials and ministers—had always been part of Mussolini's dubious practice of government, by which he sought to remain the sole arbiter of the management of power. Moreover, the enormous popularity of Balbo, especially after the transoceanic flights, combined with his exuberant personality, risked overshadowing the image of *Il Duce*, the unique and irreplaceable leader. Thirdly, it is not inconceivable that Balbo, on his return from America, had discussed his ideas on the reform of the armed forces in person with Mussolini, plans which envisaged a conspicuous increase in the budget of the air force at the expense of the army and a highly prestigious role for himself.[37]

In essence, Mussolini could no longer tolerate a 'cumbersome' and ambitious character like Balbo and preferred to confine him to Libya because he would have affected his balance of power and could have even become a formidable political opponent. What the nature of their relationship was (and how power functioned in the fascist regime) is evident in an extraordinary letter from Mussolini to Balbo, dated 12 November 1933:

> Dear Balbo, on your farewell visit on the 7 you told me you would leave me a total of 3125 aircraft. This number also appears in the delivery note signed by you and Valle. I made the necessary checks and discovered that the actual number amounts only to 911 aircraft that are ready for war, as of today. Let me say straightaway that I consider this situation satisfactory. Best regards, Mussolini.[38]

So, even if Balbo did not hesitate to 'inflate' the numbers, Mussolini explicitly made quite clear to him that he could blackmail him if he did not accept the 'changing of the guard'. Mussolini's way of exercising power is shown here in its clearest light: the determining factor for him was always the politics of prestige, to the great detriment of the country on which he claimed to bestow a questionable historical greatness.

The Air Force during the Years of Giuseppe Valle (1933–39) and Francesco Pricolo (1939–41)

The coming to power of Adolf Hitler in Germany (30 January 1933) upset the post-war European balance and caused commotion in diplomatic circles. The ruthless power politics of the German chancellor, who became absolute dictator and head of state within little more than a year, ended up becoming a foreign policy inspired first by the most aggressive revisionism and finally by the most radical expansionism, in search of the *Lebensraum* (living space) necessary for the survival of the Germans.

In 1935, contrary to the provisions of the Treaty of Versailles, Hitler reinstated compulsory military service and secretly began to rearm. In a secret memorandum of 1936, the German chancellor expressed the desire that the German armed forces should be ready to fight within four years, which is exactly what happened.[39]

Hitler's dynamism led the other powers to react, and even though the Four-Power Pact promoted by Mussolini in 1933 did not help to restrain Hitler, the *Duce* reacted promptly to the failed Putsch fomented by the Nazis in Austria in July 1934 by sending some army divisions to the Brenner. In April 1935, he promoted the 'Stresa Front', an agreement between Italy, France, and Great Britain for anti-German purposes and for the defence of Austrian independence.[40]

In this way, Mussolini hoped to be able to attack and annex Ethiopia, as he had been planning for a long time, without having to fear retaliation from the other powers. The war in Ethiopia (3 October 1935 to 5 May 1936), which ended victoriously with the proclamation of the 'Empire', was a propaganda triumph for Mussolini, who consolidated his prestige and popularity at home and gained enormous popular support; in the field of international relations, Mussolini's belated colonial enterprise initially led to a worsening of relations with France and Great Britain, also following the economic sanctions decreed against Italy by the League of Nations, and ended up drawing Italy into the dangerous orbit of Hitler's Germany.

The outbreak of the Spanish Civil War, on 17 July 1936, which saw the clash between the 'nationalist' rebels led by General Francisco Franco and troops loyal to the government, led to a closer collaboration between the two fascist regimes: both Mussolini and Hitler, albeit to a lesser extent, sent economic and military aid to Franco while the Republicans were joined by international volunteer brigades and received military support from the Soviet Union. The bloody ideological war that took place in Spain and ended on 1 April 1939 with the victory of the Francoists came to constitute a sort of 'dress rehearsal' of the Second World War. It is no coincidence that, in a speech given in Milan on 1 November 1936, Mussolini spoke for the first time of the 'Rome-Berlin Axis', that is that *de facto* alliance that would later be made official by the 'Pact of Steel' signed on 22 May 1939 in Berlin.

On August 23, a non-aggression pact was signed between Germany and the Soviet Union (known as the Ribbentrop-Molotov pact named after the signatories), which diplomatically isolated Poland. On 1 September, Hitler's troops invaded Poland, after Germany had annexed Austria and Czechoslovakia in little more than a year; it was the beginning of the Second World War, in which Italy decided to participate—after a period of 'non-aggression'—with the declaration of war on France and England on 10 June 1940, just when France was about to succumb to the onslaught of German forces. Within this historical frame of reference, we now return to the activities of the Italian Air Force, with particular regard to fighter jets.[41, 42]

In Ethiopia, the air force, despite having to overcome enormous logistical and climatic difficulties, was operating against an essentially unarmed enemy, devoid of aviation and anti-aircraft batteries, and it therefore achieved conspicuous results.[43] The popularity of the air force benefited from this: even the very young Vittorio and Bruno Mussolini, sons of the *Duce*, and Galeazzo Ciano, his son-in-law, were aviators. In the climate of feverish excitement following the foundation of the 'Empire', the inhuman methods employed by Mussolini's troops were easy to ignore, with the almost general indifference of public opinion in Italy and abroad.[44]

Even the Spanish Civil War had negative consequences for the development of the air force: 'nothing was more detrimental', writes Lucio Ceva, 'to the fighter planes of fascist Italy than the sense of victory with which the Spanish Civil War ended.'[45] Much could have been learnt, continues Ceva, above all from its German ally while easy successes were achieved against the second-rate Soviet aircraft of the time.[46]

However, various factors had contributed to the lowering of the technological level of the Italian aeronautical industry 'from as late as 1937'.[47] A 'deadly combination'—to quote Minniti—'of poor design, of immediate industrial interests and ministerial indecision', which seem to go hand in hand with the progressive decline of the regime, now reduced for reasons of *Realpolitik* to grotesquely imitating Nazism.[48]

Let us now examine in order these factors that made the Italian Air Force less and less competitive. In the first place, I believe it is worth mentioning a few passages from a report entitled 'The Air Force and War', sent to Mussolini on 18 November 1941 by the top official Carlo Ravasio, who was well acquainted with the milieu and the problems of the Italian Air Force; although dating back to 1941, it describes a series of problems already obvious in the second half of the 1930s:

> The Italian aeronautical industry is currently directed, with a few rare exceptions ... by persons unfit for their task. The design is usually in the hands of a single person in every company.... Thus the industry lacks the instrument: the well-organized technical office, which could provide effective solutions in this whole complicated area, aircraft structure, engines and equipment, for which it would be essential to make use of those specific skills that alone can provide the solution to the complicated problems of modern technology.
>
> This statement is supported by the fact that the aircraft and engines we produce are on average several years behind compared with the best friendly and enemy production. On the other hand, the predominantly financial and speculative mentality of the industry prevails over all technical and patriotic considerations.... The aeronautical industry has kept its original character, that is craft-based. It is pointless to look for organization in this industry, mass production, the selection and unification of models.
>
> The Italian aeronautical industrialist, not being a great technician but owing his fortune to the fact of having been one of the few to look towards this type of industry, generally has not bothered to seek improvements, to keep up to date, ... finally to equip experimental departments.... Indeed, industry has no incentive to introduce innovations in its programmes and transform its methods of production, because it knows that any of its products can be sold to the State, which, to quote an expression in fashion in the circles of the aeronautical industry: 'buys anything at any price.'[49]

The Ravasio report provides a very good summary of the problems later highlighted by Fortunato Minniti and Lucio Ceva: the substantial oligopoly of the producer companies (Macchi, Caproni, Fiat, Breda, etc.) made them able to set their conditions or even 'blackmail' the ministry (threatening the dismissal of the workers in the absence of orders), imposing their own deadlines and methods of production, without bothering at all to promote and encourage research and innovation.

Hence some inevitable, damaging consequences: orders fragmented and often divided between various companies, under-utilisation and low productivity of the factories, production of too many prototypes and models—whereas abroad the emphasis was more and more on producing a few but improved types of aircraft on an industrial scale—overlong production times (up to 21,000 hours for the manufacture of an aircraft), and finally excessive modifications required by the ministry during construction. To all this should be added the chronic shortage of raw materials and the slowness of the bureaucratic machine that delayed delivery to the companies.[50] Here we see one of the most obvious weaknesses of the fascist regime, which never had the power to coordinate and direct the industrial world towards the political objectives set by Mussolini, but rather was subject to its pressures and conditions in favour of easy and lucrative orders.

On the eve of the Second World War, the Italian Air Force had therefore in the space of a few years lost its 'primacy.' The ambitious 'R programme' (renewal) presented by Valle to Mussolini in 1938, which involved the planned production of over 3,000 aircraft, resulted in a resounding failure: many of the aircraft did not go beyond the prototype stage; others were soon withdrawn due to design and construction problems and defects.[51, 52] Despite the progressive increase in budget appropriations to support the war effort, neither the industrialists nor the regime were able fully to understand the concept of mass production on a large scale, which required standardisation of procedures and models, rational use of plant, and constant innovation.[53, 54] In essence, a modern industrial culture was lacking in Italy. The same directorate for Higher Studies and Experiments in Aeronautics, founded in 1935 in Guidonia, despite being a centre of excellence in aeronautical experimentation, failed to make up for the reality of the deficit in industrial production.

The situation was such that ten of the seventeen aircraft models, chosen between 1933 and 1936 for a huge production of about 900 planes, were cancelled by the new aeronautical undersecretary and chief of staff, Francesco Pricolo, who took over from Valle in November 1939, during Italian 'non-belligerency'. Those that remained could no longer compete with the equivalent foreign models.[55] Valle, in the delivery documents to Pricolo, had calculated the strength of the air force at 8,528 aircraft; Pricolo considered only 840 to be fully usable.[56]

It was only with Pricolo that, after discarding models that were no longer competitive, the Italian aeronautical industry was able to produce, albeit with a serious delay, the first modern Italian fighter, the Macchi M.C.202 Folgore, to which this volume is devoted. Introduced in 1941, one year after the country entered the war alongside Germany, just over 1,000 were produced. The Folgore was the first Italian fighter to have an engine of over 1,000 hp, like its best foreign competitors, at first of German manufacture and then produced under licence by Alfa Romeo.

In the end, what contributed to the backwardness of the Italian Air Force was not only the flawed and opaque relationship between those at the top in politics and industry and the consequent dramatic falling behind in production and technology, but also the mentality of the fighter pilots, still to a large extent associated with their conception of acrobatics and 'chivalry'. This dated back to the times of the air duels of the 'aces' of the First World War, which meant the lack of a modern doctrine of aerial combat.[57]

The ultimate result of all these factors has been well summarised by Richard Overy:

> It was Germany's misfortune to be allied in the Second World War with two states whose ability to produce and deploy the new technologies of war was *limited to the extreme* [author's italics]. Neither Italy nor Japan developed large armoured forces; neither was effectively motorised; Japanese aircraft production, like Italian, was restricted by shortages of raw materials and industrial capacity. Though both states could produce designs of high quality, they lacked the technical means to turn them into large numbers of battlefront weapons that could compete on equal terms with the enemy.[58]

Ultimately, Italy lacked the capacity to mobilise the masses and make use of the scarce resources available for a 'total war'. In fact, the Land of the Rising Sun, despite suffering from the same problems as Italy in the industrial field, succeeded despite everything in producing 10,954 Mitsubishi A6M Zero fighters, almost ten times the production of the Macchi C.202.[59, 60] What could be a more definitive epitaph for the fascist myth of aviation modernity?

2

The Schneider Trophy and Agello's Record

Macchi's participation in the Schneider Trophy, and Fiat's research and development of a very high-performance inline engine, failed to have a significant impact on the development of a modern fighter plane in Italy. While this might seem a paradox, the efforts made by Italy to win the cup did not give the desired results for a series of factors that still today are the subject of discussion among historians.

The history of modern aviation began with a prize won by the Wright brothers at 10.35 a.m. on 17 December 1903 in Kill Devil Hills, North Carolina.[1] The relationship between the sponsors and the construction of the first working single-engined plane, as well as the subsequent prizes that supported the improvements in design and engineering in order to beat the speed, distance, and altitude records, played a considerable role. We will mention some of the many factors that contributed to increasing the pace of technological innovation in these flying machines.

The International Michelin Cup, followed by the British Empire Michelin Cup, the first Pegasus trophy and the Winged Blacksmith Trophy all helped to bring about, by means of their 'policy of records', an increase in international competition and also improvements in aviation technology.[2]

A little later, air races followed: the Prix de Lagatinerie, the Gordon Bennett Aviation Trophy, the London–Manchester flying challenge, the Paris–Madrid air race, and, last but not least in this list of aviation events, the Circuit of Europe that began on 18 June 1911, leaving Paris and travelling through Brussels, Calais, and London before ending back in Paris.[3]

Starting in 1910, hydroplanes and seaplanes made their appearance, along with new races dedicated to them: the Schneider Trophy is the best-known competition, running from 1913 until 1931, when the British won the trophy. Jacques Schneider succeeded in convincing the Principality of Monaco to host the first competition.

The aim was to combine the passion for seaplanes—which were considered the aircraft of the future, since they had three-quarters of the planet to land on—with Monaco, which offered a calm and elegant setting by both day and night, one of the most charming of the time. We need to bear in mind that the spirit of the initiative was nineteenth-century romanticism and, before the outbreak of the First World War, exactly the opposite of what it would become later, with the arrival of national propaganda. Monaco, in fact, was the ideal location for the first race since it could appeal to and attract many enthusiasts from every corner of Europe and the world.

A few days after the first meeting with the president of Monaco's Yacht Club, as a result of a new decree by Prince Albert, a new committee was set up to plan the first competition for the Schneider Trophy and approve the regulations, which Jacques Schneider himself had drafted. It specified that the competition was to take place on 16 April 1913 in the bay in front of the Principality, weather permitting. The participants had to cover a 270-km circuit after passing various tests involving take-off, airworthiness, and sea-landing. The competitors were required to take off and perform manoeuvres by themselves, while there were no limits on the number of engines, their horsepower, or the structure of the aircraft.[4]

Various steps were taken to give the greatest possible importance and credibility to the event: Schneider offered to fly his own plane from Beaulieu to Rome (with stops in Genoa, Portofino, Civitavecchia, and Lido di Roma).[5]

Apart from a single American participant, the first time the race took place, the Schneider Trophy remained an essentially French event, but it had the merit of launching a competition that would become the world's most famous air race, as well as an international contest to set an important record, involving some of the most technologically and scientifically advanced nations. The Italians, along with the Americans and the British, were the main protagonists of this story.

The year 1919 saw the first participation by Italy; France was racing with two aircraft, and Great Britain had three. Italy registered only one plane, a Savoia S.13 built by SIAE and fitted with an Isotta Fraschini 6V-cylinder engine sporting 250 hp.[6] That year's race did not have a winner, but one team—the Italian team—was disqualified, and due to the questionable circumstances under which it happened, the Italians were at least granted the right to host the next running of the competition, which then took place in Venice.

In 1920, Italy won the trophy with Macchi's first ever participation. Its models M12 and M19 were two different aircraft; both the former and the latter were withdrawn from later years of the competition because of technical problems. The latter was equipped with a large Fiat A.14 V19 engine producing 650 hp, probably the most powerful Italian engine at that time.

The year 1921 saw another Italian victory while the three competitors, rather than teaming up, chose to push their respective aircraft's performance to the maximum, risking technical problems. Two out of the three planes (the ones specifically prepared for the race), were in fact forced to give up and the competition was won by De Briganti, who commanded one of the two M7s registered for the race.[7]

The technical aspect devoted to speed gave way to the reliability of the plane during the race, and that is how a lower-performance, but well-proven aircraft not specifically designed for racing could win. Most of all, it convinced the engineers to ask the organising committee for a change in the rules. In future races, the goal would be simple:

> ... to direct the manufacturers towards engineering planes that, by having a maritime use in mind, could also have the maximum payload per hp, and which could reach the maximum speed by using that power and minimizing passive resistance—as far as possible. Once this was achieved, the issue for the engineers would simply be to find the best relationship between wing loading and the type of wing.[8]

The turning point came in 1922, when the English won with an aircraft whose manufacturing took two years of work, the *Sea Lion*. The British seaplane was equipped with a 450-hp engine, way ahead of the other planes, which did not go beyond 280 hp. The race, which took place in Naples, ended with an English victory and, despite all the *bravura* and the effort of the Italian pilots, the trophy did not go to Italy (we should remember that a third consecutive win for a team in a five-year span would have meant the end of the race).

The Victory of the United States

In 1923, the trophy was hosted by England as laid down in the regulations (which stated that the winning country should host the race), and the chosen location was traditionally famous for its sailing regattas. Even though the race was marred by various incidents and by the fact that the Italians eventually pulled out (their seaplanes were not ready) and the French could not deploy a single aircraft of the six registered for the competition, the Americans put in a great performance. They took part with a plane designed with innovative lines, the Navy Curtiss CR3s 'Racer', mounting a Curtiss D12 465-hp engine, registered with two models.[9]

Even with the biplane formula, it had remarkable flying qualities. The central-hull flying boat formula, used by England and France, had proved to be a losing one. In 1924, the Schneider Trophy did not take place. The Americans found themselves alone mainly because of the aftermath of the 1923 victory, which revealed that the technological gap was too big and could not be filled in a short space of time. The Americans therefore had to give up taking part in the race and to allow the other participants to get ready, thus preventing the competition from ending in 1925.

By now, the Schneider Trophy had become a big international competition, so the governments decided to intervene directly by subsidising their manufacturers and deploying armed forces personnel. As far as Italy was concerned, the government opted for the allocation of funds to Aeronautica Macchi, which had manufactured the M33 seaplane, a project of the engineer Mario Castoldi. This, too, was a race without any excitement, which ended in a victory for the Curtiss piloted by James Dolittle with an average speed of 373.5 km/h. De Briganti, racing at a significantly lower speed, came third.[10]

The Success of Macchi

The predictable failure in the United States had brought with it more experience and a determination to do well. In fact, shortly after returning from the USA, in the early days of 1926, Castoldi was tasked by the Ministry of Aviation with building a new plane for the Schneider Trophy, to be modelled around an 800-hp Fiat engine, the AS2. After a short time, the preliminary plan was for the M39 (the new plane) to be equipped with technical solutions that would later be adopted by all seaplane manufacturers taking part in this and other races. Castoldi was inclined towards a seaplane with a fuselage and double floats, as well as the shape of a monoplane, sporting lowered and wind-bracing wings fastened to tie rods.

Moreover, the system of surface radiators for cooling the engine and oil was addressed, the first consisting of radiating elements that completely wrapped the wing and the second adhering to the shape of the whole aircraft and placed in the lower part of the bow. After the first tests inside the wind tunnel and the realisation of the load lines during experiments in a water tank, the aircraft was finally built, and on 30 August 1926, the M39 made its maiden flight. The choice of the pilots belonged to the ministry, which selected De Bernardi, Ferrario, Centurione, Bacula, and Guasconi as a backup. The favorites were De Bernardi and Ferrarin, who had distinguished records and enjoyed international fame.[11]

The training of the pilots started almost immediately, with just a brief stop caused by the sudden death of Centurione on 21 September, who crashed shortly after take-off on his maiden flight and was killed in the incident. On 27 September, De Bernardi returned to flying, and the group focused on engine tuning, with attention paid to carburation, which still needed improvement. The engineering and preparation of the aircraft for the race almost broke a record, since it took only seven months. In the same way, the training of the pilots continued, perhaps in too great a hurry, since the management was relying on the pilots' skills rather than on an extensive training programme. In fact, on 12 October, the Italian team sailed off to the United States aboard the *Conte Rosso* liner, and arrived in New York City ten days later. After finally getting to Norfolk, on 3 November—ten days before the official date of the race—the first of the three M39s was ready for the first test on American soil.

The trial went badly. Here I shall quote the words of Valfredo Fradeani:

> De Bernardi floated, put himself in take-off position and then slowly went to full throttle. The manoeuvre was perfect, but … he had just enough time to climb a hundred metres before a backfire generated a contrail of black smoke covering the tail of the aircraft. De Bernardi … immediately performed a perfect landing in the sea in the bay of Hampton and, as soon as the seaplane stopped … he went up to the engine that was showing signs of catching fire, removed the covering … and after getting a fire extinguisher he managed to put out the fire.[12]

The local news highlighted how the Achilles' heel of the Italian machines was their engine carburation. A similar setback was experienced by Ferrarin, who had to abort his flight due to power supply issues. The problem was overcome only thanks to the American commander of the base, who offered the Italian team some special spark plugs for the AS2 engines, to replace the ones used until then with such disappointing results. The races started and two among the favourites had to withdraw: Ferrarin and the American pilot Cuddihy. De Bernardi instead got better and better, gaining first place with an average speed of 396.689 km/h (the new world speed record for the 100- and 200-km). The competition therefore ended with Macchi being placed both first and third.

The Return of the British

The race in Venice was a bitter disappointment to Macchi, which had prepared a much better plane than the one used in the previous competition, this despite the fact that the English had trained for three full years before registering for the race again. In fact, Macchi had produced a great machine, but the flaws all came from the engine: the Fiat AS3, capable of generating 1,000 hp. Trying to get the best performances out of the engine, the engineers adopted for the first time ever pistons made of elektron, the lightest aluminium alloy, but they turned out to be the main cause of the engine seizures suffered during the race.

The British victory caused some discontent with Balbo (the Italian aviation minister from 1926 to 1933), who promptly asked to get the aeroplane ready with the modifications needed to challenge the speed record. The new symbolic Italian victory did not exhaust the national enthusiasm for the improvement of the aircraft. Balbo opened the centre for testing and research in Desenzano, but things did not go any better.[13]

In 1929, in Calshot, England, four Italian firms (Fiat, Macchi, SIAI, and Piaggio) built prototypes that were to take part in the race. Almost all of them were destroyed by engine fires, crashes, and other misfortunes. Dal Molin obtained second place with an old Macchi M.52R, a modified version of the model that had won in the United States in 1926. The English were one step away from winning the trophy—another victory would be enough to retain the trophy. However, both in Italy and in the other countries, the race was under fire for the costs sustained by the governments.[14]

Balbo defended the commitment to the Schneider Trophy as an opportunity for technological progress and a practice exercise. Along with France, he asked England for more time to prepare but the English refused, thus making Macchi and Fiat work together once again for the production of the M.C.72. The aircraft was equipped with an AS6 engine (two AS5 engines paired together), which set contrarotating propellers in motion. The solution had been adopted to overcome the problems with the engine torque since the engines produced a whopping 1,000-plus hp.[15] The production proved very difficult, and after the death of the pilot Monti, the Italians withdrew; the last race ever held was won by England, which competed alone and conquered the Schneider Trophy for good.[16]

Agello's Record and Some Considerations on the Effect of the Schneider Trophy on the Italian Aviation Industry

The English conquest of the trophy did not stop the Italians. In fact, it led to a reorganisation of the *Scuola Alta Velocità* ('High Speed School') in Desenzano. Furthermore, the Italian prototype seaplane was capable of breaking the record set by the Supermarine S.6B, at least in theory. The *Scuola Alta Velocità* was turned into *Reparto Alta Velocità* ('High Speed Department') and Colonel Bernasconi was confirmed as its head. He was entrusted with the development of the M.C.72. The programme was based on four points: to beat the overall speed record; to achieve the record for the 100-km; to enable Italy to win the Blériot Cup for the first time; and to take part in international speed races using speed racers of the department.[17]

The goals of the programme were fully attained: the 700-km/h speed barrier was broken in 1934, as reported in the following public annoncement from the Ministry of Aviation:

> On October 23, at the Desenzano sul Garda seaplane base where the *Scuola di Alta Velocità* is based, Marshal Francesco Agello on a Macchi-Castoldi M.C.72 aircraft, equipped with an AS6 3000 hp engine, broke a previously held speed record by performing the four regulatory passages at an average speed of 709.202 km/h ...[18]

In a biography of Balbo published in 1988 and written by Claudio Segrè, it is stated that how much the air force benefited from the Schneider Trophy races is still a matter of debate.[19] Actually this comment, apart from Castoldi's statements, remains rather isolated; in fact, most military historians are inclined to think that the opportunities stemming from the research of *Reparto Alta Velocità* were ignored. Agello's record was not particularly celebrated by the fascist regime; in fact, it was soon obscured.

Might it be that Balbo's fall from grace made people believe that celebrating or ensuring the continuity with what could be seen as another success of the *quadrumviro* would certainly annoy Mussolini? Why, otherwise, would one take nine years of research and development on engines, fuel, cooling systems, and flying techniques, only to put them aside and move to air-cooled radial engines?

The planes that were engineered for the Schneider Trophy were so cutting-edge that it took almost five years before aviation engineers could keep up with that; we still do not have a satisfactory answer to these questions, especially since Britain, on the contrary, made good use of its experience. In fact, from the development of Rolls-Royce Merlin came the Spitfire and the American Mustang.

Having lost precious time, in 1940, the Italians were forced to rely on German Daimler-Benz DB601 A1 liquid-cooled engines, manufactured under licence by Alfa Romeo.[20] Segrè writes that Balbo cannot be blamed if his successors could not benefit from the opportunities offered by the competition to win the Schneider Trophy, and he adds:

> The Schneider was also important from another point of view: in an era in which the budget for aviation was meagre, the races engaged the public and made it focus on flying. Benefits like this can be intangible; nevertheless, when we evaluate the role played by Balbo in the context of the Schneider competitions, they cannot be ignored.[21]

Our point of view, although not based on available documentation and thus expressed using the conditional tense, is the opposite of Segrè's: as far as the aviation triumphs are concerned, the 'policy of races and records', as it has been called, was discontinued by Valle and most of all by Mussolini both because the *Duce* could not really appreciate its results, and because of the unwillingness of Balbo's successor to reap the rewards.[22, 23, 24] A partial explanation can be found in the previous chapter. Basically, Balbo was found guilty of not working towards the *Duce*.'[25]

Castoldi was asked to evaluate the impact of the Schneider Cup on the future developments of the fighter planes. His reflections are collected in the following interview from the magazine *l'Ala d'Italia*:

> Something we have been wanting to ask engineer Castoldi for a long time is by what miracle he succeeded in creating a perfect and very fast fighter plane all of a sudden, when he had seemed to focus almost exclusively on seaplanes in the last few years. (We can mention the single-engine sea patrolling C. 77, the double-engine amphibious C. 94 for civilian operations, the triple-engine bomber C. 99 and the triple-engine commercial C. 100).
>
> Engineer Castoldi responded to our question with a smile, then pointing to a scale model of the M.C. 72, the famous seaplane piloted by Agello, he said: 'The contemporary fighter aircraft C. 200 and C. 202 are direct descendants of that quite long series of racing seaplanes which from 1925 to 1931 it was part of my task to study thanks to the participation of Italy in the Schneider Trophy'.
>
> By following the history of these seaplanes, one sees the progress of speed from 400 to more than 700 km/h.

The aircraft that won the Schneider in 1926 had a maximum speed of a little more than 400 km/h. It is with the record of De Benardi in Venice, on April 30, 1928, that we got past the 500 km/h limit for the first time. In 1931 the first flights of M.C. 72 (from 'Macchi-Castoldi 72') went beyond 600 km/h, then finally a speed in excess of 700 km/h was reached by Agello with M.C. 72 on October 23, 1934 (the count was 709.209).

The study of these seaplanes, many years ago, made the solution of some of today's contemporary problems imperative. The contemporary fighters have many points of contact with the racing aircraft of yore, most importantly the speed. Just compare the photographs of the M.C. 72 with one of today's fighters, and you will notice they are closely related.

These racing seaplanes have also had a very positive effect on the global progress of aviation, by highlighting the advantages that can be reached with improving the shapes and suppressing passive resistance.

– Will the fighter be able to benefit further from these experiences? For example, by adopting the double propellers, one of the most interesting features of the M.C. 72?

– The first studies on the two contra-rotating coaxial propellers were started by me in 1921, when I was at the *Istituto Sperimentale Aeronautico* ('Experimental Aviation Institute') in Rome. The wind tunnel tests had yielded some flattering results, which had convinced me of the benefits of the system. A first project of mine of an aeroplane equipped with coaxial propellers dates back to that period.

The first practical application was made on the M.C. 72, a huge risk that we took under my responsibility. The first flight was completed on 22 June 1931, prior to all the other tests which were carried out abroad.

The double propellers have their field of action limited to great horsepower and very high speed. The advantages over the common propeller are substantial, since with the pairing of the propellers, from a certain form of blade one can obtain the minimum possible diameter, lower than that of a four-blade propeller absorbing the same power. The system is therefore used to reduce the peripheral speed of the blades, an indispensable condition for higher performance. These advantages are better seen on 2000–3000 hp engines, or even more powerful engines (horsepower figures for contemporary engine manufacturing are rising rapidly) mounted on very fast aircraft.

The two propellers of the M.C. 72 were set in motion separately by two engines paired together. This made keeping the two propellers' rpm constant difficult. It was noted, though, that the performance was still good, as the slight rpm variations of the propellers did not go beyond 2 or 3 %.

In future manufacturing, it would be good if the two props were tied to one another so that they can have the same rpm, and if engine power is applied to the tied propellers system.

Another benefit of the double propellers is that of abolishing the effect of the engine torque, which in racing seaplanes was bothering pilots, especially at take-off. Overseas, especially in the United States, this solution is starting to be seriously taken into account. Nevertheless the system still needs study and testing, because the two propellers should be of variable pitch during flight, since discarding this useful improvement does not seem appropriate to me.

Another development of the double coaxial propellers could be the increase in the number of blades of a single propeller from two to three, or even four. This enhancement deserves some study.

– The Aer. Macchi C. 200 had a radial engine, while the C. 202 had an in-line one. Which one do you deem better for a fighter plane?

– There is little doubt that the in-line engine is to be preferred, thanks to its reduced frontal section that permits a greater finesse, all in the interest of the overall characteristics of the aircraft. Thus, the C. 202 is a remarkable improvement on its predecessor and the resounding successes obtained in war which are also confirmed by, the headquarters, are the best proof of that. If we are heading, as is expected, towards more powerful engines, adopting this solution proves essential, since the radial engine cannot reach great horsepower due to its limited frontal space.

The problems with the engine cooling system are very important. The cooling of an engine with liquid circulation on a fighter plane, which tends to reduce volumes to a minimum, presents certain difficulties. In the M.C. 72, however, I had to face and solve even more stringent requirements, which was done in a very brilliant way. By then cruising at 700 km/h meant burning more than 600 calories per square metre every minute, with a total weight of the circulating water of just 15 kg. The water circulation was the result of the work of four centrifugal pumps moving 900 litres of water every minute, i.e. the same amount of water flowing almost eight times through the radiators.

The circulation of water functions with a pressure maintained by some special extra-sensitive valves, controlled by a series of barometric capsules. Without the valves, as the water temperature nears 90° C the pumps switch off and reduce the mass flow rate. Keeping the circuit under pressure means that water does not boil and the pumps are still functioning even with a temperature over 100° C; the temperature is correlated with the pressure at which the valves are calibrated.

I think that the cooling system with pressurised water circulation was first used only on the M.C. 72.

– Could the system so brilliantly adopted on the M.C. 72 find an application on fighter planes, too?

– That would be desirable, but unfortunately a war plane has different needs than a racing plane. The work done on the M.C. 72 by using hollow laminated elements applied on the wing, on the floating hull and on other parts of the aircraft can hardly be replicated on fighter planes, due to its vulnerability to bullets.

The use of intubated radiators is now catching on. They deserve study for their full development.[26]

3

Mario Castoldi

This chapter owes a great deal to an article by Enrico Rebora published in the *Rivista Aeronautica* and to other articles on the decisions made by Castoldi during his tenure at AerMacchi. Specifically, we introduce unpublished documentation regarding Castoldi's educational path, and the course of studies he followed at the *Politecnico di Milano*.

The *Politecnico di Milano*

Mario Castoldi (Zibido San Giacomo 1888–Milan 1968) graduated from the *Politecnico di Milano* in 1913. In the record of his studies, subjects concerning the development of aircraft took precedence over all the others.[1]

Giuseppe Colombo, one of the key figures in the founding and development of the *Politecnico di Milano* and its second director, in addition to being a prominent industrialist, had shown a precocious and well-documented interest in aviation—i.e. the science that studies the technology of heavier than air objects, since the end of 1860. Colombo's relationship with Enrico Forlanini, one of his first students at the *Regio Istituto Tecnico Superiore* and a prominent figure on the Milan aviation scene for many decades from the end of the nineteenth century to the early twentieth century, shows the involvement of the leading figures in the academic field.

The introduction of the first preparatory course for aviators, taught in 1909 by Giorgio Finzi, which Castoldi attended, was supported, as in other universities, by the members of the Italian Aeronautical Society, also responsible for bringing Léon Delagrange in Italy in 1908 to conduct the first flight in an aeroplane. Finzi was a physicist, an enthusiast experimenter in the field of fluid dynamics, on which in 1903 he had published a memoir that detailed the results of intense experimental activity.

Along with Finzi there were figures such as Nicola Soldati, co-author with Finzi of the above-mentioned memoir and others.[2] However, it was Cesare Dal Fabbro, an engineering officer in the Italian army, who consolidated the teaching on aviation. He, thanks to his close contact with Forlanini, was able to improve the course, even if it relied on a totally external teaching staff, having just been established.[3] In the preliminary print edition of the course reported in the academic schedule of the school year 1909–10, it is stated that the main goal is:

> ... to show the students of the Institute how vast a field of scientific research and technical activity air navigation is... In other words the course, more than being a really detailed course, aims to make the vision of the boundaries of air navigation clear, and explain the conditions suitable for studying it.[4]

The events of the First World War saw Dal Fabbro, by then a lieutenant in the Engineers Corps, move to Turin to be appointed technical director of the air force. After the war, he was promoted to the rank of general and later he would go back to Milan, even if it was as a senior engineering, motor industry executive, only marginally involved with activities in the aviation sector.

The war effort deprived the *Politecnico* of some of its teachers, and from the beginning of his career, Castoldi was sent into the armed forces, in the same institution directed by Dal Fabbro. The *Politecnico*'s curricula during the war years were patchy, and sometimes they were not even published. This problem was in part solved thanks to the contribution of Silvio Bassi, who graduated from the *Politecnico* in 1911 as an industrial engineer with a degree in electrical engineering. Bassi was asked to flank Dal Fabbro with the role of dedicated coordinator. Therefore Bassi was conceivably among the first students to attend the aviation course, and he managed to keep the interest in aviation studies alive during the years of the First World War. On the whole, only the armed forces received an education as newly specialised engineers and technicians, resulting in the deprivation of the companies of part of their staff. On the one hand, then, there were rapid developments in the aviation industry in Lombardy; on the other hand, few Milan graduates took part in it.[5]

The efforts of a few teachers resulted in the attempt to establish a real graduate school in the early 1920s within the *Politecnico di Milano*, an unsuccesful attempt since, after a long period of marginalisation, only after the Second World War (in the 1950s) did aeronautical studies experience an expansion.[6]

The Beginning

After a brief military education, Castoldi's aviation engineering activity started in Turin in 1915 as a reserve officer in the Technical Direction of Military Aviation (DTAM). He was sent immediately afterwards to Turin as a 'surveillance officer' tasked with monitoring the project at the Pomilio company, which led to his becoming head of the technical department towards the end of 1916, and later to his return to DTAM to solve manufacturing and technical issued raised by the ongoing war. During the First World War, he went on a mission to France and Great Britain, where he could deepen his knowledge by visiting a few aviation factories and airfields.

In November 1919, after being released from military service, he joined the '*Direzione Sperimentale*' as a civil engineer, at what is today known as Guidonia airport (then Montecelio airport), where studies and practical tests on aerodynamics were being carried out. It was during the period spent in Guidonia that Castoldi designed for Breda Aeronautica a four-engined bomber carrying the initials 'BC' ('*bombardiere Castoldi*', i.e. Castoldi bomber), thus starting the construction of an experimental model and the first study on contra-rotating propellers, which would be resumed later for the Macchi M.C.72, in 1929. In 1922, he became an Aeronautica Macchi designer in Varese, and later its technical director, at first signing his work on the Macchi M.24 at the firm together with engineer Tonini, but soon becoming the only manager responsible for all Macchi's projects, from Macchi M.26 to Macchi M.C.206. The role of chief designer in Italy, and particularly that of Castoldi, given the great human and professional skills required, needed to resemble more that of a skilled craftsman than of a scientist.

In the above-mentioned report by the fascist top official Carlo Ravasio, who reported on the productive capacity of the whole Italian aircraft industry, the part dedicated to assessing design reads as follows:

> With rare exceptions, the Italian aviation sector is led, both as regards design and when it comes to production, by people unfit for their task. In any firm the design is usually done by a single person, thus concentrating

> such an amount and complexity of work that, to be well performed, it would require an encyclopaedic knowledge and a Leonardo-like mind. The industry has total confidence in this person, for he has generated remarkable profits, though it is well known that the product could have been better. It is the emerging role of *progettista* (designer), someone who has an interest in keeping for himself all the responsibilities.... The result is that highly cultured and well trained technical staff are kept in the dark and unable to engage in any profitable activity. The industry is therefore lacking the tool: the *well organized technical staff*, capable of presenting efficient solutions in the complex fields of aicraft structure, engines and equipment, for which it is indispensable to use the specific expertise that alone can guarantee the solution of the complex problems of modern technology.[7]

The responsibility for this state of affairs certainly did not lie with Castoldi, but overall with the directorate of the armed forces, the fascist government, and an industrial oligopoly more interested in dividing up the commissions equally among the firms than in entering into rivalry and real competition.

Aircraft Design

To the long list of aircraft designed by Castoldi, it is fair to add the studies and the unfinished projects, including that of the Macchi M.C.207, a project that was in an advanced state, with construction drawings already completed.[8] Castoldi's activity can be divided into two main strands: the racing seaplanes (1925–31) and the fighters (1935–43). His remaining professional activity can be considered as dedicated to the manufacturing of a series of seaplanes, flying boats, and land-based aircraft for both civilian and military purposes. The list of the achievements of this third professional phase is as follows:

a) Biplane central-hull seaplanes equipped for war (*idrocaccia*):
   M.26—construction year: 1924—prototype only;
   M.41—construction year: 1927—prototype only;
   M.41bis—construction year: 1928—built for the Italian and Spanish military air forces;
   M.71—construction year: 1930—prototype only.
b) Biplanes:
   M.40—a metal, embarqued, catapult-launched seaplane, construction year: 1928;

M.70—land and sea-based two-seater, for tourism, construction year: 1928;

M.C.73—land and sea-based two-seater, for tourism, construction year: 1930;

To these we should add, although a monoplane, the M53, due to its aerodynamic analogy with the M.40's wing (same profile family, justified by the identical purpose of the aircraft) and many very similar structural elements (the windbracing of the wings, the body, and the floats), resulting from the same indispensable folding wings used by both the aircraft. M53 – submarine-borne seaplane, one-seater, mixed-building. Construction year: 1928.

c) The third family, consisting of large and medium-sized monoplanes, central-hull seaplanes, designed for military and civilian use:

M.77—single-engined wooden reconnaissance plane, construction year: 1935;

M.C.99—twin-engined wooden reconnaissance, construction year: 1937;

M.C.100—three-engined wooden plane, for civil transport, construction year: 1938;

Here we consider also the amphibious aircraft:

M.C.94—twin-engined wooden seaplane, for civilian transport, construction year: 1936.

Castoldi's work in manufacturing aircraft for the Schneider Trophy and his research on greater speeds is the subject of a later chapter devoted to the prize, but as Castoldi recalled his experience with racing seaplanes:

> It was in the autumn of 1924 that a contest among all Italian firms was organized in order to manufacture the aircraft to compete for the Schneider Trophy the following year. In designing the lines of what would become the M33 I found myself facing the problems of building a racing seaplane for the very first time.... Among the indispensable requirements are the stability of the machine, the perfect centring, the manageability, good performance on water at take-off and landing at sea. If these requirements are necessary for every aircraft, they must be especially taken into consideration on racing planes...[9]

Castoldi went on to address the priorities in manufacturing a high-speed aircraft, and state its main difficulties:

> We need to reduce the dimensions of the aircraft's parts to a minimum, since they are exposed to the air—thus opposing resistance to forward

> movement—and give them the most appropriate shape to reduce this resistance. When it comes to the engines, one that generates its power along with the smallest possible weight, fuel consumption and front section is preferable. Every achievable weight reduction in turn allows us to increase speed, because it enables us to reduce the dimensions of some parts of the aircraft, for example the wings and the floats. Almost all the parts of a seaplane have undergone an evolution while reaching higher and higher speeds, and most of all the wings, the floats, the radiators and the propellers. The wingloading has been rising year after year. The outlines of the wings most suitable for racing planes are the symmetrical biconvex ones, which have a minimum resistance at high speed, allow the inclusion of good-size longerons and enjoy a constant point of application of the resultant force. Even the floats have been constantly improving their shape and dimensions, but this reduction has a limit. The seaplane must be able to float, and it needs to take off, too. Now since the take-off is becoming more and more difficult and the smaller the floats, the greater the engine power it requires, the result is a decrease in the volume of the floats, limited by the weight of the aircraft and the power of the engine.[10]

Let us now consider the development of fighter planes, which despite having completely different features in terms of materials and intended purposes, have to some extent benefited from past experience. The development of fighter planes in the mid- to late 1930s happened with the ending of a formula (in the case of the fighters that of the open cockpit biplane with fixed landing gear and, sometimes, still with an adjustable pitch propeller). This formula had been at the centre of doctrines, traditions, schools, mentalities, and habits for over fifty years (in Italy from the Nieport 'Bebé' to the Fiat CR.42).

The shift to low-wing, closed-cockpit monoplanes equipped with flaps, retractable landing gear, and variable pitch propellers, and with an additional 60 mph at top speed, set new piloting standards and deployment practices, and the training of new 'average' pilots, rather than people showing outstanding skills.

The Macchi M.C.202

An account by Carestiato reported by Rebora of the first flight of the prototype of M.C.202 helps to show the professional relationship existing between the designer and the test pilot: 'In those days Castoldi had kept close to his test pilot and had talked to him at length, and in detail ...

about the plane, about its limits, about what to expect from it, about the remaining doubts'.[11]

Then, on 10 August 1940, after a few delays for technical reasons or because of the inopportune presence of some unwanted 'bystander', the prototype finally had its maiden flight. The engineer was too afraid to look at his aircraft while it was leaving the ground, and so he was informed immediately after the take-off was complete. The account continues:

> In the meantime Carestiato, who was aboard the 600 km/h fighter prototype, could ascertain that at the first take-off everything went in a way that seemed perfectly familiar to him, just as he had already flown that plane, and that everything was unfolding exactly the way engineer Castoldi had told him it would during those days of anxiety and hope.[12]

At the end of the Second World War, when Macchi had to convert its production, Castoldi designed a threshing machine, about fifteen of which were later produced. After his retirement from AerMacchi, he kept studying and consulting.

His last studies led him to draw sketches of the C.209, a supersonic jet fighter plane. He died in his home in Trezzano sul Naviglio (near Milan) on 31 May 1968.[13] The last time that Macchi produced aircraft designed by Castoldi was for the Egyptian Air Force, when some parts of the M.C.202 were modified to produce forty Macchi M.C.205 Veltros.

4

The Macchi M.C.200 Saetta

In 1937, the *Direzione Generale Costruzioni Aeronautiche* (DGCA) issued the tender specifications for bids to build a solid monoplane fighter sporting a retractable landing gear and carrying 'sufficient armament'.[1] The engine on which the competition was based was the Fiat A74 RC38, sporting just 840 hp, inadequate compared with the specifications of the fighters deployed by the other main European industrialised countries and in a stark contrast with the aircraft previously designed by Castoldi, the M.C.72 carrying a Fiat AS6 3,000-hp engine.

The first Macchi prototype flew on 24 December 1937 over Lonate Pozzolo (Varese), piloted by Giuseppe Burei, a test pilot for the firm. Subsequently, the organisation responsible for the evaluation of the aircraft, the first *Centro Sperimentale Aviazione* (CSA) of Guidonia, near Rome, appointed *tenente* Adriano Mantelli to conduct further testing. During tests, some problems emerged, among which was the tendency of the aircraft to fall into a spin during particular stalling maneuvres, caused, according to the CSA, by a spontaneous phenomenon brought about by the airfoil of the M.C.200 'being too sharp on the leading edge and having a constant and not variable profile'.[2]

The introduction of retractable landing gear, although it enabled the aircraft to keep up with its direct competitors, was the first cause of some incidents (namely belly landings), because the pilots were so used to the fixed gear that they forgot the new feature.

Another issue linked to innovation aboard the aicraft was that of the closed cockpit. The open cockpit had been in use for a very long time on the aeroplanes of the *Regia*, yet the Macchi C.200 and its twin aircraft Fiat G50 sported a glazed canopy, with a hand-operated sliding door.

Besides the fear that in the event of an emergency the cockpit would not open (opening and closing were not that easy), there was also an actual reduction in visibility because of the poor quality of the 'rodovetro' plexiglass in use, which over time crystallised and easily became opaque. Hence the decision to recondition the glazed-canopy aircraft produced and replace them with an open cockpit.

The first Macchi M.C.200s to receive their baptism of fire were those of the 6° *Gruppo Autonomo CT* (*Caccia Terrestre*), of pilot *tenente colonnello* Armando François, based at the Sicilian airport of Fontanarossa di Catania, which on 11 June 1940, after moving to the airfield of Comiso (province of Ragusa), formed direct and indirect escorts for the S70 bombers of the 2ª *Squadra Aerea*, which were sent to Malta to perform their first military actions.

That same day saw the first ever air combat between Italian and English fighters, and also the first of the Macchi C.200:

> The eighth and final raid came at 19.25 that evening, the Gladiators being scrambled to intercept. Flg Off. Woods (N5519) was again involved, and on this occasion dog fought, Woods believed he had shot down the fighter but in fact, the Macchi had not even been seriously damaged. Evasive action and the black exhaust smoke from a hastily-opened throttle had apparently misled him into thinking he had inflicted damage to the Macchi's engine.[3]

During that day, no plane was lost by either side.

If at first the pilots were apparently not happy with the new machine, after a few adjustments made in the early days of warfare, things changed. In fact, in February 1941, the journalist and pilot Giulio Lazzati wrote in his novel, which is nonetheless quite accurate technically due to his personal experiences:

> We are making the move to the new fighter planes we have just received: the Macchi 200s. The first days we saw them, many of us were puzzled. A single-wing fighter, what the hell!; and one keeps going back to the nostalgic memories of our CR. 42 biplanes, that were marooned in Libya.[4]

Lazzati goes on:

> After a ten-day trial, the formation is moderately happy: the Macchi is a bit less acrobatic than the C.R., but turns out to be as solid, and

> very fast: about 490 km/h. It has an at least decent radio system, areat visibility on all sides, retractable gear (getting the wheels in and out is the only new maneuvre for us pilots used to the 42's fixed gear). The only disappointment is the equipment: frankly, we expected a little more than the usual two 12.7 weapons. The English are piloting fighters with four, six, eight machine guns. Oh well![5]

After he became familiar with the aircraft, Lazzati wrote about Macchi 200 flight characteristics before the war. The pilot wrote:

> Today I tried to dive, I took it up to 4000 metres, and then went back down. What a dive, folks! The needle of the speed gauge was racing, four hundred, four hundred and fifty, five hundred, six hundred; the aircraft wasn't diverging from the straight line, no signs of vibrations: it is definitely a good plane. After the round-out I let it speed in horizontal flight.... The 200 cruises the air like a charm; one might forget to pilot it.[6]

Against these considerations, we should be aware of the situation of the fighter divisions that were equipped with biplanes, where if Macchi 200 could certainly not compete with the more recent aircraft of the Allies, it was nonetheless true that it represented a considerable improvement on the biplanes manufactured by Fiat and had more reliable features than the similar G50. Here is another account by Lazzati regarding the 200's performances, this time in combat:

> Malta stinks. The first months, well, everything went smoothly enough. They only had a few fighters, almost all Glosters, but then day after day you could find yourself facing more and more numerous formations of Hurricanes and Spitfires, and then on with the acrobatics, because if you were not able to make the most of that, considering their speed and their munitions, you were screwed for real. Luckily enough, with the 200, you can wear it out however you want, and it won't play tricks on you. Therefore, whirling, 90-degree dives, tonneaux, turns so tight that you fear the aircraft will break apart right under your arse. And all of this only to manage to get close to one of their tails just enough to shoot them with our two 12.7.[7]

In part, the limits of the aircraft in comparison with the more gifted enemy fighters explain the reasons for the tendency showed by the Italians to engage in acrobatic combat as if they were still in the First World War (a tendency highlighted in the memoirs written by Allied pilots).

The Macchi M.200s were deployed—except for CAI and Eastern Africa (the Channel front, where the Fiat CR.42s and the G50s were entrusted with the fighting role; in AOI the same happened with the CR.42s and the more than obsolete CR.32s)—in all Italian operational theatres, from the war in North Africa to Russia, where although it was proving more and more reliable than the twin aircraft Fiat G50, the Macchi was to suffer various defeats.[8]

It is difficult today to grasp why the open-cockpit Macchi was chosen for the Russian campaign and deployed in an environment that turns remarkably hostile in winter. We can assume that, just as a mistake was made in evaluating the endurance of the British in 1940, another error of judgement was committed as regarded the Soviets' defensive capacity.

The Russian front was not the setting for that quick victory pictured by the German command, and the Italian stay was particularly painful because of the freezing Russian winter and the usual unpreparedness of the fascist troops.

> [The Macchi C200] was severely tested by the unfavourable weather conditions that laid a grip on weapons, engines, mechanisms and above all personnel. The severe temperatures that often reached 30 degrees below zero equally affected the technicians and pilots.... The latter withstood indescribable temperatures in flight in their semi-enclosed cockpits, without electro-heated flying suits or effective protective equipment.[9]

Subsequently in 1942, underwing gunpacks for small-calibre weapons, mostly used against Soviet light targets, were fitted to some Saettas. In May 1943, the operational life of the Macchi ended in Russia, then to continue later at home, albeit only for secondary tasks. Among the last roles played by the Saetta was that of a training aircraft: the Macchi became an instructor plane, though a two-seater version was never developed. Overall, the production ran to about 1,176 aircraft. The twenty-five series manufactured by the three firms AerMacchi, Breda, and Sai-Ambrosini, denoted by Roman numerals, resulted in aicraft with few technical and engineering differences.

During production, only the canopy was subject to modifications; in the end, it became half-closed thanks to two moulded closing gears, made entirely of metal. The tail wheel was made fixed together with the closing doors, the Piaggio propeller replaced the original Hamilton-Standard and the protective nose cone was abandoned and removed; under the wings, it should be remembered, were placed the bomb racks for light weapons. The mother factory planned and produced two prototypes, the C.201

(MM436 and 437), removing the 'hump' and trying to sharpen the lines as much as it could; at first, they sported a Fiat A74 RC38 1,000-hp engine, then they were converted to be powered by the A74 and entered into service.

Those remained the only models ever produced. In subsequent plans, the emphasis was put on trying to provide higher drive-power ratings, and to this end Breda developed the C.200bis, which experimentally sported a Piaggio P.XIX RC45 1,175-hp engine. This plane, too, did not go beyond the usual initial test trials. Towards the end of the war, because of the lack of replacement parts, the aircraft was decommissioned.

The Macchi C.200 was undoubtedly a forerunner of the better Folgore, not to say an aircraft with very similar features, with the main difference being the new engine (or the shift from a radial engine to the more powerful Daimler-Benz in-line engine).

The Technical Profile of the Macchi M.C.200

Absolute maximum speed at 15,000 feet:	503 km/h
Minimum speed:	128 km/h
Outdistance:	245 metres in 13 seconds
Landing distance:	300 metres
Minimum speed at ground level:	143 km/h

Aircraft: Aer. Macchi C200

Unladen weight:		1,898 kg
Working load:		430 kg
Total weight:		2,328 kg
Pilot with parachute:		80 kg
Arms, weapons, and miscellanea:		128 kg
	Fuel:	197 kg
	Oil:	25 kg
Total:		430 kg
Tank capacities:	Main tanks:	220 kg
	Auxiliary tank:	80 kg

Climb speeds:
Altitude in metres: 1,000: 1 min 3 secs; 2,000: 2 mins 10 secs; 3,000: 3 mins 24 secs; 4,000: 4 mins 35 secs; 5,000: 5 mins 21secs; 6,000: 7 mins 33 secs

Theoretical service ceiling m.a.t.:	9,100 metres
Actual service ceiling m.a.t.:	8,900 metres

Autonomy (at 6,000 metres, 2,250 rpm, press. 530 mm/Hg., level flight speed of 465 km/h): 570 km (with permitted load of fuel of 197 kg)
Maximum autonomy (at the above-mentioned altitudes and speeds): 870 km with auxiliary fuel tank (total load of fuel 300 kg)
Armament: All versions: 2 × 12.7-mm Breda—SAFAT machine guns mounted above the engine and syncronised to fire through the propeller arc with 400 rounds per gun.[10]

5

Anatomy of a Plane: M.C.202's Construction and Variants

The operational history of the Macchi M.C.202 cannot be reduced to a dry narration of daily events, of flight hours, performance, planes shot down, and losses. To interpret those events and those data in a meaningful way, we need to refer to the context that enabled the plane to fly and fight. In other words, we need to look at the industrial and procurement policies that determined the production of the M.C.202, the reasons why such and such an engine and such and such an armament were installed, to examine the system that prepared the pilots that flew it, that defined their tactics and their strategic doctrine, that ensured (or failed to ensure) supply, ammunition, and spare parts, that implemented—or failed to implement—lessons learnt after the first clashes, and understand the organisation of the *Regia Aeronautica* forces in theatre. Not least, we have to talk briefly about what planes, pilots, and systems the M.C.202 measured up against. Only in this way will the narration of the day-by-day engagement, the speed, rate-of-climb, diving speed, armament, and manoeuvrability be useful for interpreting the experience of the M.C.202 in its arc of existence.

Martinoli, Lucchini, Ferrulli, Solaroli di Briona, Malvezzi, Reiner, Ruspoli, Baschirotto, Niclot Doglio, Tarantola, Omiccioli, Gorrini, Biron, Visconti, Drago, and Annoni—some of the most celebrated Italian aces of the Second World War—all have something in common: they flew, fought, and sometimes became aces on the M.C.202. This is a testimony both to the quality of this superb plane and to its generalised use, as it quickly became the backbone of the *Squadriglie di Caccia Terrestre* of the *Regia*

Aeronautica. Indeed, the M.C.202 is probably the most important and one of the best, while not the most numerous, Italian fighter planes of the Second World War, with a generally agreed number of 1,070 aircraft produced between mid-1941 and August 1943. Overall, 1,453 'Folgore' were ordered:

- Breda, 900 units, of which 649 were produced.
- AerMacchi itself, 403 units, of which 390 were produced.
- SAI Ambrosini, 150 units, of which sixty-seven were produced.[1]

The fact that a wholly outdated plane such as the CR.42 was produced in larger numbers, and until late 1943, tells us much about the Italian aeronautical industry and the *Regia Aeronautica*'s doctrine.

When we talk about generalised use, we are naturally making a qualified statement, as Italian industrial capacity in the course of the war was by no means comparable to that of Germany, not to mention that of the Allies:

Aircraft type	Production period (during the Second World War)	Number of aircraft produced
Spitfire (all marks)	1939–1945	19,898
Hurricane (all marks)	1937–1944	14,533
P-51 Mustang (A to D model, Mk I, A36)	1940–1945	15,588
P-47 Thunderbolt (B to N, and other variants)	1941–1945	15,636
P-40 (all variants)	1939–1944	13,739
Messerschmitt Bf 109	1935–1945	33,984
Focke-Wulf Fw 190	1939–1945	19,987
Mitsubishi A6M Zero	1940–1945	10,939
Macchi M.C.202	1940–1943	1170
IAR80	1939–1944	448

Suffice to say that whereas in about two years, 1,150 M.C.202s were built, the British produced 6,487 Spitfire Mk Vs, the main adversary of the Macchi in the Mediterranean theatre.

The initial chokepoint of the M.C.202 production was the engine, given the need to import the liquid-cooled inverted V12 Daimler-Benz DB601 engine from Germany. Nevertheless, the licence-produced version of the DB601, the Alfa Romeo RA1000 RC41, never reached a production rate of more than sixty to sixty-five engines per month, and it was also necessary to motorise the Re.2001.

In any case, the direct predecessor of the M.C.202, the Macchi 200 *Saetta*, also produced by Macchi, Breda, and Sai Ambrosini, motorised by the radial fourteen-cylinder Fiat Aviazione A74 RC38 *Ciclone* (which was more readily available and in production since 1935) never surpassed the relatively modest number of 1,153 fighters. This was due to the extremely complex, if very solid, structure of the plane, which required 20,000 man-hours to complete, in comparison to the Bf 109E/F, which was rated as typically requiring 4,500–6,000 man-hours per aircraft to complete. The extremely complicated structure was the result of a project unsuited to the needs of large-scale industrial production. In fact, the only important design experience of the designer Mario Castoldi was that linked to the racing seaplanes built to participate in the Schneider Trophy, which were essentially the result of aeronautical craftsmanship, albeit of the highest class, rather than the mindset of large-scale mass production 'industrial' aeronautics.[2, 3]

The M.C.202 differed from the M.C.200 in having a significantly streamlined fuselage, built to fit the new engine and to increase performance, but based on a complex semi-monocoque shell, comprising four light-alloy beams, complete with longerons and ovoidal bulkheads, and an enclosed cockpit. Being an even more elaborate plane and thus less well suited to mass production, the M.C.202 needed in excess of 22,000 man-hours to complete: 'A Spitfire V took 13,000 hours to build, a time that could be compared to that required for the production of a Macchi, due to the large number of parts that required specialized workmanship'.[4]

There were also broader problems, related to the backwardness of the Italian industrial system, which had a knock-on effect on aeronautical production and eventually on the fighter itself. The incapacity of the Italian metallurgical industry to produce the indispensable special alloys necessary for the production of high-performance aero engines made the licence-produced DB601 engines more prone to breakdowns and more maintenance-intensive. Moreover, after the Ethiopian War, the Italian chemical industry was cut off from the development of new aviation fuels that significantly increased engine power, and never managed to catch up properly either at research or at production capacity level. Only quite late (in 1939) did the Italians start producing tetraethyl lead, the additive boosting the octane rating that allowed engine compression to be raised substantially.

Until 1943, the Italian industry managed only to produce 87 octane aviation fuel, while the British moved rapidly from the 87 octane aviation fuel that powered the Rolls-Royce Merlin IIs of the Hurricane I and Spitfire I to the 100 octane fuel in June 1940, powering the Merlin XII of the Spitfire II and the Merlin XX of the Hurricane II, and later the Merlin

45 of the Spitfire V, the usual adversary of the M.C.202. Later (from 1942) models of Spitfires (e.g. Mk VII–Mk IX) used Merlin 61 engines powered by 115/145 octane fuel. This increased the gap between the M.C.202, albeit powered by a good engine, and the Allied fighters that it fought against, whose often equally good (or better) engines used higher-octane fuel resulting in significantly more power and performance.[5, 6]

Eventually, and this is a problem that concerned all the specialities of the *Regia Aeronautica*, there was a problem of budget, which prevented it from attaining the planned number of *Squadriglie* and from developing a more powerful armament for its planes.[7]

War is a collective effort, and it is an effort of numbers, of logistics, of resources, and of industrial capacity. No individual weapon system changes the course of a war (though, as far as the Second World War is concerned, the illusion of the *Wunderwaffen* has somehow lingered in the collective historical memory), nor a small number of motivated and courageous *Regia Aeronautica* aces. The Macchi M.C.202 was a fine plane, which catapulted the *Regia Aeronautica* into the era of modern air combat, and gave it the chance to face enemy aircraft on an even or superior footing. In its heyday in the Mediterranean theatre, the brief period between late summer of 1941 and the appearance of the Spitfire Mk V in March 1942 (in Malta) and July 1942 (in the Western Desert), the presence of a substantial number of Macchis could have shifted the balance, at least temporarily, by establishing and maintaining air superiority. This was not to be, simply because the Macchis were the product of a dysfunctional political and industrial system that could not produce and send to combat units more planes that it actually did. Even if it had done so, it is doubtful whether the *Regia Aeronautica* would have had the capacity to provide ammunition, fuel, and spares, and to have them serviceable in sufficient numbers. When later marks of Spitfires, US fighters, and US heavy bombers appeared in theatre, the inadequacy of both the M.C.202 and of the Italian military-industrial complex to provide more modern planes in sufficient numbers became obvious, but the writing on the wall was there well before.

'*Indubbiamente il tipo con motore in linea è da preferirsi*'[8]

In 1933, a ministerial decree established that air-cooled radial engines were the only type of engine to be fitted to newly-built Italian fighters. While the decision at the time had some sense, since radial engines were more powerful and efficient than in-line ones at this time, the unwanted result was also to inhibit the research and development effort in liquid-cooled in-line engines for mass production (with the exception of the numerically irrelevant and experimental engines for the *idrocorsa* series, which were handcraft products and one-offs).

In August 1936, shortly after the end of the Ethiopian War, drawing its inspiration from the comprehensive reorganisation and re-equipment undertaken by the *Reichsluftfahrtministerium* in Germany in 1933, the *Ministero dell'Aeronautica* launched a programme of wide-ranging improvements, both qualitative and quantitative, throughout the *Regia Aeronautica*, called *Programma R*, setting its completion date for the spring of 1938. The *Programma R* envisaged a *Regia Aeronautica* equipped with 3,170 planes by the second half of 1940, of which 750 would be fighters of a totally new design.

By early 1938, a generation of fighters of the so called '*Serie* 0', which had been designed with specifications set in 1935 and modified in 1936 were being tested in the framework of the ministerial competition for single-engined interceptors (with a radial engine, as that was virtually the only engine produced by Italian industry). The M.C.200 came out as the winner of the competition but one of the other competitors, the Fiat G50, was also ordered into production notwithstanding its mediocre performance in competition tests. The Macchi M.C.200, a sturdy and manoeuvrable plane, and the Fiat G50 were somewhat disappointing when compared to the contemporary fighters of other countries, such as for instance the Bf 109B that the Italians were fighting alongside in the ongoing Spanish Civil War, and though virtually obsolete, they were delivered to frontline units in 1939–40.[9] The culprit was in good measure the 870-hp Fiat A74 RC38 air-cooled radial engine that powered them both. The Fiat engine, with a total displacement of 31.25 litres, developed only 740 hp at take-off and 840 hp at 3,800 metres at a speed of 2,400 rpm. This engine, like all Italian aeronautical engines of the time, was not of national conception but was derived from the production under licence of foreign engines (English, American, or French).[10, 11] In particular, the A74 was derived from the American Pratt & Whitney R1830 Twin Wasp engine. The changes made by Italian technicians to the original American project in order to simplify production, significantly worsened the characteristics of the engine in terms of reliability and ease of maintenance, and the special alloys produced in Italy, which were necessary for the aero engines, were of substandard quality.[12]

The *Direzione Generale Costruzioni Aeronautiche* (DGCA) therefore gave the directives for another competition, to be launched on 5 January 1938 for a single-seat monoplane fighter, with a radial engine and a variable pace propeller and two 12.7-mm machine guns (projects were to be presented on 31 March 1938 and prototypes before 1 May 1939) to equip the *Regia Aeronautica* by mid-1940.[13] The competition proved inconclusive (as a result, it was decided to order 200 Fiat CR.42s, a rather outdated biplane that did not take part in the second competition), and yet a third call for tender—not a proper competition—with guidelines was published on 21 November 1938, which would lead to the production of the 202.

As the second competition for a fighter was opened, the DGCA on the very same date launched competitions for high-power in-line engines, with a horsepower output between 1,100 and 1,500.[14] They likewise decided, following the already well-established tradition of acquiring licences for re-elaboration and production of foreign engines, to obtain authorisation from Daimler-Benz to produce their DB601 engine, as an insurance policy should the national production bid fail or be insufficient. The move towards the in-line liquid-cooled engine was the consequence of realising that other air forces, such as the British, German, and French ones, seemed to be moving in that direction, and that the Italian fighters using the Fiat engine compared unfavourably with their liquid-cooled engined contemporaries such as the Hurricane I, Spitfire I and II, and Bf 109E. This change is to be attributed mostly to *Generale* Valle, and *Tenente Colonnello* Tondi of the 1° *Centro Sperimentale Aeronautico* of Guidonia, who wrote a memorandum about the necessity for the producers to propose airframes for in-line engines.

When the agreement was reached with the German firm in November 1939, not only was the licence obtained to produce the engine (DB601Aa), but also to import original engines (initially fifteen) that were needed to begin the delivery of the various planes that were to be motorised with it (not only the M.C.202, also the Re.2001, the Caproni Vizzola F.4, F.5bis, and F.7, the Breda 201 dive-bomber, etc.).[15, 16] 'The lack of a suitable engine led ... to the decision to purchase the licence from Daimler-Benz and entrusting its construction to the Alfa Romeo in the new plant in Pomigliano'.[17]

Mario Castoldi, the chief designer of Macchi, had come to the conclusion that the future was in in-line engines:

> ... undoubtedly the type with an in-line engine is to be preferred, given its smaller frontal section, which allows greater refinement much to the advantage of the overall characteristics of the aircraft. As we are necessarily moving towards engines of greater power, adopting the in-line engine appears indispensable, since it is not possible to achieve sufficient power and reduced frontal dimensions with the radial engine.[18]

The first six DB601 engines arrived in Italy in the second half of 1939, and in the spring of 1940, two DB601 engines arrived at the Macchi's Varese factory.

Castoldi fitted one DB601 in a modified M.C.200 airframe that kept the fighter's wings, landing gear and vertical tail and tailplanes, with a redesigned forward fuselage section. In August 1940, negotiations began for the purchase of Daimler-Benz engines for installation in the first batch of C.202s, and on 10 August, the prototype M.C.202 (MM445) powered by a DB601A-1 engine took to the air.

Still in August, Alfa Romeo, a well-established firm with an experienced workforce and a significant tradition of aeronautical engine production (of which many were licence models), was tasked with the production at its modern and efficient factory in Pomigliano d'Arco, which resulted, in the summer of 1941, in the delivery of the pre-series engines AR150 RC41s, built in Italy but with parts and precision machinery provided by Germany, and eventually with the production series engines (RA1000 RC411 Monsone and sub-version RA1000 RC411a) in 1942, which powered the Serie VII fighter onwards.

The initial production rate seems to have been of about thirty to forty engines per month, for a total of seventy-four engines delivered in 1941, not enough to motorise the fighters produced by Macchi and Breda more or less in that same timeframe.[19] Those were probably equipped with some of the 180 DB601A delivered by November 1941 (of a total of 419 engines delivered to Italy, but which were also used for other planes); later production increased to sixty to sixty-five engines per month, for a total production of perhaps 1,500 engines in the course of the war.[20,21] 'In 1943 for 1750 fighter planes [both M.C.202 and Re.2001, author's note] only 1000 engines were delivered, whereas the immediate need was for at least 2000 engines without counting the necessary reserves'.[22] Production was, in other words, insufficient compared to the needs of the *Regia Aeronautica*.

This scarcity was compounded by the limited capacity of Alfa Romeo to overhaul engines, to a maximum of about sixty engines per month; it needs to be remembered that a general overhaul of the engine was perhaps necessary every fifty hours of flight, and several operations of maintenance were necessary at about twenty-five hours. Engines in use in the punishing conditions of the African theatre required even more frequent maintenance. Ultimately, the use of domestically produced materials in the production of the Italian version of the engine resulted in lesser durability of some components, as compared to the German originals.

Eventually, tests performed on the two engines in the course of the war (probably at the *Officine Reggiane*) showed that the Alfa Romeo engine's power was inferior to the DB601, which coupled with a somehow heavier weight brought inferior performances from the planes using the Italian version of the engine.

RA 1000 RC411 Monsone Characteristics

Twelve-cylinder, four-stroke, direct-injection engine in inverted V-line with 60-degree angle, water-cooled; supercharged and equipped with cylindrical gear reducer. View from the rear, rotation of the crankshaft to the left, with that of the propeller to the right.

Each cylinder is equipped with four valves with camshaft control. Power is supplied by a Ducati-type fuel pump with gears FG3501 (corresponding to Graetzin ZD 500) or Nardi type 12 with vanes, the latter with greater capacity. The injection is supplied with an Iniex TPZ12 HM 100/11 pump or Bosch PZ12 HM with twelve inverted in-line cylinders equipped with an automatic system that regulates the flow rate according to the pressure and temperature of the air supply, as well as a stop device and deaerator commuter. The injectors are Iniex (corresponding to Bosch B94 M10) or Orange 9-2029B. The compressor is a single-stage centrifugal compressor equipped with a regulator—connected to a barometric capsule—which determines the flow rate of the pump: 0 up to 2,100 metres and then progressively growing up to the maximum, which is reached at about 7,000 metres.

The maximum pressure is 1.45 kg/cm^2, allowed for no more than one minute, and the normal recommended is 1.23 kg/cm^2. The ignition, controlled by a twin magnet Marelli MZM 12BR4 or Bosch ZM 12BR4 and using Marelli MR405 or Bosch DW240 ET8 candles with ceramic insulation, occurs in the following order: 1/8/5/10/3/7/6/11/2/9/4/12. Lubrication is guaranteed by a delivery pump and two double-gear recovery pumps while water cooling is served by a centrifugal pump that moves the water contained in the engine equal to 32 litres, to which anti-freeze and Shell oil or NP Nafta are added equal to 1.5 per cent.[23]

'*Un bell'aereo disarmato*'[24]

The evolutionary nature of the M.C.202 as compared to the M.C.200 and the underpinnings of air combat doctrine as seen by the *Regia Aeronautica* are revealed by the armament chosen for the Folgore. Like its predecessor, it was armed with two Breda-SAFAT 12.7-mm air-cooled, belt-fed machine guns, firing from a closed bolt, operated on the short recoil principle, which were placed on the forward fuselage, side by side on top of the engine, one slightly staggered ahead of the other to allow the placement of the ammunition boxes, which contained 400 rounds per weapon. They fired through the propeller disc, with propeller synchronisation—as the Macchi 202 had a three-bladed propeller, the average fire volume was 540–550 rounds per minute, though depending on the rpm, it could vary between 380 and 750.[25] This means about nine rounds per second per single MG, a fairly low rate of shooting.

In addition, provision was made for the installation of two air-cooled, belt-fed Breda SAFAT 7.7-mm, firing at 800–900 rounds per minute with 500 rounds per weapon, which could be mounted on each of the wings in a special housing between the rib 7 and 8, next to the landing gear rotation axle.

The 12.7-mm × 81-mm SR round of the Breda SAFAT was produced in several versions: a ball round, an armour piercing round, a (blue-tipped) incendiary armour piercing round, with a small charge of white phosphorus, a (red-tipped) tracer round, and a (yellow-tipped) explosive round, with a charge of 0.8 g of Pentrite, which exploded upon contact. This was the less ordinary round, as most other belligerent countries did not find it useful to have such a small explosive load on a relatively small calibre ammo like the 12.7. It was common usage in the *Regia Aeronautica* to load the ammunition belts with series of two ball, one tracer, one armour piercing, and one explosive cartridge.

The weapon aiming system was provided by a San Giorgio Type B reflector gunsight, introduced in 1939, which consisted of an optical system with a 60mm-diameter objective lens that projected two light rings and three dots on a translucid mirror slanted at 45 degrees. The three dots were used to estimate the range of the target (the interval between two of them representing a target of 7 metres length at 250 metres), and the two rings were to aim the guns for a deflection shot, the larger one to shoot at a target flying around 400km/h, the smaller one for a target flying at around 200 km/h, the pilot opening fire at the moment when the centre of the target crossed the circumference of the respective ring. It appears that already in 1940 it was known that the reflector could be problematic as its maker never remedied issues with the purity of the vitreous paste nor the quality of the lens production (obtained by frosting and not by moulding): a distortion of a few microns resulted in reflection failures of many metres.

The armament installation was completed by a pneumatic rearming system and round counter indicators in the cockpit.[26]

The reasons for the weak armament of the Macchi are various. Its roots were partially in the fact that the project had its origins in the specifications set for the '*Serie* 0' fighters' competition. In turn, those specifications showed up the level of technical development of the time. Given the relative novelty of cantilever wings with stressed skin and with relatively thin wing profiles, some care was exercised in placing weapons on the wings as concerns arose for the torsional stresses due to the firing of the weapon and the placing of them, which could have interfered with the spar structure:

> In designing the Macchi aircraft, up to the C.205N, the engineer Castoldi chose to graft the semi-wings to the fuselage by means of four hinges, instead of building the wing in one piece. The four comb-like hinges badly withstood extreme stress and required a complex construction process.[27]

The easiest solution structurally was to place the armament for shooting within the propeller's radius of rotation, even if the Italian fighters of the '*Serie* 0', especially the Macchi 200, had very high safety coefficients and legendary robustness (and consequent complexity and cost in building).

Wing-installed weapons also presented other engineering challenges, such as the freezing of the lubrication grease at high altitudes, which led to installing a heating system, in addition to the pneumatic systems necessary for the rearming of the MG bolts.

The possibility of arming the Macchi with a Mauser MGFF 20-mm cannon shooting through the propeller hub, for which the DB601A engine presented a tube in the propeller shaft, as in the Bf 109 E-3, was discounted as installing such a weapon and storing the ammunition would have implied the redesigning of the whole fuselage.

Looking for a solution for the clearly insufficient firepower, which became obvious in the encounter with more powerfully armed British fighters, the Folgore eventually received two Breda SAFAT 7.7-mm MGs (firing at 800–900 rounds per minute with 500 rounds per weapon), starting from series VII (produced from the beginning of May 1942), and the experimental placement of two Mauser MG151 20-mm cannons in underwing pods on a Macchi MM91974 of XII *Serie* in the spring of 1943. The test flights with the powerful but heavy Mausers, begun on 12 May 1943, increased the weight and drag, reducing the performance of the plane; the modification was made on only five specimens.

The additional problem was that the Breda SAFAT was not a particularly outstanding weapon, compared to the same of its class in use in enemy planes.

Breda based its original project on the Browning M2 machine gun, with several modifications, including the change of the cartridge from the US calibre 12.7 × 99-mm to the Italian 12.7 × 81-mm SR. For the 12.7, this choice entailed a reduction of propellant, which resulted in significantly lower muzzle velocities than other weapons of similar calibres, and considerably heavier ones (e.g. the energy of the Breda's round being 10,000 joules compared to 16,000–17,000 joules of the Browning). While the Breda was not *per se* an unreliable weapon, it had the worst weight-to-power ratio of all coeval machine guns mounted on Second World War aircraft. In comparison, the Japanese Ho-103, which was itself a derivative of the Breda, used the same licenced 12.7 × 81-mm ammunition, but was 6–7 kg lighter and had a fire rate of 800–900 rounds per minute—at least 20 per cent higher.[28]

Those two shortcomings made the SAFAT ineffective, though at the beginning of the conflict the inadequacy was less blatant, as the main adversaries of the Italian fighter were fighters that were somewhat inferior in some aspects, or bombers that were often not particularly robust.

Hurricanes, which were mostly equipped with the classic 8.303 machine guns could produce an impressive volume of fire since in a minute the eight weapons could fire up to 1,150 rounds per minute (weighing 10 grams at a speed of 700 m/s, compared to the Breda's weighing 38 grams at a speed of 760 m/s) The problem was that the small bullets fired could not carry enough incendiary or explosive to guarantee success, and also had insufficient penetration to defeat armour reliably, with some actually slowed down or blocked by the fuselage skin, as shown by a series of ground tests carried out by the British.[29, 30] Despite the fact that the weapons were aimed so as to have maximum effectiveness at a distance of 90–110 metres from the aircraft, a more effective shooting distance is often indicated for the 303 of 50–60 metres. The M.C.202 being a rather solid plane, with an armoured seat as standard equipment and a *blindovetro* (bulletproof glass) from the VII Serie, stood more than an adequate chance against the Hurricane.

The P-40C Tomahawk's armament of two .50-inch (12.7-mm) Browning AN/M2 'light-barrel' dorsal nose-mount synchronised machine guns and two .303 Browning machine guns in each wing was clearly superior to the M.C.202, and more so the P-40D Kittyhawk I's, which had two .50-inch (12.7-mm) guns in each wing, but the M.C.202 was overall a superior plane, even at parity of pilot skills.

Therefore the dissatisfaction of Italian M.C.202 pilots towards the fighter's armament was limited until the fighters equipped with 20-0mm guns appeared in the Mediterranean in March 1942, such as the Spitfire Mk VB with two Hispano-Suiza 20-mm cannon and four Browning 0.303-inch machine guns, which outclassed the M.C.202's armament, and even more so with the later appearance of heavy US four-engined bombers. *Tenente* Attilio Sanson, who flew the Folgore with the 22° *Gruppo*, against USAAF bombers, called it '*un bell'aereo disarmato*'.[31] Then it was clear that an increase in the number of weapons on board, or the installation of cannons, would have been necessary:

> With regard to the armament, the good quality of the Breda-SAFAT calibre 12.7 was confirmed, but we realized to our surprise that there were still only two weapons. As for the calibre and range of fire they were fine for fighters and light twin-engine planes, but against the four-engine bombers the need was felt to have three times the number of machine guns, or even better, to be able to count on a cannon with more effective fire power. I myself noticed this when I attacked a Liberator formation over Messina, I took a real beating, I got wounded and I succeeded only in getting the engine of one of those beasts smoking.... For example, we had to hit Wellington bombers at the wing joint, but it was always a difficult aircraft for our two meagre 12.7 even if it was not very fast. I remember my first real combat with the 202: I did it together with Valtancoli against a Wellington off the coast of Pantelleria. Well, the twin-engine bomber took at least 700 bullets while, flying very low over the sea, he defended himself strenuously and sped away at full throttle. Then, suddenly, while we were about to let him go because we were short of fuel, he banked and slid into the water.[32]

Both in the Italian and the British case, it is clear that wing MGs of small calibre, like the 7.7, were rapidly becoming obsolete, so it is not surprising that the installation of the Breda SAFAT 7.7 × 56-mm MGs in the wings in a few Macchis (in 1942) was not the answer; instead of adding more firepower, the modification simply increased the weight of the fighter by 100 kg.

An increase in the weight of the plane not corresponding to an increase in propulsion lowered the performance of the plane unacceptably as far as its manoeuvrability was concerned. Acrobatics was a key tactic for which the Italian pilots were trained, and which was also necessary to ensure to land the bullets on the target: the position of the two 12.7s on the fuselage undoubtedly allowed a more instinctive attitude when shooting even without the collimator, and a longer reach, compared to all wing-mounted weapons, which had a convergence point.

On the other hand, regardless of the relative hitting power of the 12.7 MGs, their number and low rate of fire forced the Italian pilots to place themselves on the tail of the adversary and shoot at close distance, with the least deflection possible, as they knew that they could send very few bullets flying towards a target flying across their collimator for a brief instant as opposed to one they tailed. The charge of the explosive projectiles of the 12.7, 0.8 g of Pentrite, was too small to make much effect, the reason for which incendiary bullets were often preferred in the hope of setting fire to fuel fumes, but to do so a sufficient number of them needed to land on the target. We have seen that the 303 was a rather weak round too, but the arrangement of eight wing MGs gave it a good capacity for deflection shots just from sheer volume of fire. Then again, the poor training of Italian pilots in shooting compounded the difficulty of performing deflection shooting.

'Il vero caccia sano, sicuro, senza sorprese'[33]

The M.C.202 was produced from mid-1941 until August 1943, a fairly short run. Moreover, already by September 1942, its improved successor, the M.C.205, started rolling out of the factories.

Production of the M.C.202 ended with the Armistice of 8 September 1943, and when it was restarted shortly after by the Germans, the last order of fourteen XIII *Serie* at AerMacchi and thirty-three V *Serie* at SAI Ambrosini was not fulfilled. Breda delivered perhaps sixty-one or sixty-two planes, all ordered before the Armistice, apparently of *Serie* XII.[34]

The all-metal *caccia intercettore diurno* M.C.202 was, as we said, an incremental plane compared to the M.C.200. It inherited most of its virtues, such as robustness, manoeuvrability, responsiveness, and light handling and some of its shortcomings, such as light armament. Nonetheless, it brought significant improvements that the pilots of the *Regia Aeronautica* were much in need of: engine power, an armoured seat, an enclosed cabin, a radio, a resilience to enter a flat spin, which was a feature of its predecessor when turning tight. The prototype Macchi fighter inherited the wings, undercarriage, and vertical and horizontal tail units of the M.C.200 with a different, tapered cell, made to accommodate the DB601A-1 engine. It is not so surprising, given these premises, that the production and testing of the plane proceeded speedily.

The M.C.202's fuselage structure was a semi-monocoque shell consisting of four profiled duraluminium beams and stringers with stamped duraluminium ovoidal formers, upon which a skin of superavional ultralight aluminium alloy was fixed with flush riveting. The structure, and the streamlining to reduce parasitic drag, were typical of Castoldi planes as we have illustrated above, which made the Macchi a very solid plane, able to survive quite substantial damage but also to perform extreme acrobatic manoeuvres, and high-speed diving (M.C.202's pilots experienced in a few instances the hitherto badly understood effects of compressibility).[35]

On the very front of the fuselage, there were four hinges for the engine bearer on the bulkhead of the cockpit, two in correspondence with the upper beams and two resting in correspondence with frontal longerons of the centre wing box structure. The engine bearers were of steel tubing for the Macchi prototype and for series I to III and later replaced by two forged elements of light alloy for the subsequent series.[36]

The engine mounted on the initial M.C.202s was the original DB601A-1 twelve-cylinder V-injection in-line, liquid-cooled engines with 1,175 hp at take-off at 2,500 rpm and around 1,000 to 1,120 hp at 2,400 rpm between 3,600 and 4,500 metres. Germany supplied 419 original engines, but in the summer of 1941, the AR150 RC41 engines started being available (built in Italy with German components and machinery) and later still, in 1942, the RA1000 RC411 Monsone (heavier, with 1,075 hp at take-off, and less hp at altitude) started being mounted on the Macchis of serie VII. The oil radiator was placed under the nose and its tank, with a capacity of 36 litres, was placed behind the engine; it was built in duraluminium with perforated diaphragms internally. The cooling liquid radiator was placed under the cockpit, with a capacity of 12 litres.

The propeller was the three-blade metal Piaggio P.1001 with variable pitch in flight and constant speed, with a diameter of 3.05 metres.

The wing structure owed much to the M.C.200, but presented some improvements. It was a cantilever monoplane with a biconvex aerofoil section, of decreasing thickness and depth towards the trailing edge, thus preventing the stalling that the Macchi M.C.200 was initially subject to. The wing was made in three parts, the centre wing box structure that was built integral with the fuselage, carrying the housing compartments of the main wheels, the outer wing fittings and the main fuel tank, and the two half-wings connected to the central wing box structure by means of high-resistance steel hinges at the extremities of the longerons. The span and surface of the left wing was slightly higher than the right one (it was 21 cm longer) to compensate for the propeller torque; the longer wing generated more lift and so compensated for what would have been the normal tendency to yaw to the left.[37]

The wing structure was made of two longerons with ribs made in profiled duraluminium, for a total of fifty-four, of which the first two per side were wider and stronger than the others. The wing skin was of superavional alloy plates, bolted to ribs and longerons with flush rivets. The wings' leading edges were removable from the landing gear position to the end, and were fixed to the front longerons by screws.

The trailing edge was instead occupied by the split flaps from the root to about half the length of the wing, and by the ailerons from there to the tip. The flaps were entirely metallic, being made of duraluminium ribs and steel tube longerons, covered with superavional skin, while the ailerons were of ribs made of a duraluminium profile and a longeron of three parts of steel tube connected by steel hinges with ball bearings, all covered with a canvas skin.

The cockpit presented some improvement as compared to that of the M.C.200, as it was enclosed, with a tilting canopy, hinged on the right side. The cockpit fairing protected the pilot in the event of a nose-over on landing, as did the specially reinforced windscreen, though it impeded to a degree rear vision, as apart from the prototype when it was made in glass, it was all metal in the production series.

A British report of a captured Macchi 202 describes the cockpit:

> The view from the cockpit is fair in all directions. The front three transparent panels are of triplex glass and the remainder of a material of the Perspex type. No rear-view mirror is fitted. The hood can be opened from either side by a separate release handle on each side or jettisoned by using both handles at once. The front panel of each of the side windows can be slid back if required. The cockpit is comfortable and fairly roomy and has plenty of headroom. Neither the seat nor rudder bar are adjustable [they were, actually]. The pilot is well protected by armour plate from astern and, in fact, to about 40 degrees off dead astern. He is provided with a bucket seat entirely constructed from a single piece of 8 mm armour, which stretches from his shoulders almost to his knees and comes well round the sides of his body. The armour plate seat appears to be handmade. In addition there is a headpiece of 7 mm armour and a small strip to cover the gap between the two. No bulletproof glass is used on this aeroplane.[38]

In fact, armoured glass was provided on the frontal windscreen from IV series, so the model examined is probably an earlier version.[39]

The pilot position consisted of a seat, adjustable in height and length, protected by a 44-kg shaped back armour.

Immediately behind the cockpit were the additional fuel tank, the fire extinguisher tank, the compressed air cylinder, the landing gear accumulator, and the accumulator of the flaps. In the rear part of the fuselage, there were on a single support the receiver-transmitter unit, the radio booster, and the modulator, and the radio direction finder.

The radio system was an *Allocchio Bacchini* B30 shortwave R/T, consisting of a receiver, transmitter and a *Bg42* direction finder receiver—a significant improvement as early war Italian fighters had only the receiving apparatus.[40] Controls for the radio were in the cockpit on the left side, and the plug for the headset. The radio set receiver was linked to an aerial, connected between an antenna mounted on the head protection bar behind the pilot headrest, and the empennage.[41, 42, 43]

A stick placed centrally between the pilot's legs controlled the ailerons and the elevators, through push-pull rods connected by ball bearings.

Rudder control was through a pedal bar with pedals hinged on the same lower central former upon which the centre stick was placed. Flaps were connected to the oleo-pneumatic system of the landing gear and actuated through a *Magnaghi* jack, up to a maximum angle of 45 degrees.

The control of the adjustable stabiliser was via cables, actuated by a hand-wheel on the left of the cockpit, up to an upward angle of attack of 1.45' upwards and 5.30' downwards.

The other controls in the cockpit were those of the engine, the throttle and the injection pump switch, both on the left side of the cockpit, the propeller pitch control, the oil and water radiators shut controls (on the lower left instruments panel), the landing gear control, and the brake control (placed on the centre stick).

On the centre stick was the trigger for the two 12.7 MGs, and, if the 7.7 wing MGs were mounted, also a selector with three positions: 'A' for firing the 7.7-mm weapons, 'C' for the 12.7-mm, '*Tutte*' for all weapons. The weapons were armed, reloaded, and unjammed pneumatically through the system connected with the compressed air tank, by a lever on the main instrument panel.

The centre stick could also be fitted with the control for the FM-62 OMI *Nistri fotomitragliatrice* camera, which could be fitted at the root of the left wing, and that was used for the training of pilots.

Engine starting was electric with controls (fuel injector and start button) on the right instrument panel. Alternatively, the engine could be started manually with an inertia system by a crank-operated starter, with an external port.

The cockpit was provided with an oxygen system with two tanks, and the *Sala* inhaler with the distribution tube was placed on the right side, close to the armoured seat. The system was notoriously unreliable and had to be replaced.[44]

The plane's electrical system provided energy for various systems (heating of the flying suit, propeller, aiming sight, heating of pitot tube, instruments panel, fuel pump, etc.).

The fuel system was constituted by a main fuel tank in the fuselage between the firewall bulkhead and the pilot's seat, with a capacity of 270 litres, two tanks of 40 litres each in the central section of the wing, and a reserve of 80 litres behind the pilot's seat, for a total capacity of 430 litres. The tanks were made of duraluminium plate, reinforced with internal diaphragms, and received a self-sealing treatment (*SeMaPe*, from the name of the chemical firm providing the treatment) that gave them the theoretical chance to withstand 12.7-mm calibre weapons. It appears that in addition to the main system, at least from M.C.202 AS/CB of series XI, there was the possibility of installing auxiliary underwing fuel tanks of 100- or 150-litre capacity, but the iconographic evidence of such installations is extremely rare, and it is possible that this arrangement was applied after the 8 September Armistice to the M.C.202 *cobelligeranti*.[45]

The main weapons, the two 12.7 SAFAT machine guns, were positioned at the front over the main fuel tank, fixed and parallel to the aircraft's centreline and attached to supports lying longitudinally and adjustable both vertically and horizontally. On these supports were mounted adjustable shock absorbers to allow the recoil of the weapon. The weapons were synchronised with the propeller. The SAFAT machine guns had 400 rounds each and were belt-fed, one with right feed and the other with left feed. Their ammunition boxes and the boxes to collect the spent cartridge cases and the ammunition belts were placed under the weapons and between them. This was typical of the Italian fighters of the time as metal was too precious to be expelled from the plane and the burden of the weight of the spent ammunition was therefore deemed acceptable.[46] To make space for the boxes, the right machine gun was placed slightly forward of the left one, though the flash cones of the machine guns were of different lengths to compensate for this arrangement. Two doors at the top of the engine cowling allowed access and maintenance of the weapons.

The 7.7-mm machine guns in the wings were mounted one on each side and were located in a special compartment between the ribs 7 and 8, just after the landing gear rotation shaft. The left one was fed on the left side, and the right one on the right. Each weapon was equipped with 500 rounds. The weapons could be collimated both laterally and vertically, and the arming and unjamming system was the same pneumatic one as on the fuselage MGs.

All the weapons were aimed by the reflector gun sight San Giorgio type B, placed slightly on the right above the main instrument panel, but iron sights were also available.

Macchi 202's empennages were basically unchanged since the M.C.200, and were of conventional elliptical shape. The horizontal and vertical stabiliser structure was made of two high-strength steel tube longerons, duraluminium ribs and skin cover, while the elevators and rudder structure were made of a high-strength steel tube longeron, duraluminium ribs and formers, but was covered with high-resistance linen cloth.

Likewise, the undercarriage was basically the same as that of the M.C.200. The landing gear was inward-folding with hydraulic action and equipped with oleo-pneumatic shock absorbers in the main wheel struts. The landing gear rotation shaft was hinged on the longerons of the outer wings, and each strut had a lifting jack. The tailwheel, retractable on the prototype, was fixed on production aircraft and partially enclosed by a fairing, though some aircraft lacked the rear fairing.

Production Models Series, Variants, and Prototypes

Series	Serial number	quantity	factory	delivery period
Prototype	445	1	AerMacchi	-
I	7859-7958	100	Breda	July 1941–April 1942
II	7709-7718	10	AerMacchi	May–June 1941
III	7719-7858	140	AerMacchi	June 1941–April 1942
IV	7409-7458	50	SAI	September 1942–June 1943
V	7959-8008	50	SAI	June–August 1943
VI	8339-8388	50	Breda	March–May 1942
VII	9023-9122	100	AerMacchi	April–September 1942
VIII	8081-8130	50	Breda	May–July 1942
IX	9389-9486	98	AerMacchi	September 1942–March 1943
X	9500-9599	100	Breda	July–November 1942
XI	9602-9751 6560-6609	200	Breda	November 1942–May 1943
XII	91803-91951[47]	150	Breda	May–September 1943[48]
XIII	91953-91993	55[49]	AerMacchi	March–August 1943
XIV	92003-92052	50[50]	SAI	-
XV	92053-92152	100	Breda	-
XVI	95950-96099	150[51]	Breda	-

The prototype M.C.202 (serial number MM445) first flew on 10 August 1940 at Lonate Pozzolo, and its virtues and superiority to its immediate predecessor M.C.200 were immediately clear.

Macchi's test pilot Guido Carestiato, an extremely competent former military pilot with a substantial experience both of acrobatic flight and of air combat, was enthusiastic about its performance. He described it as 'the true fighter, sound safe, reliable'.[52] *Maggiore* Luigi Bianchi, who had the opportunity to test the M.C.202 on behalf of the *Stato Maggiore dell'Aeronautica*, commented:

> Very easy take-off. Flight behaviour: very stable, safe plane, perfectly manageable in every position. Easier to pilot than the MC200 because of its better aileron compensation (speed attained from 350 to 600 km/h). At low speed (from 350 to 230 km/h) the aircraft is perfectly controllable if it is well piloted. Violent manoeuvres cause significant shaking in the tail and the aircraft straightens or tends to tip over (sometimes) on the right, compensating however with the aileron for this irregularity. Spin

> is regular both when spontaneous and controlled. Very easy descent and landing with a very well balanced aircraft.[53]

The DB601A-1 engine, developing 1,175 hp, pushed the plane to 596 km/h at 6,000 metres and enabled it to reach that altitude in six minutes and twenty-six seconds. Its responsiveness and agility were excellent, equal to the M.C.200.

Shortly after the first flight, the M.C.202 was sent to the *Primo Centro Sperimentale* (First Experimental Centre) of Guidonia for further flight testing, and subsequently to the *Secondo Centro Sperimentale* (Second Experimental Centre) at the Furbara firing range where the plane was confirmed to be a stable and reliable gun platform.[54]

The *Ministero dell'Aeronautica* issued an immediate instruction for series production of 150 fighters to AerMacchi, which was formalised with a letter of 4 November 1940 (which constituted Series II and III, MM7709–7718 and 7819–7858), and was followed immediately by another request (Series VII, 100 planes MM9023 to 9122). A licenced production scheme envisaged the setting up of two separate production lines with Breda, in Sesto San Giovanni (Milan), with the placing of an order on 1 November for 100 planes (Series I, MM7859–7958) and with SAI Ambrosini, at Passignano (Perugia), with an order on 5 November for fifty planes (Series IV, MM7409–7458) and on 21 December a further fifty (Series V, MM7959–8008). The first Macchi, MM7709, Series II, produced by AerMacchi, was delivered in May 1941, just eight months after signing the first production contract, demonstrating the general soundness of the project and its evolutionary nature from an already tested design such as the M.C.202.[55] One month later, in June 1941, the first Series III, still produced by AerMacchi, rolled out of the factory, and in July, the Series I produced by Breda. SAI Ambrosini started delivering their Series IV much later, in May 1942.

The M.C.202 was built in thirteen production series, and saw relatively limited modifications in the course of its production span. It is important to underline that the concept of series refers to orders placed with the various companies, while modifications to the plane did not necessarily correspond to different series, as many Macchis were retrospectively fitted with modifications:

> During its production cycle, the C.202 underwent 116 technical modifications; many of these involved marginal details (the diameter of certain bolts, the reinforcement of the nailing, etc.), while some were more significant (fitting of armoured glass, installation of wing weapons, stabilizer with compensated elevator, etc.). Each change was entered

on a special 'Proposal Form' which accurately described the changes to be carried out and became operative after the designer's approval. It is interesting to underline two points:

1) The changes were classified according to three categories: A, B and C. Those of type A were to be made, both to all the newly produced planes as well as those already in service, by the personnel of the producer firms; those of type B, as well as on new aircraft, were to be installed also on the previous ones when they were sent for repair and overhaul; those of type C did not apply retroactively. As an example, the modification no. 74 'Application of armoured glass to the windscreen' was of type A, the number 65 'Cooling box for petrol pump' was of type B, while the number 60 'tailwheel of D type' was classified C.

2) The application of the changes almost never coincided with the start of a new series. In reality the various series distinguished the successive production orders, whilst they did not mark the introduction of particular changes in construction or fitting out: in practice they had a more administrative meaning than a technical one.

The 'Proposal Form' indicated, from time to time, the Military Serial Number starting from which the change was to be installed, giving specific instructions to each of the three manufacturers: AerMacchi, Breda, SAI Ambrosini. In fact there were no differences from the point of view of construction between the aircraft of the three companies: only the camouflage finish, interpreted slightly differently by the painters of Varese, Sesto S. Giovanni and Passignano sul Trasimeno, allowed their identification at a glance. On the contrary, efforts were made to ensure perfect interchangeability between the components. To this end, planes called 'Arlecchini' were planned, the product of the assembling of parts coming from different assembly lines. Only one Harlequin is known 'AerMacchi-Breda (MM9415)'; of others, if there were any (even a triple 'Arlecchino' AerMacchi-Breda-SAI was planned), no documentary trace has survived.[56]

Prototype M.C.202

The sole M.C.202 prototype was built using many of the C.200's components, including its landing gear, vertical tail and tailplanes, the two 12.7-mm machine guns, and the asymmetrical wing. Those were mated to an all-new fuselage, considerably more slender and aerodynamic, with a lowered upper fuselage decking without the distinctive 'hump' of its predecessor. It was powered by an imported DB601A-1 engine developing 1,175 hp, sitting on a steel tubing castle characteristic of the initial models of the plane. The prototype's configuration included a partially glazed roll-bar structure, a retracting tail-wheel and a short compressor air intake. It also had no air scoops on the engine cowling and no radio antenna. When it first flew on 10 August 1940, it was unpainted, apart from the green primer on the engine cowling, without the military serial and the type designator, as at that moment it was still the product of a private venture of the manufacturing company. When it was tested in Guidonia in the autumn of 1940, it received the camouflage painting in the three-tone scheme previously used on the majority of the Macchi C.200s (the 'poached egg' blotched pattern), and the set of insignia typical of the *Regia Aeronautica*: the *fascio* roundel on the side just before the cockpit, the white rudder cross with the national insignia, the model designator on the tailplane (Aer.Macchi C.202) and the military serial (MM445) below the horizontal stabilizers, all in light blue. By now the fighter showed some small modifications, such as a longer air intake for the supercharger and nose scoops on the side of the engine cowling.

Series I

A total of 100 aircraft were built at the Breda factory between July 1941 and March 1942 (MM7859–7958). These aircraft presented a long air intake for the supercharger and the rear cockpit glazing was replaced with alloy sheet. The retractable tailwheel was replaced with a fixed unit with fairings and the welded engine mount was replaced with a forged one. The initial radio mast was of the stub type. The planes of series I rolled out of the factory after those of series II and in part simultaneously to those of series III, produced by Macchi. Those aircraft operating in the North African theatre, which received the tropicalisation kits introduced on the series III produced by Macchi, presented a camouflage of dark sand colour (*nocciola chiaro*, pale walnut) with olive green spots, whose shape, distinctive of the whole Breda production, was called '*serpentelli*' (little snakes).

Series II

Series II (MM7709–7718) planes presented the same characteristics as the series I, though they were the actual initial production, M.C.202 MM7709 being the first one of the production series. Some, but apparently not all, of the planes of *Serie* II and III still presented the steel tubing castle for the engine.[57] Those ten planes were built by Macchi in April to May

1941. At least two aircraft of this series, MM7711 (code 378-4, which was in service in the 378ª *Squadriglia* CT) and MM7712 (originally code 97-2, 97ª *Squadriglia*, 9° *Gruppo*, until the end of 1941, then code 168-2, 168ª *Squadriglia*, 16° *Gruppo*, 54° *Stormo*, until at least the first half of 1942, and then probably 377-1, in service with the 377ª *Squadriglia Autonoma*, perhaps one of the three M.C.202s received in February 1943) were M.C.202 RF photoreconnaissance variants with a camera *macchina fotoplanimetrica* AGR 90 placed vertically behind the pilot instead of the radio, easily distinguishable by the lack of the antenna mast.[58] They retained the camouflage painting in the three-tone 'poached egg' scheme previously used on the majority of the Macchi C.200s, (the blotched pattern), and the set of *Regia Aeronautica* insignia (*fascio* roundel, rudder cross, white recognition band behind the cockpit). The model designator on the tailplane was in black and the military serial below the horizontal stabilisers in light blue. All the planes were delivered with a yellow noseband, as prescribed by the summer 1941 regulation that remained in force until October 1941.

Series III

Series III was built by Macchi from May 1941 until April 1942 (MM7719–7858). These 140 C.202 aircraft introduced changes necessary for desert conditions, including a sand filter, *presa d'aria dinamica antisabbia Corbetta*, fitted to the supercharger air intake. The aircraft so equipped were designated C.202AS (*Africa Settentrionale*). Virtually all M.C.202s produced were fitted or retrofitted with the AS filter, and the filter became standard on all operational fronts.[59]

Cooling vents in the machine-gun covers and a cockpit air intake were also added. A single aircraft, M.C.202 MM7768, was fitted in late 1941 with a coolant radiator directly under the engine, the idea being to simplify maintenance and to eliminate long and vulnerable pipes, but it was deemed to cause an unacceptable drag and so the modification was dropped.

Planes of this series started also to receive the radio mast of the longer type. One aircraft in this series, MM7844, was produced in 1942 with a fairing on each wing's attack edge to accommodate two AVIA film cameras. The purpose of this installation was to film combat scenes to be provided to newsreel and other propaganda outlets.[60] Another fighter, MM7727 (code 73-10, in service with the 73ª *Squadriglia*, 9° *Gruppo*, 4° *Stormo* CT), was built in the RF photo reconnaissance version.

Those fighters presented the usual 'poached egg' three-tone camouflage scheme until September 1941, and those produced after October 1941 were probably already delivered without the yellow noseband on the front, while those in service might have had it painted over, though those Macchis of the 4° *Stormo* and 1° *Stormo* operating in the North African theatre briefly received instead a white band.

In the summer of 1941, new regulations were issued for the painting of the fighters and were applied to those planes produced from September onwards; those planes presented a uniform dark olive green livery. Those Macchis already delivered in the AS version presented the camouflage for deployment in Africa—that is a dark sand colour (*nocciola chiaro*, pale walnut) with olive green spots whose shape, distinctive of the Macchi production, was called '*cuoricini*' (little hearts). Some thirty Macchi produced between February and April 1942 (almost all of which ended up with the 378ª *Squadriglia*, with the exception of very few to the 4° *Stormo*) received instead a scheme of *nocciola chiaro* spots over the dark olive green livery, while the few produced at the end of April 1942 (MM7851–7858) reverted to the AS scheme, but with spots of the '*serpentelli*' type. The model designator on the tailplane and the military serial below the horizontal stabilisers were light blue.

Series IV

These fifty aircraft (MM7409–7458) built by SAI Ambrosini between November 1941 and May 1942, presented the same characteristics as the late Series III Macchis.

Series V

Fifty machines constructed by SAI Ambrosini (MM7959–8008) between May 1941 and July 1942. Early examples were similar to the series IV aircraft, while late-build examples had modifications similar to the series VII. A *San Giorgio* C reflector gunsight was also fitted to replace the B model.

Series VI

Fifty aircraft (MM8081–8130) were built by Breda in the spring of 1942.

Series VII

The 100 M.C.202 of the *Serie* VII (MM9023–9122) presented perhaps the most significant changes in all the production cycle of the fighter. This series was produced between April and July 1942 and saw a substantial, if unsuccessful, increase in the weapon capabilities of the aircraft, with the introduction of a Breda-SAFAT 7.7-mm. This did little to increase overall firepower, but it did increase the take-off weight and adversely affected the aircraft's performance, so that pilots often had the wing guns removed in the field. Other modifications included a *blindovetro* armoured glass panel placed on the windsreen and additional armour plating aft of the pilot's seat. From mid-1942, a new 'D' type tailwheel was also fitted. The fighters of this series were the first to be powered by the RA1000 RC41-I engine, which had reached sufficient levels of production, rather than the imported DB601A-1. Some aircraft of this series, MM9115 and 9916, sported the fairings on each wing's attack edge to accommodate two AVIA film cameras.[61] The machines of this series sported the definitive version of the AS camouflage scheme, in *nocciola chiaro* with olive green rings, whose shape, distinctive of the Macchi production, was called '*anelli di fumo*' (smoke rings), which characterised also the 140 planes of the series IX and XIII. The model designator on the tailplane and the military serial below the horizontal stabilizers were light blue.

Series VIII

Fifty Breda-manufactured C.202s (MM8339 to MM8388) were built between March and July 1942. Twelve of those planes were sent in September 1942 to Russia to beef up the 21° *Gruppo*, which distributed three M.C.202s to each of its 4 *Squadriglie* (356ª, 386ª, 361ª, and 382ª *Squadriglia*); these were camouflaged in the typical Breda AS pattern with '*serpentelli*', but presented yellow wingtips, fuselage band, spinner, and noseband, which were distinctive to this theatre of operations, already painted in the factory. Apart from those insignia common to all Axis fighters on the Eastern Front, they also received two white triangles on the upper and lower surface of the wings, starting from the attack angle and pointing back.

Series IX

A total of 100 aircraft built by Macchi (MM9389–9490) rolled off the assembly lines from September 1941 until February 1942. Some aircraft of this series, MM9405, 9406, 9425, and 9426, sported the fairings on each wing's attack edge to accommodate two AVIA film cameras.[62]

Series X

A total of 100 machines produced by Breda (MM9500–9601) between July and September 1942.

Series XI

A total of 150 aircraft (MM9602–9753) built by Breda from November 1942 until April 1943. Minor modifications to late series XI aircraft included a new horizontal stabiliser to compensate for the flutter effect and the relocation of the *Venturi* tube from the underside of the fuselage to the starboard side of the aircraft beneath the cockpit.[63] From the series XI onwards, a plumbing system was fitted for drop tanks of 100 or 150 litres, though those were rarely used, and two bomb racks for 50-, 100-, or 160-kg bombs; this version of the fighter took the name of M.C.202 AS/CB (*cacciabombardiere*, fighter bomber).

Series XII

These 150 aircraft (MM91803–91952) were similar to the C.202 series XI (late) machines and were assembled by Breda between May and August 1943. Not all the aeroplanes of this series were completed, apparently eighty-two being on order but not delivered (five were ready but not sent to units, when the circumstances of the Armistice halted the production). To increase the unsatisfactory firepower of the fighter, especially when coming up against heavy US bombers, a single aircraft, MM91974, was fitted with two underwing gondolas for 20-mm Mauser MG 151/20 aircraft guns with 200 rounds per weapon—this version was called M.C.202EC. The problems that had emerged with the installation of the 7.7-mm MGs in the wings—increased drag, weight, and stress on the outer wings' hinges, decreased manoeuvrability—were even more in evidence when this variant was tested from 12 May 1943 onwards. Another four aircraft received this modification, but the modification was basically rejected by the *Regia Aeronautica* fighter pilots.[64] Of the eighty-two series XII, not yet produced, sixty-one or sixty-two were delivered after the Armistice when the Breda factory was under German control, before the bombing of the factory on 30 April 1944 put it definitively out of commission. Of those, twelve went to *Zrakoplovstvo Nezavisne Države Hrvatske* (Air Force of the Independent State of Croatia), eight to Germany, and none to the ANR (*Aeronautica Nazionale Repubblicana*).

Series XIII

These fifty aircraft (MM91953–92002) produced by Macchi were the last production series C.202s built during the war, from April until August 1943. They incorporated the same modifications made to (late) *Serie* XI machines. They also sported a small air intake placed immediately ahead of the windscreen. Not all the aeroplanes in this series were completed, some probably being in construction or under test when the political and military circumstances halted production.

M.C.204

The M.C.204 was a paper project of Castoldi based on the same type of aircraft cell on which was installed the DB601 engine, which eventually led to the creation of the M.C.202, but in this case with the installation of an Isotta Fraschini Asso L121 RC40. Known simply as 'C.202 Isotta Fraschini', after the production of the M.C.205, the project was later renamed M.C.204, to occupy the number that remained free.

M.C.205V (MC.20S)

These aircraft were the result of the conversion of the M.C.202 to the M.C.205 *Veltro* standards, and were born of the perilous state of the *Regia Aeronautica* after the armistice. The southern co-belligerent aviation had only thirty-seven *Veltros* available, which, after a few months of military operations, in the spring of 1944, were reduced to nine functioning machines. Wrecked or incomplete M.C.202 cells were quite abundant at all South Italian airports and therefore specialists made 'handcrafted' conversions from the M.C.202 to the M.C.205. The conversion was complex but possible to achieve, requiring the installation of an RA1050 RC58 engine on the fuselage of the Folgore. The *Regia Aeronautica* decided to entrust the reconstruction to the *Servizio Tecnico Caccia* and *Aeronautica Sannita* of Benevento, which, between June 1944 and June 1946, transformed at least twenty-one to twenty-four cells of Folgore, bringing them up to the *Veltro* standard, albeit with non-standard armament, consisting predominantly of two or four 12.7-mm guns, due to the reduced availability of 20-mm guns for installation.[65]

The conversions of the Folgore to the M.C.205 continued after the end of the war until 1948 by AerMacchi itself, as the Italian Air Force decided to update and standardise its fighters to *Veltro* standards and to roll out the order from the Egyptian Air Force for eighty M.C.205 fighters, which used them in the Arab-Israeli War of 1948.

Aeronautica Lombarda Assalto Radioguidato

The *Aeronautica Lombarda Assalto Radioguidato* (radio-controlled attack) was the result of the research carried out with the S.79 ARP, but where the control plane was to be a M.C.202. This was to guide to the target the AR drone, originally a S.79 ARP, and later a specially built large single-engined aircraft, the AR4, employing a Fiat A80 engine recovered from decommissioned BR.20s, and flight controls from an S.79s. The drone had a simple wooden structure, aimed at minimum production costs. Wings and empennages were squared and rather large, to give the drone good stability in flight. In the fuselage, there was a large inventral compartment housing the explosive charge consisting of one or two 1,000-kg bombs; exactly above, was the cockpit of the pilot where the radio-receiver complex was housed. Once the pilot performed the take-off, he discarded the landing gear to improve the aerodynamic performance of the drone, set up the receiver for the cruise flight, and then abandoned the drone by jumping by parachute.

At the end of 1942, an order for the construction of a small series of six AR was placed with the *Aeronautica Lombarda* of Cantù, which enjoyed a good reputation for its experience in the construction of wooden structures for yachts. In November 1942, a contract was signed for the supply of a prototype and five examples of a pre-series.

Meanwhile, the M.C.202 control plane equipped with a SAFAR S150 radio, was tested in the spring of 1943, by *Capitano* Giulio Martini with a S.79 ARP:

> I tried the MC202 radio control plane that Montuschi and Fermonte had already prepared for me. Flying a few kilometres to the rear of the radio-controlled SM.79, in order not to overtake it I had to lower the undercarriage, open the flaps a little and decrease the throttle. Nothing serious. In the event of actual use, however, the two aircraft would have been escorted by fighters. Nevertheless, after the expected impact on the

> target of the SM.79 loaded with bombs, the MC202 would obviously have been able to defend itself and disengage better than the Cant Z.1007.[66]

The first flight of the AR4 took place on 13 June 1943 and then it was transferred to Guidonia to the *Direttorato Studi ed Esperienze* of Guidonia where other flight tests showed the soundness of the drone; the supply order was then confirmed and mass production started.[67] In August, the second unit was ready for testing, while the remaining four were still under construction. The core of the apparatus though, the radio-receiver complex, was not yet ready at the time of the Armistice. The takeover by German military authorities resulted in the suspension of the programme and its subsequent definitive cancellation.

Apparently at the end of the conflict, among the documents requisitioned by the Allies and returned after the war to the Italian government, a drawing was found that showed a combination between an AR and a Macchi fighter M.C.202 similar to the Mistel-type configuration developed by the *Luftwaffe*.

6

The Men Who Flew the M.C.202: Training and Organisation

'*E se la morte non vuole andar via, girale intorno e fai acrobazia*': Italian Pilots' Training and Tactics[1]

The history of the Macchi M.C.202 is also a story of its pilots. Who piloted the Macchi 202? What sort of training did they receive? What doctrine did they adopt? How did they put it into practice?

It is somewhat baffling that a country offering to the world the foremost theoreticians of air power such as Douhet, and where the debate on strategic and tactical aviation was so lively (not only about the former's vision, but also those of Mecozzi, Rougeron, etc.), came to face the conflict so inadequately prepared and with so many misconceptions about how the war would be fought.[2, 3] This happened notwithstanding the ample experience accumulated in the conquest of Ethiopia, and more importantly, in the Spanish Civil War (though, admittedly, the Spanish Civil War turned out for many countries to be somewhat of a poisoned chalice in terms of lessons learnt, as far as both the deployment of weapons and of air power are concerned).

Those misconceptions had a significant impact on what planes were deemed necessary to keep the *Regia Aeronautica* ready for combat, what sort of training the pilots needed, and what sort of doctrines of deployment were to be adopted.[4]

As in most other countries, pilot training was onerous and lengthy, as it passed through multiple qualification phases with aircraft provided with intermediate flight characteristics, to ensure a gradual transition from training planes to front-line fighters. At the beginning of the war in 1940, the *Regia Aeronautica* had a total of 5,440 pilots in service, but of those, only about 2,000 were combat-ready—not a very large number; as the conflict erupted and expanded, the traning schools, the *Accademia Aeronautica* and the rather small pool of the *Riserva*, could not cover the losses and the increased needs. Moreover, if morale was relatively high, the preparation for combat was inadequate, lacking proper shooting training and night and instrumental flying skills, both because of the unsatisfactory set-up of the flying schools and because of the poor instrumentation on board Italian aircraft. This also held true for the M.C.202 pilots, who came either from the flying schools or from the *Accademia Aeronautica*.[5]

Training

In line with the pattern of most other air forces of the time, pilots of the *Regia Aeronautica* could be either officers (*Ufficiali*) or NCOs (*Sottoufficiali*). In the system established in 1938 by the *Ispettorato Generale delle Scuole*, officers could be either professional soldiers (*Ufficiali in Servizio Permanente Effettivo* or SPE), coming from the *Accademia Aeronautica* at the Royal Palace of Caserta or *Ufficiali di Complemento* (short-commission officers called up by draft), trained at the 9 *Scuole di Volo di 1° Periodo* and then at the 7 *Scuole di Volo di 2° Periodo*.[6]

The bulk of the *Regia Aeronautica* pilots were *Ufficiali di Complemento* and *Sottoufficiali*, but the main difference between all categories was the theoretical component of the curriculum, as the practical part, at the various flying schools, was quite similar for all. The *Ufficiali in Servizio Permanente Effettivo* at the *Accademia Aeronautica* followed a curriculum of three years, and about 200–300 pilots per year were breveted. The *Ufficiali di Complemento* on the other hand could become part of the permanent officer corps—for instance, as a result of meritorious conduct in combat.

After completing his basic military training, the flight training of a *Regia Aeronautica* pilot was based on two phases, *Periodi* and the *Scuola di Specialità* (Specialised Flying School).

The *1° Periodo* flying school turned the aspiring pilot into an actual breveted *pilota militare d'aeroplano* (military pilot). The *1° Periodo* was before the second half of the 1930s left mainly to civilian flying schools, but was thereafter concentrated in specific military schools, though having previous civil flight experience remained a preferential route to the pilot's curriculum. In the case of *allievo ufficiale pilota di complemento* Pier

Paolo Paravicini (who was already a pilot in civilian life), the *1° Periodo*'s course, starting in June 1941 at the military airport of Pescara, consisted of the following:

> ... dual controls flight on the Breda 25 and after four hours I am taking off alone. The flight schedule includes: turns, airfield laps, double laps, altitude climbs, navigation, reconnaissance for a total of thirty hours. Then I switch to another Ba.25, a biplane built for acrobatics with a radial engine (Alfa Romeo D2) with two carburettors for inverted flight. I use the Breda to spin, right and left, as well as the first acrobatic figures, full looping, then right and left wing loop, tonneau and upside down with both right and left wing.[7, 8]

Fighter training programmes were never particularly rich in flying hours compared to other countries' programmes. In March 1939, for example, sixty hours of flight time were necessary to complete the *1° Periodo* and obtain the brevet of *pilotamilitare*, which allowed the passage to the *2° Periodo*. Of those, thirty could be on the Breda Ba.25 biplane or on the AVIA FL.3 (that became available in October 1940).[9, 10] The remainder was often divided between several aircraft types—twenty hours on the SAIMAN 202 (from October 1940) and ten hours of aerobatics on either the CANSA C.5, SAIMAN 200, or the Caproni Ca.164, or on the IMAM Ro.41.[11, 12, 13] RA pilots Galbusera and Paravicini experienced: 'I am promoted to move on to a Ro.41, an aircraft conceived as a light fighter.... On October 10th 1941 I give an official demonstration of acrobatics and I become a military aeroplane pilot'.[14] Later on, by mid-1942, the *1° Periodo* flight hours increased to eighty-five.[15] It is significant that the *Ufficiali in Servizio Permanente Effettivo* came out of the Accademia Aeronautica with seventy-two hours of flying, but spread over three years, compared to the sixty hours of the *Ufficiali di Complemento*, who flew in a much more concentrated period of time.

It took the trainees roughly nine months to reach this point in the syllabus and get certification; with this, the trainees would be posted to one of the *Scuole di 2° Periodo* for advanced pilot training, where they would pilot the more powerful and challenging Fiat CR.30 or CR.32 biplane fighters, for an initial total flight time of twenty hours in 1939, increased to forty-four in 1941, fifty-six in 1942, and sixty-five in 1943.[16]

On the *2° Periodo* and the *Scuola di Specialità* for fighters, Paravicini recollects:

> ... having gone through the first brevet period, I became a sergeant cadet pilot ... the pilots' environment is made up of many veterans from Spain

> who were sent to Gorizia to rest and to pass on, as instructors, their war experience to us raw recruits. The aeroplanes are all, except the Cr.32, modern combat planes ... I am starting the new acrobatic programme solo on the Cr.32. It is an exciting biplane, with exceptional manoeuvrability features, forgiving even in extreme manoeuvres; especially in the first flights in an acrobatic pair. In order to perform the acrobatic pair well, the trainee must position himself three metres to the side of the patrol leader, with his wing slightly inside the area between the wing and the tail of the patrol leader. This position must be maintained at all costs, otherwise you risk a collision ... the course continues with patrols of two and three. At the end of each flight cycle on a given aeroplane an acrobatic patrol programme is run with five aeroplanes in wedge formation and in single file, that is one after the other.... Once I have finished the prescribed number of hours on a Cr.32, the course on biplanes ends. The time has come to prove that one is a fighter pilot able to enter the operational units.[17]

In the course of this curriculum, the first rounds are fired at hydrogen-inflated tethered balloons, part of the weapon training. Both trainees at Gorizia, Gianfranco Galbusera transitioned from CR.42 to his monoplane fighter (the Fiat G50) after a total of 100 hours of training.[18] So did Paravicini who had little fondness for this problematic fighter:

> ... the beginning of this course is very difficult. Acclimatization flights with a series of more complicated manoeuvres for us, coming from experience of the biplanes: the lowering of the landing gear, use of the flaps, the speed of gliding and landing ... after a few hours of acrobatics on the field with much fear due to the risk of autorotation ... we perform the whole regulation programme [of acrobatic pairs], looping, tonneau, imperial [half looping, when reaching the top of a tonneau after which you are in level flight], reverse turn, left and right ... finally to finish the course one must move on to the MC200, which has no two-seater versions and therefore one takes off immediately on the single seater ... we are training in an acrobatic team of five ... all's well. FINISHED. I have become a military pilot and officer. It is October 1942.[19]

At the end of this phase, being awarded their crowned eagle badge, the *Sergenti Allievi Ufficiali Piloti* became *Sottotenenti Piloti* at the officers' schools, while the *Primi Avieri* became *Sergenti Piloti* at the NCO pilots'schools, like for instance Giuseppe Ruzzin, still at Gorizia, a few years earlier in 1936.[20]

Short-commission officers and NCOs completed this training in about fourteen months and then transferred to an operational unit, where they received acrobatic and combat training on the planes they were to fly in the front line, about thirty to fifty hours of aerobatics, and an intensive series of simulated combat situations (*Finta Caccia*), spread over a period of about four months. This final part of the syllabus was not always made available, at least to the same extent, to all novice pilots, as it wholly depended on the resources of the operational unit and the leadership and skills of the individual squadron commander. When the war started, the refining of novice pilots put an excessive burden on operational squadrons, for the wear and tear of the machines, the commitment of instructor staff and for fuel consumption.

Combat tactics in a strict sense were not really taught—though combat experience was transmitted by combat-experienced or veteran pilots and through simulated combat situations.[21] In 1941, six fighter *Gruppi Complementari* were established, to which some of the newly breveted pilots would be assigned after the *Scuola Specialità* and would complete their training next to experienced pilots, and undertake low-risk operational missions, such as air defence for the fighter units' bases and patrols.[22]

In the case of Paravicini, at Rome Ciampino Airport, between October and December 1942:

> In the Gruppo complementare of 51° Stormo caccia I immediately began military training first with the Macchi 200 and after four to five hours I took off on the famous MC202, a first-line monoplane fighter.... Acrobatics first of all, forget the autorotation, reach the limits of the aeroplane's possibilities at all altitudes. The MC202 really is a wonderful machine, it manoeuvres as one wants ... now one has to get used to the high altitude, 5–6000 metres and in addition make simulated aerial combat, fly in combat formation, get used to keeping looking back to see if anyone is coming on your tail. Performing rapid overturns, paying attention to the speed limits in nose-dives.... Heated flight suit, oxygen mask, gloves, helmet, radio, life jacket, padded boots, flare gun strapped to the leg, fluorescence bag (dye for identifying the pilot in the water) strapped to the other leg, lifebuoy under the seat and parachute. Piloting with all this kit on is not easy.... Everything that is normal training for a fighter pilot is a surprise to begin with, nobody has ever told me anything, for example that you are obliged to be lumbered like this, under the August sun in Africa or Sicily, perhaps in the cockpit with more than 40° waiting to scramble on alarm, and then get to make a cruise flight at 5–6000 metres where you find outside temperatures of -15 or -20.... I am training myself at 8000m, I have to run through the acrobatic programme, turn as tightly as possible while trying not to lose

> altitude. With our instructors we do mock high-altitude combat. We fly to the Furbara range to carry out firing exercises with weapons on board ... our flight activity continues with a very tough programme. Mock combat at high altitude (it starts at 8,500 and then ends at 1,500) and increasingly tight turns, during which you often see black for a moment: this training is very important for us as both Brits and Americans turn tighter than us.[23]

The curriculum of the *Ufficiali in Servizio Permanente Effettivo* was different, as it took three years to train permanent officers at the Academy of Caserta and the flying school at Capua airport, north of Naples, but their training path was not privileged compared to the *Ufficiali di Complemento*. On the contrary, the cadets who went to war in 1943 received a total of 128 hours of training, of which only thirteen hours were of combat training.[24]

There are a number of significant conclusions to be drawn from the way the *Regia Aeronautica* structured its training programme.

In the first place, it was short of flight hours: this aspect was blatant in the pre-war period (when the enormous expenses incurred in keeping the *Regia Aeronautica* operational, first in Ethiopia and then in Spain, diverted resources from training) and the corrective measures adopted—with the increase in total training hours for the *1°* and *2° Periodo* from eighty in 1939 to 104 in 1941 to 150 in 1943, including about thirty on combat planes—paled in comparison to other air forces.

In September 1939, German training consisted of about 240 hours, including about ninety on actual front-line fighters, while a British pilot received about 200 hours in the same period, including about fifty on combat models. While the German fighter training programme saw a decrease in flight hours (210 and fifty in October 1942 to 175 and twenty-five in July 1943 to 130 and twenty in July 1944) as a consequence of the deterioration of the situation, the Allied forces intensified their programmes steadily until the end of the war: the British, 340 and seventy-five hours in October 1942, 330 and eighty in July 1943, and 320 and ninety in July 1944; and the Americans 270 and seventy-five, 310 and 120, even 390 and 150 in the last period of the Second World War.

When the war started, the reduction in fuel allocations to flight schools contributed to keeping the planes on the ground (during the course of 1942, they contracted by 35 per cent and more so in the last year of the war to meet the needs of the war effort). Likewise, the disorganisation and the misuse of material and personnel was such that by the end of 1942 each of the 777 aircraft available to the *Scuole di 1° Periodo* flew on average eighty hours per year, and each of the 829 aircraft available to the

Scuole di 2° Periodo flew on average seventy-eight hours per year, less than seven hours per month.

In the second place, there were significant shortcomings in the training programme. The pre-war syllabus aimed at producing pilots with excellent acrobatic skills, in particular good 'collective' acrobats.[25] Giuseppe Ruzzin, having experienced combat in Spain, observed on the quality of Italian pilot training:

> What at that time, exactly one year before the German attack on Poland, was the main characteristic of our training? To tell the truth, mainly acrobatics. Our school was capable of producing great *manici* [expert pilots], as we used to say jokingly: skilled pilots for sure, and here I'm talking about the fighter arm. The preparation did not focus on navigation and the improvement of firing skills. Navigating and knowing how to fire with precision are the elements to be added to acrobatic ability. These requirements are absolutely necessary to create a combat-ready pilot ... we would become aware of some serious gaps when the moment of truth came and we had to fight. On the other hand, personally I had already had experiences in this regard in the skies over Spain. Almost all had proved themselves to be skilful in acrobatics, but not as effective in gunfights. My flight log records that from January 1938 to 10 June 1940, so in almost 29 months, I carried out about 800 flights. Of these, almost all of them were in acrobatic formation with three, five and even seven aeroplanes. An acrobatic 'solo' flight was already a reward. This type of flight was exhausting and did not exceed thirty minutes. Navigation training missions in formation took place very rarely.... Operating in formation is very useful ... certainly only continuous training could take us to this high level of confidence in and mastery of the aircraft. But the facts proved that in real combat all this was not enough.[26]

Acrobatic training had very little value in combat situations, and was unnecessarily dangerous, causing the loss of many precious pilots in peacetime drills. Three of the top ten Italian aces of the Spanish Civil War, *Sottotenente* Bruno di Montegnacco and *Capitani* Enrico degli Incerti and Giuseppe Majone, lost their lives while performing aerobatics after the war. Majone was killed in a mid-air collision with *Capitano* Alfiero Mezzetti (another prominent *Aviazione Legionaria* pilot). Giuseppe Ruzzin observed that the losses suffered by the *Regia Aeronautica* to non-operational causes, in good measure in training, even before the start of the Second World War, were significant.[27]

Nonetheless, it was not until the end of April 1943 that the *Regia Aeronautica* Chief of Staff General Fougier indicated to the *Comando*

Generale delle Scuole that 'collective acrobatics must be considered as redundant for the war training of the speciality' for the *scuole di 2°* *Periodo* and *Addestramento Caccia*.[28] As Ruzzin pointed out:

> ... the military pilot must also know how to fire and navigate. Often after a fight in an area far from his base, the pilot finds himself alone, disorientated and just as often does not know how to return home. Besides, how many scored no successes because of their limited knowledge of how to use their own weapons?[29]

While this might seem a platitude, the gunnery training for Italian fighter pilots was weak, to say the least: '... actual firing training, which was rare to tell the truth', which prepared the pilot for strafing runs, 'consisted in flying a given circuit and being able to fire at bunches of balloons, tied to the ground, from a set direction. In the final dive we let rip our fuselage machine guns, 7.7 mm Breda SAFAT sing'.[30]

The 'simulated firing tests using bunches of balloons that were released by ground personnel' to train the pilot in aerial combat, seemed to take place without actually firing rounds, at least in 1935 when Ruzzin experienced it:

> We had to simulate tailing an enemy plane, on which we imagined releasing a burst of machine-gun fire at close range ... sometimes a camera was installed on board the plane to verify the accuracy of the bursts and the quickness of the pilot's reflexes.[31]

There was no drogue or moving target shooting, nor deflection shooting training:

> [It was] particularly mystifying when one considers that all armament in Italian fighters consisted of two machine guns mounted above the engine [which] obviated the problems associated with wing-mounted guns and the variable accuracy of their converging fire, thus making deflection shooting considerably easier.[32]

The *Regia Aeronautica* pilots had to learn by themselves, mostly in combat, whereas those skills should have been the very core of their speciality.

The lack of a RT system on pre-war fighters (another aspect of the modernisation of the *Regia Aeronautica* buried under the burden of the enormous expenses incurred by intervening in the Spanish Civil War) hampered communication and therefore coordination in flight.[33] It meant that no training and doctrine for its use in combat had been developed by the time the conflict broke out: 'It should not be forgotten that for us the radio was still a futuristic dream. At most, the formation leader beckoned with his finger. In more complicated situations the patrol leader also used the palm of his hand'.[34]

Navigation and instrument flight training were equally weak spots of the syllabus, contributing to the fame of Italian fighter pilots as 'fair-weather' fliers and seriously hampering the fighter force's effectiveness during the early years of the war. Prewar training was lacking in navigational basics as much as the early Italian fighters were lacking in navigational equipment:

> No actual theoretical programmes had been drawn up for the training schools ... the real theory of navigation and the functioning, as well as the interpretation, of the few instruments of that time ... were not addressed. Proficiency in the use of geographical maps assumed great practical importance; yet no one ever provided them, we bought them in bookshops, always for ourselves. In Spain, for example ... if the commander announced a navigation in formation, we wingmen followed him. On the other hand in a Cr.32 we only had the compass and, for those who could afford it, the wristwatch. If we then came across fog banks, we were suddenly in the dark ... at the time, at least for us in the fighter arm, the principle to be applied was 'leave with the sun on the right, return with the sun on the left.' That wasn't enough.[35, 36]

Instrument navigation training was not introduced into the programme until June 1941, and even then it consisted of five hours initially on the SAIMAN 202.[37] It was increased subsequently to ten hours, some time between the second half of 1941 and the second half of 1942, when Paravicini received his training:

> There is a gap to be filled, and that is the suitability for instrument flying with an aircraft adapted for flight without visibility. The aeroplane is a Nardi FN305, with the trainee's cockpit modified for blind flight (it is obscured by green curtains). The trainee has on his dashboard a three-degree yaw string, a precision compass and a chronometer, plus the other instruments: altimeter, variometer, speed indicator and engine instruments. Once a given route has been chosen, at a given altitude, keeping the plane level, the instructor who is behind communicates a change of course. At this point the trainee in the cockpit must start the turn, keeping his eyes fixed on the variometer (the indicator of ascent and descent), on the meter (inclination indicator) calibrated to the chosen degrees of freedom, and press the button of the chronometer (as

> the degrees of deviation are a set amount per second) keeping an eye on the compass for the new course angle indicated by the instructor ... the course lasts ten hours and is very useful for everyone.[38]

In 1943, this part of the curriculum was increased to fifty hours, but the lack of adequate onboard instrumentation and radiolocation installations on the ground, and an underdeveloped conception of ground-directed interception, ultimately relegated the *Regia Aeronautica* to challenge the enemy in the air mostly when meteorological conditions allowed it.[39, 40, 41]

Output and Replacements

At the start of the war in June 1940, there were 2,146 combat-ready pilots, a number barely sufficient to ensure a reduced operability of the units. There were 2,500 pilots in the *Riserva*, but of those, only 600 were considered competent for combat operation, and only 300 without further training, which fell on the *Scuole*.

The training programme faced several bottlenecks that had a negative impact on the output of trained fighter pilots. In ideal conditions, it took fourteen months to complete the curriculum, including nine at the *Scuola di 1° Periodo* and five at the *Scuola di 2° Periodo*. The lack of fuel and the inefficient allocation of aircraft and personnel together with the insufficient number of qualified instructors often prolonged the course unduly, in some case very significantly. Later, in the final months of the war, it was also necessary to move some schools from southern Italy to the north to avoid the encroachment of Allied aircraft, adding further discontinuity (the *Accademia Aeronautica* was transferred from Caserta to Forlì on 20 August 1943).

When Italy entered the war, it actually saw a decrease in the number of pilots coming out of the *Scuole di 1°* and *2° Periodo*, exactly at the time when qualified personnel became more necessary. In 1936, the pilot schools produced 1,765 breveted pilots, 1,528 in 1937, 1,414 in 1938, 1,535 in 1939, an undetermined number in 1940, 1,079 in 1941, and 1,017 in 1942.[42] In 1943, there was no output due to the circumstances of the Armistice, but the available places were 800 for *Ufficiali di Complemento* and *Sottoufficiali*, and it was intended that the regular course of the *Accademia Aeronautica*, 'Vulcano' for that year, would produce about 250 pilots. Notwithstanding the adverse turn of events in the conflict, the competitions for accessing the pilot training courses never ran short of men, as in 1942, for 250 places available for *Ufficiali Piloti* and 300 for *Sottoufficiali*, respectively 986 and 2,778 applications were received, while in 1943 for 430 places available for *Ufficiali Piloti* and 370 for *Sottoufficiali*, a total of 1,230 applications were received. Nonetheless, the difficulties mentioned above and the expansion of the curriculum, which increased the flight hours, including training on front-line fighters, prolonged the duration of the course and limited the output as compared to the shorter pre-war courses.

The result of this situation was that the *Regia Aeronautica* was not able to compensate, in the course of the war, for its losses of qualified personnel: three years of conflict consumed a large part of its human resources, wearing down the rest, including those produced before the war, the intake from the school being insufficient to redress the situation.

Ultimately, and despite the efforts of the *Ispettorato delle Scuole*, and later of the *Comando Generale delle Scuole* (from 1941), the new pilots proved to be inadequate for the needs of war, both in terms of number and preparation.

Morale

The *Regia Aeronautica* entered the Second World War with the buoyant spirits of military and sporting achievements. The pre-war record-breaking flights had proven the nation's ability to produce effective aircraft and skilled pilots. In combat, the *Regia Aeronautica* pilots performed well in Ethiopia, against no enemy air activity whatsoever, and in Spain, where aerial combat was intense, and usually the Italians came out best in fights with the Republican air force, so much so in fact, that some erroneous lessons were drawn from that experience. The regime's propaganda of the *Arma Azzura* built up the image of a battle-hardened, modern, and well-trained force. Being a *Regia Aeronautica* pilot was a much sought-after career path for many.

This image was dispelled after the first months of war alongside and against major world powers, when circumstances showed that the resources available to the Italian air force were far from allowing reasonable prospects of success, not to mention survival, in a long-lasting conflict, and when the training of the pilots showed itself lacking in many areas. Discouragement and demoralisation arose as a consequence, along with distrust of the chain of command's capacities, as testified by the reports reaching the *Capo di Stato Maggiore* Fougier from his subordinates.[43] Of all the *Regia Aeronautica* though, the least affected by this collapse in morale seems to have been the fighter arm, mostly because of the aggressive *esprit de corps*, the achievement of some tangible results, and the atmosphere of the operational units, and the younger pilots, in particular the very motivated ones coming from the regular courses of the *Accademia Aeronautica*.[44]

The introduction of the M.C.202, concomitant with the Italians gaining the upper hand in the Malta campaign, gave a boost to the morale of the fighter pilots:

> It was clear not only from the number of new aeroplanes flying in, but from the calibre of the aircrews, that the High Command was serious about winning, and that was a big boost to everyone's morale. We knew we had the English badly outnumbered and we didn't see how we could possibly lose. There was a feeling that the whole thing would be over by the end of the summer at the latest. Our morale could not have been better. We were certain we were going to crush Malta and win the war. I can remember listening to Rome radio every night, hearing about yet another Axis victory. Whether it was us, the Germans or the Japanese, we were winning everywhere. It was uncanny.[45]

For the fighter pilots, a serious crisis in morale came relatively late in 1943, as testified by Paravicini and others, when the overwhelming odds and the superiority of Allied fighters started to tell.

In an attempt to motivate the pilots and counteract what was euphemistically called 'moral tiredness'.[46] From March 1942, Fougier reintroduced the title of 'ace' for fighter pilots with more than five acknowledged individual air victories.[47, 48, 49] The *Regia Aeronautica* subsequently laid down clear procedures as to how an official victory was to be confirmed.

Unit commanders were also requested to report individual aerial victories, also retrospectively, to establish a coherent combat record (which never materialised because the Armistice of 8 September 1943 intervened). In certain cases, aerial victories of the 1940–41 period were assigned collectively, which meant they were registered as shared kills. In September 1942, the system was revised and all the claims of the previous two years re-examined, with the result of awarding of individual kills to many of those pilots previously credited with shared victories. Furthermore, from May 1943, it was decided to pay cash awards for pilots credited with an aircraft kill or a ship sinking, the amount of the prizes being relative to the importance of the target (5,000 lire for the downing of a single-engined or twin-engined enemy aircraft, 15,000 lire for a four-engined aircraft, 150,000 lire for the sinking of a merchant ship or a minor war unit, 250,000 for a cruiser, and larger sums to be specified for the sinking of a battleship or an aircraft carrier).

Tactics

Given that operations in Ethiopia were virtually useless in terms of lessons learnt for modern aerial warfare, it is in the Spanish Civil War that the *Regia Aeronautica* fighter arm was shaped for its next conflict.

The Italian participation in the Spanish Civil War resulted in the modernisation of fighter tactics and widespread operational experience among pilots. However, it also exhausted the moderate resources that the country could dedicate to its air forces; for three years, Italy had to maintain an operational force of around 600 aeroplanes in Spain and Ethiopia, while struggling at home to expand and modernise itself. Moreover, while some lessons were learnt (and not all of them, as the Spanish Civil War in this respect was a poisoned chalice), they were not applied to update doctrine and training.[50]

The *Regia Aeronautica*, or rather the *Aviazione Legionaria*, entered the conflict in Spain with a tactical doctrine inherited in good measure from the experiences of the First World War, although in this respect, it did not differ significantly from the air forces of other countries in that period. In very broad terms, this meant that a *Squadriglia* would fly in line abreast or in a V formation, with the commander in the centre or at the apex of the V, each pilot scanning the sky to locate the enemy. Once in contact, since the planes lacked any RT, communication would be delegated to hand signals or flapping wings, and the *Squadriglia* would break formation and merge with the enemy with each aircraft engaging in an individual dogfight, without any particular coordination. Once the combat was over, the *Squadriglia* would regroup in order to return to base together, again with all the difficulties related to primitive navigation instruments and lack of RT communication.

In such circumstances, the concept of leader and wingman as a combat unit was informal, and dependent more on relations between the pilots rather than on a rational division of tactical tasks, the more so as all incentives were to go for the individual kill rather than covering the wingman. In fact, the various units of the *Aviazione Legionaria* used quite indifferently the pair or trio as the basic tactical unit.

It should also be emphasised that in the initial phase of the Spanish Civil War, large-scale air combat was relatively rare and planes mostly rather obsolete, so little need was felt for doctrine developments; this changed once the opposing sides became organised and external intervention made its weight felt. In those circumstances, various *Gruppi* of the *Aviazione Legionaria*, the *Cucaracha*, *Asso di Bastoni* and *Gamba di Ferro* all came up with different solutions to respond to the more robust formations of Republican fighters, but always involving substantial numbers of planes, usually at least a *Squadriglia*. In common to all those solutions was the deployment of the *Squadriglia* or the *Squadriglie*, or the whole *Gruppo*, in different types of tight groupings of columns or lines, echeloned in height, and usually structured on the couple (*coppia*) or trio (*pattuglia*) as a basic tactical unit.[51, 52]

All in all, those approaches were equally successful since the doctrine of deployment of the republican fighters was outdated and inefficient, and the Italian fighter arm usually scored highly regardless; in fact, even too much, as the conclusions were that 'contrary, however, to common belief, the combat formation must be tight ... the fighter pilots must therefore be used to a tight formation, which they must maintain automatically and tirelessly ... the tight formation is in the instinct of each of our fighters'.[53] Future Air Force Chief of Staff General Francesco Pricolo stated in a 1938 report for the *Scuola di Applicazione della Regia Aeronautica* of Florence that 'all the pilots that I have been able to question have expressed to me their conviction, which I share, that the usefulness of collective aerial acrobatics has had the most resounding confirmation in the Spanish Civil War.'[54]

The Germans, in comparison, who entered the war with equally traditional doctrines, even when the brand new Bf 109 monoplane fighters entered action in April 1937, came out of the war (thanks in good measure to Werner Mölders) with a veritable revolution in fighter deployment, based on a section of four aircraft (*Schwarm*), formed by two pairs of fighters (*Rotten*), constituted by a leader and a wingman to protect him, exactly as in the *Schwarm* the second *Rotte* would protect the first; faster planes required ampler space for manoeuvre, therefore looser formations, which in turn implied that command and control could only be exercised with RTs on board. The innovations introduced by the Germans were noticed and the deployment in February 1939 of an experimental unit of the new Fiat G50 fighters for operational evaluations suggested the need for a new approach to air combat.[55]

Yet no change was made to the *Addestramento dell'Aviazione da Caccia* 1936 and *Addestramento Formazioni Volo* manuals, both dating from 1936, as a consequence of the Spanish experience. A summary in an article written for the *Regia Aeronautica*'s official magazine, *Rivista Aeronautica*, in May 1940 recommended that the basic formation of the fighter force should be changed from the *pattuglia* to the two-aircraft *coppia*, while the tactical unit to enter battle should be increased from the nine-aircraft *Squadriglia* to the twenty-seven-strong *Gruppo*, but Italian tactics born in Spain remained conceptually more akin to the patrols of the First World War than to the agile German tactics.

After all, aircraft without RT required tight formations and prearranged procedures to keep a minimum of control and coordination; even after the RT sets were installed, their quality and reliability were poor, forcing the pilots to continue relying on plane and hand signals, thus drawing attention away from the surrounding environment. Once the fighting started, the high manoeuvrability of the biplane fighters made the dogfighting approach a natural choice.

It was the acrobatic fighting techniques that worked so well in Spain, mostly due to the failure of Republican pilots to fully exploit the capacities of their low-wing monoplanes (such as their new I16) rather than doctrine that influenced the perceptions of the pilots regarding the plane they needed, provoking an undue and anachronistic disposition for biplanes in the *Regia Aeronautica*, which was slow in updating to monoplanes (and continued to produce the CR.42 until 1943).[55,57]

After the Spanish Civil War, the *Regia Aeronautica* started re-arming with monoplanes, more in imitation of what other air forces were doing than from understanding that such a shift had fundamental implications for the way air combat would take place. The best approach with the high speed of the monoplanes was to bounce the enemy fighters possibly by surprise, exploiting height, firing with hard-hitting onboard armaments for the brief moment of contact and then disengaging equally fast, ideally on the vertical plane. To exploit the monoplane characteristics in full, acrobatic capacity was much less relevant than good shooting, skills of collective combat, instrument flying, and navigation, since the interception would be ground-directed.

In Italy, there was an attempt to find a compromise between the increased capacities and speed of a monoplane and the manoeuvred combat techniques more fitting to the biplanes, and acrobatics kept being taught even when a training more suited to the new aircraft should have been devised, as the German example had shown. Moreover, no RT, no heavier guns apart from the two fuselage 12.7-mm MGs were usually available, so as not to compromise manouvreability. Undoubtedly, *Regia Aeronautica* fighter pilots excelled in acrobatics, and there is ample testimony to the fact that acrobatic skills had allowed them to escape from dangerous situations or allowed them to score victories. Neverthess, while German tactical doctrine forbade pilots from becoming involved in individual dogfights, recommending rather to evade manoeuvred combat with a sharp dive, followed by a climb and a new dive, the Italian fighter pilots started their combat in the Second World War as they did in Spain.

In fact, for a good part of the Second World War, the *Regia Aeronautica* stuck mostly to what it had learnt in Spain, and the first taste of the new 'German' tactics (which the Allies adopted as well in the course of the war as 'finger four'), was introduced in Italy for the first time in the summer of 1944 when the Germans, while supplying Bf 109G fighters to the *Aeronautica Nazionale Repubblicana* (ANR) took the opportunity to teach the ANR pilots the *Rotte/Schwarm* concept. The pilots of the *Regia Aeronautica cobelligerante* in southern Italy, on the other hand, did not receive any novel tactical teaching from the Allies.

The British did the same at the beginning of the war, but evolved quickly by measuring up to the Germans:

> We flew in 'fluid sixes' or fours, all weaving.... The standard German attacks were either to dive and climb, or to dive, fire, and continue down through the formation.... The German pilots did seem to work much better in pairs than the RAF, and this team work was most effective.... The Italian pilots were much more inclined to engage in dogfights than the Germans but the lower performance and greater manoeuvrability of their aircraft accounted for this. They were certainly very fine acrobatic pilots but seemed to enter combat more in the spirit of a medieval joust than of a life and death struggle. They appeared to have many problems with inter-aircraft communication in the air and were consequently easier to bounce.[58]

Malta's top ace, George Beurling, had the chance to discuss tactics with an Italian M.C.202 pilot, *Sergente* Faliero Gelli, whom he had shot down shortly before scoring a kill on the Italian ace and commander of 151[a] *Squadriglia Capitano* Furio Niclot Doglio, who did not survive:

> The gent was a flight sergeant by the name of Cino Valentini [Gelli either gave a false name or was misunderstood] who had been in the Air Force since 1936 and the last five months in Sicily, during which time he had shot down three Spitfires.... He asked me what I thought of Italian pilots and I said: 'You're pretty good, but your tactics stink.' He asked what I meant by that and I replied: 'Well, for one thing, your formations are too tight. You have to spend so damned much time concentrating on the formation, keeping out of the other guys' slipstreams and away from wingtips that you don't get a chance to look around.' Valentini said that's the way they teach it in the Italian Air Force, as if that made it right. I gathered he didn't think I knew what I was talking about. To him I was just a stiff who had been lucky enough to shoot down a real pilot.[59]

Before Niclot and Gelli, Beurling had already shot down Sergeant-Major Francesco Pecchiari, Lieutenant Romano Pagliani, and Sergeant-Major Francesco Visentin, a veteran of the Italian Air Corps in Belgium in 1940, and commented:

> The Eyeties are comparatively easy to shoot down. Oh, they're brave enough. In fact, I think the Eyeties have more courage than the Germans, but their tactics aren't so good. They are very good gliders, but they try to do clever acrobatics and looping. But they will stick it even if things are going against them, whereas the Jerries will run.[60]

Fiorenzo Macchi, a Re.2001 pilot, remembers clearly how the British tactics compared to Italian ones:

> When we were fighting against the British we were inferior not only numerically but also technically. I remember the constant stiff neck I had in flight, always looking for the Spitfires or the Hurricanes that jumped us from nowhere like devils. The British pilots preferred the swoop to the dogfight and came down like hailstones. We fired wildly from the two wing machine guns; the British, in addition to having the radio on board, spewed an incredible volume of fire from the wings: a real firestorm.[61]

The tight formations and acrobatic combat were actually dissipating the qualities of new generation fighters, but were also inconvenient for bomber escort, as they gave little space of manoeuvre to engage the enemy and, once engaged, dragged the fighters into dogfights that separated them from the bombers.

The German allies were also unimpressed by Italian tactics. Rudolf Sinner, a technical officer of II./JG 27 observed: 'The Italian pilots on average were better acrobats than the Germans and British. In combat they had nothing to offer, even after equipment with excellent aircraft like the MC202!'[62] Friedrich Körner, *Oberleutnant* with I./JG 27, commented:

> For us the Italian air force was a great disappointment after the 'fame' of the Italians before the war. Their equipment was very bad, their aircraft obsolete. Some outstanding Italian pilots with dash and lighting spirit (aerobatic flying in low-level flight) could not alter that impression.[63, 64]

By 1942, the *Regia Aeronautica*, faced with better Allied tactics, had acquired significant combat experience, if at a heavy price, but it updated its doctrines slowly, and 'any changes that did occur were usually driven by individual squadron commanders in the field and not from any systematic change in the training syllabus', such as probably the adoption of the conventional leader/wingman pair formation, and speed tactics.[65] *Maggiore* Giuseppe D'Agostinis, an experienced pilot of the 4° *Stormo*, had taken part in combats along with Hans-Joachim Marseille and had observed the effectiveness of German tactics:

> The tactic of keeping in line to ensure the safety of the patrol leader and the possibility of exploiting his ability as the best marksman was clear. It is a tactic that requires strict patrol discipline, coming together again after a fight, rather than breaking up as is typical of our patrols, whose wingmen often engaged in individual duels.[66]

Sergente Arnaldo Mauri, M.C.202 pilot of the 86ª *Squadriglia*, 7° *Gruppo* of the 54° *Stormo*, commented about in-squadron training:

> … on the concepts of attack and manoeuvred combat, there were no directives from above: what was done was worked out in the Squadron on the initiative of the commanders. I have to say that my commander, Capitano Gostini, made us experience 'book' manoeuvres, mock fighter combat, pairs, flight in single file and some other manoeuvres, but I repeat, all were the result of local initiatives. For the tactics on intercepting bombers we received only vague indications, more a digest of previous experiences than something based on specific information.[67]

Fighter tactics of the *Regia Aeronautica* were heavily influenced by the relative delay in developing efficient ground control techniques. On-board RT were one aspect of the problem, which we have already discussed above, but the ground component was equally relevant:

> At the end of 1940, after six months of war, for our fighter arm to scramble on alarm and be able to intercept the enemy was still a matter of luck rather than effective coordination: in practice there was no organized air defence. According to a directive of Superaereo of 27 December 1940: 'it turns out that the planes, both those in cruise and those that scrambled only rarely succeed in intercepting the enemy bombers before they reach the objective. Usually the fighters only have the possibility of pursuing the enemy when he has completed his attack…. If it is not possible to have an observatory particularly suitable for the purpose, the r.t.f. transmitter station (R.T.800) can be placed at the airport which is the fighter unit's base…. It will therefore be necessary to widen the field of observation connected to the use of the r.t. station, by placing a series of signaling posts in a suitable position and connecting directly, or via the DICAT Command, the signaling posts with the station itself. The personnel in charge of the transmissions will thus be informed of the situation regarding a large area of sky around the objective, an area that will try to match up, roughly, with the field of activity of the fighters.'[68]

This held true on national territory and in the colonies, where a DICAT network was present.[69] Later German radars supplemented the antiquated Italian systems, when in 1942 the first DETE radar system, which could be used to track air targets, was installed on the CT *Legionario*. Those were used as a rudimentary *guida caccia* centres, as Costantino Petrosellini remembers:

> After returning home, [in early 1943] the 8° *Gruppo* initially reconstituted itself in Albenga.... Here we were in charge of the fleet escort. Radios were mounted on board, and we finally entered into contact with the *guida caccia*. The first radiolocalizers were mounted on our ships. They were German RADARs, quite precise, so for the first time we didn't go blindly into the skies, looking for a hypothetical opponent. A *guida caccia* was on the cruiser *Duca degli Abruzzi*.[70]

On 21 January 1942, *Superaereo*, encouraged by the positive experiences of coordination between *Regia Aeronautica* fighters and *Luftwaffe* radar guidance taking place on the African front, issued a directive to procure Freya and Wurzburg radar sets, and pondered the development of an Himmelbett system for Northern Italy.[71] The Germans provided Freya and Wurzburg radars, operators, and training to the Italian personnel to man them. In the course of 1942, the first *cellule* radars were created, first in the prealpine area to protect the northern Italian cities, then around Rome, and eventually around the main naval and air bases. By 12 December 1942, there were twenty-four radar stations on national territory, plus six in construction.[72] By 1943 in Italy, there were, in addition to the few radiolocalizers of Italian construction, 164 Freya (for long-distance interception from 40 to 75 km), Riese, and Wurzburg models (with a range of 30 km). German radars operated in close collaboration with the Flak and DICAT—*Artiglieria Contraerea* (Anti-aircraft) batteries, thus constituting a system of warning and response to an enemy air attack, and providing a fairly precise *guida caccia*.[73,74,75,76]

In operational theatres, the *Regia Aeronautica* relied, for the *guida caccia*, on the German radar network and on field RT systems, such as the RT300, RT800 and, subsequently, RT310 (with a power of about 250 w for medium range communication) and RT1000 (with a power of about 1 kw for long-range transmission). All the devices were designed to be used as field radio-transmitter complexes; the smaller RT300 was installed on a single-axle trailer, the so-called *biga-radio*, while two trailers were needed to set up the RT800 complex. The two more powerful complexes, RT800 and RT1000, both built by SAFAR, were also installed in fixed positions, in buildings specially set up as radio centres. The first examples of the

RT1000 in a radio-truck field set-up entered service in late 1941. Towards the end of the war, updated installations of the RT310 *biga-radio* complex were brought into service, also on the SPA *Dovunque* truck. *Sergente* Mauri explained how the system worked:

> On certain occasions we received indications from our biga [RT300 or 310] about the presence of enemy planes in a certain sector, specifying it with reference to the squares of the geographical map. For example, in the jargon received on the intercom that in the small square X a blonde of fifty years was arriving it meant that in this sector a formation of fifty planes was coming. It is likely that our Carro 1000 [RT1000] also received information from German radiolocalizers. If you didn't have precise instructions, instead you would fly on a certain course and would be sure to come across something.[77]

7

The M.C.202 in Combat, 1941–45

M.C.202 Distribution in *Regia Aeronatica* Units[1]

1941

1° *Stormo* C.T.	
6° *Gruppo*	79ª, 81ª, 88ª *Squadriglia*
17° *Gruppo*	71ª, 72ª, 80ª *Squadriglia*
4° *Stormo* C.T.	
9° *Gruppo*	73ª, 96ª, 97ª *Squadriglia*
10° *Gruppo*	84ª, 90ª, 91ª *Squadriglia*

1942

1° *Stormo* C.T.	
6° *Gruppo*	79ª, 81ª, 88ª *Squadriglia*
17° *Gruppo*	71ª, 72ª, 80ª *Squadriglia*
2° *Stormo* C.T.	
13° *Gruppo*	77ª, 78ª, 82ª *Squadriglia*
3° *Stormo* C.T.	
18° *Gruppo*	83ª, 85ª, 95ª *Squadriglia*
23° *Gruppo*	70ª, 74ª, 75ª *Squadriglia*
4° *Stormo* C.T.	
9° *Gruppo*	73ª, 96ª, 97ª *Squadriglia*
10° *Gruppo*	84ª, 90ª, 91ª *Squadriglia*

51° *Stormo* C.T.	
20° *Gruppo*	151ª, 352ª, 353ª *Squadriglia*
155° *Gruppo*	351ª, 360ª, 378ª *Squadriglia*
54° *Stormo* C.T.	
7° *Gruppo*	76ª, 86ª, 98ª *Squadriglia*
16° *Gruppo*	167ª, 168ª, 169ª *Squadriglia*
21° *Gruppo* Autonomo C.T.	356ª, 361ª, 382ª, 386ª *Squadriglia*

This *Gruppo* was reinforced to comprise four *Squadriglie* when on the Russian front. When the unit returned to Italy, in the spring of 1943, the 382ª *Squadriglia* was disbanded, but by the summer it returned to operations.

24° *Gruppo* Autonomo C.T.	354ª, 355ª, 370ª *Squadriglia*
153° *Gruppo* Autonomo C.T.	372ª, 373ª, 374ª *Squadriglia*
161° *Gruppo* Autonomo C.T.	162ª, 163ª, 164ª *Squadriglia*
153ª *Squadriglia* C.T.	3° *Gruppo* C.T. *Diavoli Rossi* (Red Devils)
377ª *Squadriglia* Autonoma C.T.	

1943

1° *Stormo* C.T.	
6° *Gruppo*	79ª, 81ª, 88ª *Squadriglia*
17° *Gruppo*	71ª, 72ª, 80ª *Squadriglia*
2° *Stormo* C.T.	
13° *Gruppo*	77ª, 78ª, 82ª *Squadriglia*
3° *Stormo* C.T.	
18° *Gruppo*	83ª, 85ª, 95ª *Squadriglia*
23° *Gruppo*	70ª, 74ª, 75ª *Squadriglia*
4° *Stormo* C.T.	
9° *Gruppo*	73ª, 96ª, 97ª *Squadriglia*
10° *Gruppo*	84ª, 90ª, 91ª *Squadriglia*
51° *Stormo* C.T.	
20° *Gruppo*	151ª, 352ª, 353ª *Squadriglia*
155° *Gruppo*	351ª, 360ª, 378ª *Squadriglia*
53° *Stormo* C.T.	
151° *Gruppo*	366ª, 367ª, 368ª *Squadriglia*
153° *Gruppo*	372ª, 373ª, 374ª *Squadriglia*
54° *Stormo* C.T.	
7° *Gruppo*	76ª, 86ª, 98ª *Squadriglia*
16° *Gruppo*	167ª, 168ª, 169ª *Squadriglia*

3° *Gruppo* Autonomo C.T.	153ª, 154ª, 155ª *Squadriglia*
21° *Gruppo* Autonomo C.T.	356ª, 361ª, 382ª, 386ª *Squadriglia*
22° *Gruppo* Autonomo C.T.	359ª, 362ª, 369ª *Squadriglia*
24° *Gruppo* Autonomo C.T.	354ª, 355ª, 370ª *Squadriglia*
154° *Gruppo* Autonomo C.T.	395ª, 396ª *Squadriglia*
161° *Gruppo* Autonomo C.T.	162ª, 163ª, 164ª, 371ª *Squadriglia*
167° *Gruppo* Autonomo C.T.	303ª *Squadriglia*
377ª *Squadriglia* Autonoma C.T.	

Various '*Gruppi Complementari*'—designated by the letter 'C.'

Regia Aeronautica, 1941–43

Macchi started delivering M.C.202s in June 1941, Breda on 2 October, and Ambrosini on 20 October. The first M.C.202s were operational by the summer of 1941, and were delivered to units in the following order:

- 17° and 6° *Gruppo* of 1° *Stormo*
- 9° *Gruppo* of 4° *Stormo*
- 10° *Gruppo* of 4°
- 155° and 20° *Gruppo* of 51° *Stormo*
- 23° *Gruppo* of 3° *Stormo*
- 153° and 21° *Gruppo* Autonomo
- 151° *Gruppo* of 53° *Stormo*
- 16° and 7° *Gruppo* of 54° *Stormo*
- 150°, 154° e 24° Gruppi Autonomi
- 18° *Gruppo* of 3° *Stormo*
- 22° *Gruppo* Autonomo.

In addition, M.C.202s were assigned as replacements to various units: the 13° *Gruppo* of the 2° *Stormo* received some from the 4° *Stormo*, and the 161° *Gruppo Autonomo* received some second-hand ones.[2]

North Africa, 1941–43

The first Macchi-built M.C.202s were delivered from the end of May 1941 or June (sources are contradictory).[3, 4] The first unit of the *Regia Aeronautica* to convert to the M.C.202 was 17° *Gruppo*, 1° *Stormo* C.T., which transferred to Campoformido near Udine, for conversion training to the new machine. The unit was completely re-equipped with the new fighter only in the autumn, and, with aircrew training completed in October, the unit moved first to Ciampino (Roma), where they were to be provided with the characteristic dust filter, and later to Comiso (Ragusa) in Sicily, as intermediate stages for deployment to the North African front. The 6° *Gruppo* of the 1° *Stormo* received the M.C.202 more or less at the same time.

The 9° *Gruppo* of the 4° *Stormo* received its first M.C.202s in July 1941, six Folgores assigned in Lonate Pozzolo to a few chosen pilots of the 97ª *Squadriglia* led by *Capitano* Antonio Larsimont Pergameni.[5] One of those, *Maresciallo* Vanni Zuliani, commented about the new aircraft:

> The Macchi 202 also had a beautiful line, was well centred and stable, especially at critical speeds, both at take-off and landing, and did not give the pilot much to do. At high altitude, although it did not have a wing surface, it behaved very well because of the well conceived wing profile and good lift. It had a 1.175 HP Daimler-Benz engine built by Alfa Romeo, and was fitted, for the first time in history, with direct injection with a Bosch pump. With this system ... the drawbacks of the common carburettor supply were eliminated: that is, it was possible to make a rapid take-off without danger of engine failure and without having to wait for the engine to reach a given temperature. Moreover, during violent manoeuvres the flooding of the fuel supply system didn't take place and a good stretch of inverted flight could be made without particular precautions and without the trail of black smoke caused by the arrival of too much petrol in the engine cylinders and the consequent misfunction. In the event of a belly-up landing the danger of fire was eliminated because, with the propeller stopping, the feeder pump automatically stopped, closing all fuel access to the cylinders.[6]

By 27 September, the *Gruppo* was completely re-equipped and left Gorizia for Rome Ciampino, and then, with the congratulations of the watching *Duce*, for Comiso, where they would operate against Malta in preparation for transfer to North Africa. It is no wonder that the brand-new fighter was assigned first to the 1° and 4° *Stormo*, the most prestigious fighter units of the *Regia Aeronautica*.

The baptism of fire of the M.C.202 happened just three days later, in the early afternoon of 30 September, when five Hurricane Hurribombers from No. 185 Squadron RAF, based in Malta, arrived over Comiso to bomb and strafe it, carrying six 40-lb bombs and two 25-lb incendiaries; they were covered by other six planes from the same squadron. Three M.C.202s from the 97ª *Squadriglia*, 9° *Gruppo*, scrambled to intercept, piloted by Spanish Civil War veteran *Sottotenente* Jacopo Frigerio, *Tenente* Luigi Tessari and

Sergente Maggiore Massimo Salvatore.[7, 8] They jumped the Hurricanes after their strike and Frigerio, piloting M.C.202 MM7712, code 97-2, shot down at 2.10 p.m. Pilot Officer Donald William Lintern, flying Hurricane IIB Z5265, code GL-B, who baled out over the sea just north of Gozo. To find him, a Fulmar of the Rescue Flight of Kalafrana was sent (Lintern was never found and was reported missing), escorted by five No. 185 squadron's Hurricanes. Some 10 km off Capo Scalambri in south-eastern Sicily, it stumbled upon three M.C.202s of the 97ª *Squadriglia* which were escorting a Cant Z.506C of the 612ª *Squadriglia Soccorso*, sent from the Marsala-Stagnone base with the same purpose. The Macchis, piloted by *Sottotenente* Jacopo Frigerio, *Tenente* Luigi Tessari, and *Maresciallo* Raffaello Novelli, attacked the Fulmar, Tessari, and Novelli, bringing it down; the aircraft crew (Lieutenant Eyres and Sub-Lieutenant Furlong) were later picked up by a Rescue Flight's Swordfish seaplane, without further Italian interference.[9]

The first M.C.202, belonging to *Capitano* Pericle Baruffi's 71ª *Squadriglia*, 17° *Gruppo*, 1° *Stormo*, arrived in the North African theatre on 23 November 1941, having departed from Ciampino Sud Airport and landing in Castel Benito Airport (Tripoli) after intermediate stops, in Sicily and Pantelleria; the rest of the 17° *Gruppo* (72ª and 80ª *Squadriglia*) arriving by 27 November and being deployed to advanced airfields in the east, Uadi Tamet, Benina, and Martuba.[10] The aircraft still presented some initial problems, given that of the thirty-seven planes that left Rome only thirty-two arrived in Libya. The 17° *Gruppo* was joined in Martuba some days later, on 10 December, by the 1° *Stormo*'s 6° *Gruppo* (79ª and 81ª *Squadriglia*, the 88ª not having completed aircraft tropicalisation) led by *Tenente Colonnello* Vezio Mezzetti, so that by early December 1941, virtually all the 1° *Stormo* was in Libya for its second cycle of operations in Africa, though its command remained in Italy, and it was put under the control of the 5ª *Squadra Aerea*, responsible for the North African theatre.[11] The 88ª *Squadriglia* reunited with its group on 14 December at Benghazi K2 airfield, because the *Stormo*, having been involved in the battles of Operation Crusader, leading to the British relief of Tobruk, retreated along with German and Italian troops in Cyrenaica in mid- and late December, redeploying also to the airfields of Benina, Barce, Benghazi K2, Sidi Magrum, and eventually to Tamet (or Wadi Tamet) in Tripolitania, in late December.[12]

Meanwhile, the 9° *Gruppo* of 4° *Stormo*, under the command of *Maggiore* Antonio Larsimont Pergameni, arrived from Comiso to Libya on 25 November, two of its *Squadriglie*, the 96ª and 97ª, deploying at Martuba with eighteen M.C.202s, while the 73ª *Squadriglia* would remain at Comiso to continue operations over Malta.[13]

The late arrival of the Macchis in theatre, when the situation on the Libyan front was already under threat due to the British offensive, was the source of controversy and one of the causes of, or perhaps the pretext for, the removal of *Generale* Pricolo from the *Capo di Stato Maggiore* of the *Regia Aeronautica* and his replacement by *Generale* Rino Corso Fugier on 14 November 1941. Pricolo had delayed the forwarding of the new aircraft and therefore disobeyed orders from above, as he deemed that the personnel were not yet fully familiarized with the new fighters and that tropicalisation (e.g. the sand filters) was not complete.

The loss of Axis air superiority during the British offensive enabled the RAF to harass the Axis ground forces, though it is questionable as to how much two semi-trained *Stormi* or parts there of, equipped with a new aeroplane whose teething problems were not fully resolved, without adequate supply assets would have changed the course of the battle. Ultimately, the Folgores of the 96ª and 97ª *Squadriglia* of the 9° *Gruppo* of 4° *Stormo* were sent to North Africa without filters, undoubtedly shortening the lifespan of their engines and seriously complicating maintenance work in a theatre were logistics were already problematic.

The baptism of fire of the M.C.202s fell indeed to this latter *Gruppo*, on 26 November, when the *Regia Aeronautica* pilots claimed eight enemy planes shot down, both Hurricanes and P-40s. In reality, ten Macchis from 96ª and 97ª *Squadriglia* led by Larsimont Pergameni and *Capitano* Ezio Viglione Borghese (commanding officer of the 96ª) took off at 11 a.m. from Martuba, for a free hunting sweep over the Sidi Rezegh–Gambut area. They were split into two patrols of five aircraft each (one patrol from the 96ª *Squadriglia* and one from the 97ª *Squadriglia*). After about twenty-five minutes of flight, while at an altitude of about 5,000 metres, two enemy formations came in sight, one of which was identified as twelve Hurricanes at an altitude of 3,500 metres, and a second one escorting it, of P-40s, above 5,000 metres. Both Macchi patrols jumped the lower formation, breaking it up. The higher formation intervened in the battle, which lasted about ten minutes:

> *Capitano* Larsimont got on the tail of an enemy aircraft and attacked it (firing 94 rounds) but was immediately set upon by another enemy fighter which hit him from behind. He managed to get away and bring home his damaged fighter. *Maresciallo* Raffaele Novelli (97ª *Squadriglia*) fired on some enemy fighters in successive actions and claimed one shot down using a total of 675 rounds. *Sottotenente* Giovanni Barcaro (97ª *Squadriglia*) fired on eight enemy aircraft in the ensuing action. He got on the tail of a P40 and hit it with a long burst. The aircraft came down and crashed into the ground. His MC202 was short on fuel so he landed

> at Tmimi to refuel before returning to base. He had used 275 rounds in the combat. *Sottotenente* Jacopo Frigerio (97ª *Squadriglia*) fired on three enemy fighters over several clashes without being able to notice any visible effects, using 102 rounds. *Sergente Maggiore* Massimo Salvatore (97ª *Squadriglia*) got on the tail of an enemy aircraft and shot it down after hitting it with a long burst. Then he fired on a second one, shooting this down as well. In total he used 575 rounds before returning to base with the windscreen of his fighter smeared with oil from the oil tank of one of the Hurricanes he had shot down. By the end of the combat, the Italian pilots claimed eight enemy fighters destroyed and an additional one as probably destroyed using 3000 rounds of ammunition with two MC202s damaged (*Capitano* Larsimont and *Capitano* Viglione's). Four P40s and a probable Hurricane were credited to the 96ª *Squadriglia*; *Capitano* Viglione, *Tenente* Emanuele Annoni, *Tenente* Fernando Malvezzi, *Maresciallo* Manlio Olivetti and *Maresciallo* Dante Labanti (1 probableHurricane). Four enemy fighters were credited to the 97ª Squadriglia; *Sottotenente* Barcaro (1 P40), *Maresciallo* Novelli and *Sergente Maggiore* Salvatore (2 enemy fighters).[14]

In reality, they had engaged the Hurricane Mk IIcs of No. 229 (the higher, escorting formation of twelve planes) and 238 Squadrons (the lower one of eleven planes), which, having taken off from LG07 and 92, were carrying out a defensive patrol for the ground forces. Misidentification took place on both sides apparently, as No. 229 Squadron pilots deemed they had been attacked by twelve Bf 109s (after all, it was the first appearance of the M.C.202s on that front), of which they claimed to have shot down two, presumably the damaged planes of Larsimont and *Capitano*Viglione. No. 238 Squadron's formation suffered the loss of Sergeant Robert Arthur Knappett (Hurricane Z2355/L), KIA; of Flying Officer King (G), crash-landed; of Sergeant Kay (BV170/N), who was shot down and made it back to British lines on foot; of Pilot Officer H. G. Currie's Hurricane (Z5222/Y), crashed on landing at Tobruk; and of Sergeant Fairbairn, who landed at Tobruk wounded and with his Hurricane (E) badly damaged.[15]

While not as high as the *Regia Aeronautica* pilots claimed, it was an auspicious result and the demonstration of the M.C.202's qualities and its superiority over the Hurricanes; the *Regia Aeronautica* pilots had once more the sensation of flying a competitive plane:

> In flight, the 202 forgave so many things, certainly many more than its younger brother [the M.C.200]. The engine undoubtedly behaved better both at altitude and take-off; at the beginning of 1942 there was the feeling of having something similar or better in the hands of the

> opponents of the RAF or of the German allies and, as we know, morale is fundamental to the fighting spirit of a good fighter pilot. There was no difficulty whatsoever in making the transition from the 200 to the 202; everything was known and had been improved. Having to give an overall judgment on the Folgore, I could confirm that it always behaved very well; the weapons didn't jam on me once. The radio apparatus, the only non-positive aspect of this evaluation of mine, did not shine in its general power and quality. The cooling system had no problems whatsoever.... The various on-board items of equipment, collimator, roof release, etc., were perfectly normal and trouble-free to use.[16]

On 1 December, twenty-one German and eight Italian Ju 87s (from the 239ª *Squadriglia*) were in action attacking British concentrations 20 km north-east of Bir El Gobi at shortly before midday, escorted by ten Bf 109F (of JG 27) and seven M.C.200s of the 153° *Gruppo* in close cover and twelve M.C.202s from the 9° *Gruppo*—six from each of the 96ª *Squadriglia* and the 97ª *Squadriglia* under the command of *Capitano* Larsimont Pergameni.[17] One of the 96ª *Squadriglia* aircraft returned early because of engine trouble. As they were getting ready to return, about twenty enemy fighters, identified as Hurricanes and Tomahawks, were sighted at 4,000 metres; they were the escort of twenty-three Blenheims of Nos 14, 45, 84, and 'Lorraine' Squadrons, heading west of El Adem, and consisted of the Hurricanes of No. 1 SAAF Squadron, flying close cover, and No. 274 Squadron, providing top cover.

The *Regia Aeronautica* commander manoeuvred to gain altitude and launched into the attack:

> *Capitano* Larsimont machine gunned some enemy aircraft (using 155 rounds of ammunition). It was thought that one of them was hit by a long burst on the tail and was claimed as probably shot down. *Maresciallo* Rinaldo Damiani fired a burst at the tail of an enemy monoplane which then lost height leaving a long trail of smoke and crashed into the ground and was burnt out. He returned after having used 105 rounds of ammunition claiming two Hurricanes destroyed. *Sottotenente* Frigerio fired a long burst at a Hurricane, saw it start to catch fire and claimed it as destroyed. Subsequently he machine-gunned another two without managing to notice any visible results (in total he used up 249 rounds). *Sergente* Alfredo Bombardini machine-gunned two enemy aircraft hitting them with effective bursts but without noticing any visible results and returned claiming both as probably destroyed with the use of 303 rounds. *Sottotenente* Giovanni Barcaro machine-gunned three enemy aircraft in successive episodes but wasn't able to

> see any results. Subsequently he got on the tail of an enemy aircraft and hit it with long bursts until he saw it leaving a long trail of black smoke losing altitude in a spin. He then got on the tail of another Hurricane and machine-gunned it with long bursts from close in. The enemy aircraft left a long trail of whitish smoke coming from the water radiator.... Finally, *Maresciallo* Otello Perotti machine-gunned some enemy aircraft, hitting them with long bursts; one of them was believed to have probably been shot down with the use of 188 rounds.[18]

The battle lasted ten minutes, and 97ª *Squadriglia* claimed four aircraft shot down, another five probable, and ten machine-gunned. The 96ª *Squadriglia* also claimed to have shot down four fighters (and a fifth damaged), so attributed: *Capitano* Ezio Viglione Borghese (one Hurricane), *Tenente* Fernando Malvezzi (one Tomahawk), *Maresciallo* Dante Labanti (one Hurricane), *Tenente* Emanuele Annoni (one Tomahawk), and *Sergente* Maggiore Bruno Spitzl (one damaged Tomahawk). The Germans also claimed three Hurricane IIs as being shot down. No German fighters were lost and it seems that none suffered any damage.

No. 274 Squadron in fact suffered three shot down Hurricanes and a fourth a forced landing:

> Pilot Officer Weeks was shot down but was picked up by ground force and returned, Sergeant G. W. F. Pearse (Z2817) was shot down 25m south-west of El Adem at 13:00 and WIA (he was picked up by armoured cars and returned on 3 December) and Sergeant Alman (Z2510) was shot down and became MIA. Lieutenant W. H. Hoffe (Z5310) made a forced landing after his Hurricane had been hit in the glycol tank, causing the engine to blow up. Flight Lieutenant Owen Tracey (BD821), one of the 274 Squadron flight commanders, landed and picked him up, flying him back to base.[19]

No. 1 SAAF Squadron did not engage as it was busy with bomber escort, and remained unscathed. The Italians had two planes damaged, that of *Tenente* Annoni of the 96ª *Squadriglia* and that of *Sottotenente* Barcaro, who had been hit in the water radiator and made a crash-landing with the engine seized up 12 km from Ain El Gazala.[20] It is most probable that both the Macchis and the Bf 109s participated in the same combat, and the actual share of claims is not easy to attribute. What is significant about this combat, apart from the usual overclaiming from all sides and misidentification of enemy fighters, is the fact that *Regia Aeronautica* pilots appeared to try to shoot the enemy by putting themselves close on their tail, a result of the lack of deflection shooting training, of the mediocre firepower of the two 12.7-mm Breda SAFAT, of the inferior turning radius of the M.C.202 as compared to the Hurricane, and of the acrobatic training of the pilots.

The baptism of fire of the 1° *Stormo* in the African theatre took place on the morning of 4 December 1941, when eleven M.C.202s of the 17° *Gruppo*, six from the 71ª *Squadriglia*, three from the 72ª *Squadriglia*, and two from the 80ª *Squadriglia*, led by *Tenente Colonnello* Bruno Brambilla, took off to fly top cover for a formation of Ju 87-R5s of the *Regia Aeronautica* and then make a free sweep over Bir El Gobi, along with the Bf 109Fs of JG 27.[21,22] They encountered an enemy formation estimated to be thirty P-40s and Hurricanes fighters, in poor weather 12 km south-west of El Adem at an altitude of 4,000 metres. They were actually twenty-two Hurricane IIs of No. 1 SAAF and No. 274 Squadrons, based probably at Ain El Gazala or M'sus, the first unit making a free sweep above El Adem, while the second flying a defence patrol for its own armoured vehicles above Trigh Capuzzo. As No. 1 SAAF Hurricanes started climbing to attack, the Italians attacked the flanks of the formation and bounced from above with both Macchis and Bf 109s:

> No 1 Sqn., SAAF, received instructions from 258 Wing RAF to carry out a wing sweep with No. 274 Sqn., RAF, over our troops in area 4237, 4736 and 4533 (Purple grid map: 250.000 Egypt and Cyrenaica Sollum-Tobruk Sheet 3). The leaders of the formation of No. 1 and 274 Squadrons agreed that No. 1 should provide the top cover for the sweep. The Hurricane MK.lls of No. 1 took off from L.G. 124 at 9.15 hrs. flying in formation, i.e. pairs in line abreast. They flew at 10,000 feet, and above No. 274 Squadron's formation. Owing to engine trouble (oil pressure dropping) one Hurricane returned at 9.45 hrs. After approx. one hour ten minutes of flying the leader of No. 1 [Captain Cornelius Arthur van Vliet], (who was then flying in a northerly direction) observed about 8 E/A approaching. The E/A were to the left (about 10 o'clock) and slightly above our formation. The 8 E/A, which were in no particular formation, dived towards the rear of our formation and shot down a straggler [2nd Lieutenant Meek]. Then they appeared to break up on either side of No. 1 and climbed into the base of the clouds, at 12000 feet, where they joined other E/A. Another large group of E/A (about 16) were seen to the right and slightly above.
>
> These aircraft did not take part in the general dogfight for several minutes, but remained milling about on their own, while No. 1 was attacked on both flanks by single aircraft. Pilots estimated between 20 and 30 E/A. Most of them were C.202s, but some pilots identified Me109Es with their square wing tips.... The leader of No. 1 turned into

> the 8 E/A that attacked by a climbing turn to the left. But single E/A made attacks from both sides almost at the same time as the climbing turn was begun, and the formation broke up and general dog fighting took place.[23]

The Italians claimed eight victories: *Capitano* Tomaselli (72ª *Squadriglia*), *Sergente Maggiore* Gabriele Romagna (72ª *Squadriglia*), *Sottotenente* Renato Bagnoli (80ª *Squadriglia*, *Tenente Colonnello* Brambilla, *Capitano* Pericle Baruffi (71ª *Squadriglia*), *Tenente* Pierfrancesco Conti (71ª *Squadriglia*), *Tenente* Ottorino Cappellini (71ª *Squadriglia*), and *Sergente* Egidio Buogo (71ª *Squadriglia*) all claiming one enemy fighter (in some cases misidentified as a Tomahawk) and *Sergente* Carlo Ermo (71ª *Squadriglia*) claiming a probable.

In fact, they managed possibly to shoot down the Hurricane II of 2Lt Thomas Albert Meek, who crash-landed at some considerable distance to the north-west of LG124.[24] British sources seem rather more inclined to attribute the loss to the action of one of the Bf 109s of JG 27, perhaps that of *Oblt* Gustav Roeder. There is also the possibility that the M.C.202s might have clashed with the Tomahawks of No. 250 Squadron, in which case the number of thirty fighters encountered would add up. In that case, it is not impossible that they had shot down at least one of the other aircraft declared lost in that area.[25] Italian losses were *Sottotenente* Lorenzo Chellini's (72ª *Squadriglia*) M.C.202 MM7864/72-3, which was hit in the water radiator and made an emergency landing near El Duda, about 8 km south east of El Adem, resulting in a total write-off; *Maresciallo* Marcello Lui's (71ª *Squadriglia*) M.C.202 MM7874, which landed off the airfield because of engine trouble; and two other Macchis damaged, that of *Tenente Colonnello* Brambilla in the empennages and *Tenente* Conti in the control panel.

By now, the Commonwealth pilots (especially those of No. 1 SAAF and 274 RAF Squadrons, who had run into them already) started recognising the M.C.202s and its main characteristics 'painted in a dark green livery and ... a wide broad white band round the fuselage towards the tail ... wings have rounded tips'.[26] Most importantly, they started analysing the tactics of the *Regia Aeronautica* pilots, as demonstrated in the after-action report of this specific combat:

> The attacks were made generally by single aircraft diving out the base of the clouds, between 12,000 and 13,000 feet [those could have been the Bf 109s of JG 27, as this was more of a German combat tactic]. No enemy aircraft attempted a head-on attack. The presence of a large group of E/A that remained for several minutes slightly above and to

> the right of our formation without taking part in the fight worried our pilots. This group of aircraft frequently distracted their attention from the single aircraft that were making repeated attacks from out of the clouds. Several pilots commented on the astonishing aerobatics that the enemy pilots carried out during the dogfight. Several of them were seen to loop, stall turn, and roll off the top for no apparent reason. One C.202 was attacked when it was inverted at the top of a loop and the tail plane was shot to pieces [most likely *Tenente Colonnello* Brambilla's plane, claimed as shot down by Lieutenant Vivian Penberthy]. Another C.202 was shot down when it was in a stall turn. It is presumed, because of the aerobatics, that the enemy aircraft were flown by Italians. If they were Italians they had learned from the Germans how to take advantage of the clouds and to pounce immediately on any stragglers in a formation.[27]

The improved performance and qualities of the M.C.202 were immediately obvious, as compared to previous Italian fighters, such as for instance its robustness allowing it very long steep dives:

> The C.202 is a highly manoeuvrable aircraft, but the general opinion of the pilots of No. 1 Sqn. who dogfought with them was that the Hurricane MK. II could outturn them. One pilot dogfought one for several minutes, but neither aircraft fired because at no time could one of the pilots get the other in his sights. Three Hurricanes that chased a Macchi which had a start in a 5,000 feet dive, failed to catch up with it. The A.I.S. of the Hurricane was 340 mph, but in the level chase at 2,000 ft above the deck, the C.202 pulled away from it.[28]

Another combat, occurring a few days later, confirms the preference of the *Regia Aeronautica* pilots for dogfighting. In mid-morning of 8 December, eight M.C.202s of the 9° *Gruppo* led by *Capitano* Viglione Borghese from the 96ª *Squadriglia*, were patrolling the Ain el Gazala-Trigh Capuzzo-Tobruk area, when they clashed with enemy aircraft, misidentified as about twelve P-40s (but more probably Hurricanes, perhaps Mk Is of No. 80 Squadron or Mk IIs of No. 274 Squadron, sources are contradictory).[29, 30]

> *Sottotenente* Frigerio (97ª *Squadriglia*) attacked four enemy fighters several times; he then had to land at Z because his Macchi had run out of fuel. On spotting the enemy aircraft, *Sottotenente* Giovanni Barcaro (97ª *Squadriglia*) closed in to *Capitano* Viglione to warn him and together they attacked and shot down one enemy aircraft in flames. He subsequently fired on four more aircraft (using in total 184 rounds) before landing at Z.2 for refuelling. *Maresciallo* Otello Perotti

> (97ª *Squadriglia*) fired on two enemy aircraft (using 263 rounds) but couldn't observe the effects. He landed at Z for refuelling and claimed a probable Hurricane. Another two enemy aircraft were claimed by *Sergente Maggiore* Bruno Spitzl (96ª*Squadriglia*) and Vittorio Pozzati (96ª *Squadriglia*). *Tenente* Fernando Malvezzi (96ª *Squadriglia*) hit a P40 with a long burst but couldn't assess the result because he was attacked from behind by another P40.[31]

The 9° *Gruppo* claimed four Hurricanes shot down (by Spitzl, Pozzati, Bombardini (97ª *Squadriglia*) and one shared between *Capitano* Viglione and *Sottotenente* Barcaro) and ten more damaged (three by *Sottotenente* Barcaro, two by *Maresciallo* Perotti, four by *Sottotenente* Frigerio, and one by Malvezzi). One M.C.202, *Sergente* Bombardini's MM7739, was damaged and had to land at Ain el Gazala but it became a total loss when the airfield had to be evacuated and the Macchi had to be destroyed.

The same morning the 17° *Gruppo*, which had taken off shortly before midday with eleven M.C.202s (six from the 71ª *Squadriglia*, two from the 72ª *Squadriglia*, and three from the 80ª *Squadriglia*) was flying a protective patrol of Axis troops retreating along the coastal strip between Ain el Gazala and Tobruk, along with some Bf 109Fs of I/JG27. The M.C.202s were flying at 4,000 metres in Vic formation in echelon right, when they encountered eleven Hurricanes IIBs from No. 274 Squadron (as usual, misidentified as P-40s); those were the top cover of an Allied formation of eighteen Blenheims of No. 84 Squadron, which had been (successfully) targeting a very important concentration of vehicles in the area of El Adem, which had also a close escort of No. 1 SAAF Squadron. The latter, not seeing the Italians, continued to fly towards base with the bombers, while the returning No. 274 Squadron's Hurricanes engaged the enemy. The 17° *Gruppo* claimed six enemy planes shot down, by *Tenente* Renato Talamini (80ª *Squadriglia*), *Sottotenente* Renato Bagnoli (80ª *Squadriglia*), *Tenente* Mario Carini (72ª *Squadriglia*), *Sottotenente* Vittorio Bacchi Andreoli (71ª *Squadriglia*), *Maresciallo* Achille Martina (71ª *Squadriglia*), and *Sottotenente* Guido Modiano (72ª *Squadriglia*). *Sottotenente* Ottorino Capellini (71ª *Squadriglia*) and *Sergente Maggiore* Mario Host (80ª *Squadriglia*) claimed a probable each, for the loss of *Tenente* Carini's Macchi MM7758, which was hit in the cooling system and crash-landed at Bir El Fa, and for the damage of *Tenente* Talamini's M.C.202 to the left wing.

No. 274 Squadron in fact lost three Hurricanes: Hurricane IIb BD885 of Flight Lieutenant Owen Vincent Tracey, Hurricane IIb Z5066 of Sergeant Haines, who was declared missing, and Hurricane IIb BE347 of Sergeant John Paterson McDonnell that was hit and crash-landed at Tobruk, being a total loss. Pilot Officer Thompson's Hurricane IIb Z5130 was also forced to land in Tobruk.

It is probable also that the Bf 109Fs took part in the combat, and the RAF pilots remarked, significantly, that the Italians preferred to dogfight while the Bf 109s fought on the vertical plane on energy tactics, and dived continuously.

Those encounters set the pattern of deployment in theatre for the M.C.202s for the month of December, combat taking place on a daily basis for the M.C.202s employed in different types of missions: on 9 December, nine Macchis of 17° *Gruppo*, from 71ª and 72ª *Squadriglia*, scrambled to intercept nine Maryland bombers from No. 12 squadron SAAF; on 11 December, ten Macchis from 71ª, 72ª and 80ª *Squadriglia* of 17° *Gruppo*, led by *Tenente Colonnello* Brambilla took off to escort four Bf 110s over Acroma, and engaged a group of Hurricanes (probably Tomahawks of No. 4 SAAF Squadron) flying at 250 metres through the clouds, perhaps shooting down one.

On 12 December, ten Macchis from the 6° *Gruppo* of 1° *Stormo* took off for their first action in theatre, led by *Tenente Colonnello* Vezio Mezzetti. Shortly after, they clashed with twelve Hurribombers of No. 80 Squadron attacking the road to Derna, escorted by as many RNFS Hurricanes flying close escort, while provided top cover by nine Tomahawks of No. 250 Squadron. The *Regia Aeronautica* pilots managed to shoot down one Tomahawk and four Hurribombers—it is unclear whether there was any German participation in the fight—for the loss of the M.C.202 of *Sergente* Renato Saiani and *Capitano* Domenico Camarda.[32]

In the afternoon of the same day, another combat involved eleven M.C.202s of the 17° *Gruppo* (six from the 71ª *Squadriglia* and five from the 80ª *Squadriglia*) led by *Capitano* Aldo Felici, and a mixed enemy formation estimated at thirty Curtiss P-40s and Hurricanes. The confused and lengthy fight, which saw the intervention of various Commonwealth squadrons at different moments (No. 4 SAAF and No. 2 SAAF Squadron, No. 3 RAAF Squadron, and No. 112 Squadron) and probably of three additional M.C.202s of the 81ª *Squadriglia* (6° *Gruppo*), led by *Tenente* Giorgio Falchi, cost the Italians three Macchis damaged, that of *Capitano* Clizio Nioi hit in the cooling system and forced to land, the MM7871 of *Tenente* Glauco Vatta, crash-landed on base and the MM7861 of *Tenente* Pierfrancesco Conti, who was slightly wounded and belly-landed. A fourth Macchi, of *Sergente Maggiore* Remo Broilo, was slightly damaged. They nonetheless managed to shoot down one Tomahawk of No. 4 SAAF and two of No. 2 SAAF Squadron, three of No. 112 Squadron, one of No. 3 RAAF Squadron, and damage two more of No. 4 SAAF Squadron and one of No. 112 Squadron.[33, 34]

The M.C.202s of 79ª and 81ª *Squadriglia* scrambled to intercept Blenheims IV escorted by Hurricanes on 17 December, and later, the 6° *Gruppo* intercepted some Hurribombers of No. 80 Squadron escorted by Hurricanes IIcs of No. 229 and 238 Squadron. The same day, the 6° *Gruppo* lost in combat its commander, *Tenente Colonnello* Vezio Mezzetti, during an escort mission to Ju 87 R5 of 209ª *Squadriglia Aut. B.aT.*[35] Italian M.C.202s units suffered in this period serious losses not only from air combat, but also from the bombing of its bases, such as Barce on 17 December, and by commando assault on airfields by the SAS, such as the Wadi Tamet airfield, which was attacked on 28 December, with the loss of nine M.C.202s of 17° *Gruppo* and one of the 6° *Gruppo*.[36] At the end of 1941, 88ª *Squadriglia* of 6° *Gruppo* retreated further by redeploying to Ara Fileni airfield; the 9° *Gruppo* with 96ª and 97ª *Squadriglia* left its Macchis to the 1° *Stormo* and returned to Italy.

When the British Crusader offensive petered out at the beginning of January 1942, the Folgores of 1° *Stormo* were deployed at Tamet (17° *Gruppo*) and Ara Fileni (6° *Gruppo*).[37]

The general offensive starting in January 1942 that took the Axis forces beyond the Egyptian border, and almost in sight of Alexandria, was the most successful period for the Folgore in Africa. On 21 January, Rommel began his attack, which forced the British out of western Cyrenaica. Benghazi fell on 29 January, and the British retreated east. This retreat stopped at Gazala, to the west of Tobruk. Both sides began to build up their forces, in preparation for their next offensive. In this lull, from January to May, the M.C.202s of the 6° and 17° *Gruppo* operated almost on a daily basis as escort for fighter bombers, flew fighter sweeps and intercepts, but also strafed enemy airports, such as the 88ª *Squadriglia* did at Agedabia on 21 January, or on El Adem and Acroma by the 81ª and 88ª *Squadriglia* on 22 February. On 15 March 1942, *Capitano* Giuseppe Pesola scrambled from Martuba airfield to intercept Boston bombers escorted by P-40 fighters:

> When the first bombs started falling on Martuba 2 airfield, occupied by the Germans, several MC202 aircraft of the 6° Gruppo departed from Martuba 1. I quickly boarded the aircraft numbered 79-5 and was the sixth to fly to intercept the opposing formation on its return route. Given the nature of the scramble on alarm it was not possible to start in regular formation, nor to implement it in flight because each pilot tried to make the most of the climbing and speed qualities of his machine without waiting for the others.... I came over Tobruk at an altitude of 4,000 metres and only then with the shadows on the ground, did I finally catch sight of the enemy formation that was still compact as it flew towards

> the airfield of Bu Amud.... The fighters were arranged in a wide circle around the Bostons that were flying even lower than the former. Below a thousand metres I opened fire on a fighter that I hit directly on the cockpit with a long burst. I stopped firing when I was almost on him, slipping to his left side, I dodged him and pushed the plane up, giving it full throttle. I plunged back down and attacked a second fighter on the back like the first and with an identical manoeuvre a third one I found almost in front ... before leaving the attack I decided to hit a fourth in a more advantageous position than the third. I took myself to the east of the formation of fighters and hit the fourth aircraft with a long and precise burst at the back from the left side. While manoeuvring, having to keep a close eye on opponents, I did not have the opportunity to see if any of the four planes hit, including three rather well, had fallen. Without wasting time, I swerved around the fourth aircraft, turning left to north-west. Pleased with myself, with one last manoeuvre I intended to escape my adversaries, but one of these was ready to give me pursuit. In fact I was almost at the end of making the last turn when some tracers of greater calibre than my 12.7 went a little high slightly to the right. Having tested the engine after the departure from Martuba during the climb, with little success, I decided to evade the adversary not by climbing, as I would have done with another aircraft with a more efficient engine, but by pulling down, exploiting the very penetrating profile of the MC202.... The bullets continued to arrive at me, sometimes below sometimes above, on one side and on the other, still without hitting me. I operated the overspeed and the +100 and arrived a few metres above the sea.... Almost touching the waves I flew a few minutes, until I was hit in the lower part of the backrest. I was not injured because the armour had protected me. The machine was damaged, most likely the water cooler. After a few more miles of flight, I turned back and the opponent was gone.[38]

Pesola crashed behind enemy lines shortly after and was taken prisoner. While four Kittyhawks and Tomahawks had been damaged, some of which possibly by Pesola himself, none were shot down.

The Macchis were deployed often in this period for ground attack (as again on El Adem airfield on 27 February), a use that was ill-suited to the characteristics of this plane. First, the in-line engine was more sensitive than the radial one and prone to catastrophic failures if the cooling and oil lines were severed by ground fire.[39] Secondly, the two Breda SAFAT 12.7-mm MGs (admittedly the same was true of the M.C.200, which on the other hand could carry bombs, while only from SERIE XI—that is, from November 1942 on—would the M.C.202 be capable of carrying bombs) were a rather weak weapon for strafing; usually the fighter-bomber role was reserved for CR.42s and M.C.200s. On 20 March, the M.C.202s of the 6° *Gruppo* along with all the other available air assets, CR.42s and M.C.200s, repelled a British attack on the Martuba Airfield by acting as fighter bombers and strafing the three attack columns:

> The armoured vehicles on the ground quickly scatter and fire upwards with all the weapons at their disposal. The Macchi do not deviate, down and down, towards the tanks and armoured vehicles. Fire! The plane shudders, tracer tracks criss-cross in the air, looking for one another, the mortal combat has begun, the merry-go-round of the aeroplanes is uninterrupted: as soon as the pass has been made, low on enemy vehicles, with weapons that spew bullets, a pull-up turn and the jousting starts again.[40]

Matruba airfield would be the focus of Commonwealth bomber attacks on a virtually daily basis, and the M.C.202s of the 1° *Stormo* would provide continuously intercept and alarm patrols.[41]

In preparation for the new offensive, between 21 and 24 May, the 4° *Stormo* from Sicily returned to Africa for its third operational cycle with its 9° and subsequently 10° *Gruppo* C.T.

Both were deployed at Martuba to join there the 1° *Stormo*.[42] Meanwhile, on 15 May, at Mirafiori Airport, the 3° *Stormo* was reorganised on 18° and 23° Gruppi, the latter transitioning on M.C.202 in preparation for the deployment to Africa.

In May, the Axis offensive picked up momentum again with the battle of Gazala (26 May–14 June 1942). This renewed offensive reoriented the Axis main efforts and siphoned off resources from Malta and Operation C3, including Italian air assets. On 17 May, a meeting between *Generali* Bastico and Marchesi, *Generalfeldmarschall* Kesserling, and other Axis officers established the guidelines for the deployment of the air assets in the perspective of the new offensive. High-performance fighters such as M.C.202s and Bf 109s would be tasked with free hunting, interception, and indirect escort. Tactical assault would be the task of Ju 87s, Me 110s, and CR.42s. M.C.200s would be flying close escorts and strafing runs.

The offensive opened on 26 May with the attack on Gambut airfield by fifty-nine Folgores, of the 1° *Stormo* and 4° *Stormo*—this was basically the total number of Macchis available at Martuba (in fact, sixty) to the 1° *Stormo* and 4° *Stormo* and for the Italians a very substantial effort. The order of operations indicated 'the 4° and 1° Stormo, free hunt over Gambut airport, with indirect escort duties to aircraft of the 150° Gruppo Assalto, engaged in strafing on the ground of the airport itself', though in reality the M.C.202s came down to strafe as well.[43] The attack was deemed by the Italians an enormous success, but it probably caused the destruction of only a couple of Kittyhawks of No. 250 Squadron.

On 29 May, eight M.C.202s from the 4° *Stormo* led by *Maggiore* Antonio Larsimont Pergameni (CO 9° *Gruppo*) flying a free sweep at an altitude of 4,000 metres stumbled across nine Tomahawks IIbs from No. 5 SAAF Squadron (together with eleven Hurricane IIcs from No. 274 Squadron over Acroma (3:40–5:20 p.m.), and engaged them, some Bf 109s apparently also intervening. The combat tactics of the Axis fighter were analysed by Major John Frost of No. 5 SAAF Squadron: '8 or 9 EA were seen diving out of the sun. They were 109E, F and 202s. Turned to face them and a general dogfight followed, the 109 staying above and doing dive attacks, while Macchis came down and fought'.[44] This combat involved *Regia Aeronautica* ace Teresio Martinoli (73ª *Squadriglia*), who claimed one enemy shot down (in fact, none were lost by the Commonwealth forces, while one M.C.202, MM7824/73-5 of *Sottotenente* Mario Massa (73ª *Squadriglia*) was shot down with the pilot killed).

Rommel broke through the Gazala Line, and once again the British were forced to retreat on 14 June 1942. Most of the British troops reached the Egyptian border, while a garrison was left in Tobruk. Accompanied often by the German Bf 109s of the JG 27, Macchis of 1° *Stormo* and 4° *Stormo* were particularly active, escorting bombers against the fortress of Tobruk, intercepting bombing raids and on free interdiction missions along a rapidly fluctuating front line.[45, 46]

So far, the Macchi M.C.202 had enjoyed a clear superiority over all Commonwealth fighters present in theatre, Hurricanes, Tomahawks, and Kittyhawks, but ominously in early June the first Mk V (trop.) Spitfires started appearing in combat, having already arrived in Egypt in April and being deployed at Gambut in late May; their baptism of fire in Africa was on 1 June, and in the following ten days, the first encounters with M.C.202s took place, though early claims by *Regia Aeronautica* pilots probably refer to Kittyhawks.

Equally ominously, on 9 June, the first USAAF bomber unit, the so called HALPRO, arrived in Egypt signalling an increasing commitment of the US in theatre.[47]

However, by then, the defences of Tobruk had been somewhat weakened and Axis forces took over the fortress on 21 June. The 4° *Stormo* redeployed eastwards following the Axis advance, first to El Adem and then Sidi El Barrani on 25 June. The challenges presented by the war in the western desert came not only from the enemy, but also from the very extreme environment. *Tenente* Emanuele Annoni remembers the effect of the *ghibli:*

> The transfer of part of the 9° *Gruppo* from Martuba to El Adem took place at the moment when the *ghibli* coming from the interior reached El Adem airport. When the '202' of the 9° arrived in El Adem the sand blown by the *ghibli* had already covered the southern edge of the airport. A quick turn around the field and everyone made for the ground as fast as possible. By the time the last planes touch the ground the dust front is completely covering the airfield. The pilots taxi in the dust fog with the utmost caution until the outline of a specialist guiding them to the parking area emerges.[48]

The 1° *Stormo* that had been depleted by the short but intense tour of duty was sent back to Italy with the exception of the 88ª *Squadriglia* of the 6° *Gruppo*, under the command of *Capitano* Dante Ocarso, which was attached to the 4° *Stormo* of *Tenente Colonnello* Armando François; this unit also reached the Sidi El Barrani airfield, where it was joined on the 28 June by the 10° *Gruppo*, to prepare for the further push forward. In fact, the Axis offensive finally petered out at El Alamein on 30 June—one of the main reasons being problems of supply over long and exposed routes. The Axis advance had been rapid, and although the flying units were able to bring with them certain essential supplies, bulk deliveries had to come by road behind the advance. On the eve of the battle of El Alamein, Folgores of the 4° *Stormo* deployed from Fuka airfield, where the 10° *Gruppo* joined it on 1 July, while the 88ª *Squadriglia* of 6° *Gruppo* moved to Mumin Sbusak airfield on 6 July, with very few M.C.202s.[49] On 1 July, the first USAAF fighter unit arrived in Egypt; the 57th Fighter Group, with sixty-eight P-40E.1s belonging to the 64th, 65th, and 66th Squadrons.

The whole month of July was spent by Macchis of the 4° *Stormo* taking off several times per day for bomber interceptions, escorts, and fighter sweeps as the operational tempo increased. Both the Axis powers and the Allies were building up forces for the forthcoming clash and the Commonwealth was attempting to regain air superiority, with a significant increase in the number of planes, including the contribution of USAAF units, and with the improved quality of the machines available.

On the *Regia Aeronautica*'s side, the 23° *Gruppo* on factory-new M.C.202s arrived in theatre by 16 July and deployed at Abu Aggag, after a lengthy transfer starting from Mirafiori the 8 July.[50] The 23° *Gruppo* was led by *Maggiore* Luigi Filippi, while its components, the 70ª, 74ª, and 75ª *Squadriglie* were led by *Capitani* Claudio Solaro, Giorgio Tugnoli, and Mario Pinna respectively. The *Gruppo* was put under the command of the 4° *Stormo* while waiting for the rest of the 3° *Stormo* (to which it originally belonged), led by *Tenente Colonello* Tito Falconi, to complete its deployment to Africa.

Mid-July 1942, with the arrival of the 23° *Gruppo*, was the peak of M.C.202 presence on the African front, with ninety-three aircraft on strength in four groups: the 9° and 10° *Gruppo* of the 4° *Stormo*, the 23° *Gruppo* of the 3° *Stormo*, and the 150° *Gruppo Autonomo*, which had been provided with a few M.C.202s in the spring of 1942 alongside its M.C.200s to fulfil the mission of protecting the harbour of Benghazi and the naval traffic to Italy.[51] In early August, the 13° *Gruppo* of 2° *Stormo*, based at Bu Amud, received three M.C.202s, with the mission of protecting the harbour of Tobruk.[52] Between the start of the year and September 1942, just before the start of the El Alamein battle, the availability of combat-ready M.C.202s fluctuated from a minimum of thirty aircraft in January to a maximum of seventy-four aircraft in September.[53,54]

The appearance of new Allied planes in the theatre was experienced by *Sottotenente* Livio Ceccotti of the 97ª *Squadriglia*, 9° *Gruppo*, who was flying a protection patrol over the port of Bu Amud on 19 July, and stumbled upon a formation of six B-17Ca of No. 160 Squadron RAF, which he engaged, with the result of being raked by the heavy defensive fire of the .50-calibre (12.7-mm) MGs and crashlanding. He had just had a preview of what would be the crucible of M.C.202 pilots a few months after—that is, attacking well-armed and very robust US heavy bombers, a task for which the fighter he flew would prove sadly inadequate. A couple of days later, on 21 July, the pilots of the 23° *Gruppo* led by *Maggiore* Filippi engaged a flight of six Mk V Spitfires, managing to shoot down one. It was one of the first combats against this plane, which had been deployed for about one month, and it was an even match for the Macchi. Luigi Gorrini, of the 85ª *Squadriglia*, 18° *Gruppo*, observed: 'The Spit was a very tough nut to crack ... it had a cluster of machine guns, plus two 20 mm guns and it was also faster. The 202 was decidedly inferior in speed and weaponry'.[55] The arrival of the Spitfire spelled the end of the easy superiority of the Macchi over Allied fighters.

On 14 August, *Sottotenente* Antonio Canfora and five other M.C.202s of the 97ª *Squadriglia*, 9° *Gruppo*, 4° *Stormo*, together with some Bf 109Fs of II/ and III/JG27, engaged for the first time US fighters—P-40E Warhawks of the 57th Fighter Group (along with other Allied fighters, Kittyhawks of No. 2 SAAF Squadron and Mk Vc Spitfires of No. 92 Squadron)—escorting some bombers on Fuka airfield.[56] On 19 August, No. 92 Squadron was providing top cover to the Hurricanes of No. 274 and No. 1 SAAF Squadrons when, at 9.15 a.m., the unit ran into a formation of Bf 109s and Macchi C.202s west of Hammam. The M.C.202s of the 73ª *Squadriglia*, 9° *Gruppo*, piloted by *Tenente* Rinaldo Gibellini, which fell to Sqn Ldr Wedgewood, was among the claims. US bombers also started to show up more often, such as for instance on 14 August when a pilot of the 13° *Gruppo*, 2° *Stormo*, scrambled to intercept a formation of four-engined bombers, probably USAAF B-24Ds, over Tobruk, and again a few days later, on 23 August when five *Regia Aeronautica* pilots claimed a B-24D (no B-24Ds were shot down in fact).[57] A few days before, around mid-month, the 12th Medium Bomber Group USAAF, equipped with B-25Cs and Ds, started operating on the frontline as well. The American presence on the frontline started to tell.

At the same time, the Italian fighters began to benefit in August 1942 from the Freya Radar network that the Germans had set up for *guida-caccia* to intercept enemy formations.[58]

When on 30 August the Axis ground offensive started, the M.C.202s found themselves immediately involved, flying fighter sweeps, escorts, strafing missions on enemy airfields (e.g. the mission of 31 August involving twenty M.C.202s of the 10° *Gruppo* to strafe three enemy airfields in the Burg el Arab area), and protection patrols for ground troops. The intense pace of operations lasted into September, when the *Regia Aeronautica* pilots often flew multiple missions per day, encountering more and more often Mk V Spitfires, its *Squadriglie* being progressively whittled down by the continuous combat, and difficult spares and supplies situation (by 20 September, the 10° *Gruppo* had twenty-seven M.C.202s left, as did the 9° *Gruppo*, while the 23° *Gruppo* had only twenty).[59] On 19 September, the 4° *Stormo* was visited at Fuka by newly promoted *Hauptmann* Hans-Joachim Marseille, at that time already a very famous ace. He was greeted by *Tenente Colonnello* François, the *Stormo*'s commander, and then Marseille asked to try an M.C.202. François asked *Tenente* Annoni to satisfy Marseille's request:

> Col. François, who was occasionally present at the command post, turns to me and asks me to let him fly an aeroplane from my Squadron. He recommends that I choose an aircraft that is definitely efficient, flawless and safe. Knowing Marseille's fame and wanting to make a good impression, I assure François that I will let him fly my personal aircraft, the no. 10. We go to the dispersal area of the '96'. I show him the layout of the various controls and instruments by means of an interpreter. I have him write down some speed and altitude data and I let him take off. After circling above the airfield, Marseille prepares for landing: he does a lap of 150 metres and then lines up. After the last turn, when it is in line with the airfield he pulls down the undercarriage. While the undercarriage is coming out the engine fails. He puts the undercarriage back in and lands the plane on its belly 300 metres from the boundary of the airfield. He crashed the most beautiful, balanced, perfect aeroplane I've ever had. What had happened? That series of the '202' had the magneto switch

> consisting of a lever that ended in a knob and moved from the bottom (contacts off) to the top (contacts on) and *vice versa*. This lever was placed to the left, under the instrument panel, next to the lever of the undercarriage which also moved from the top to the bottom and *vice versa*: lever up, undercarriage inside, lever down, undercarriage out. By lowering the lever of the undercarriage to get it out, Marseille, either by mistake or without realizing it, also lowered the contact lever bringing it to the 'contacts off' position. So the landing gear came out and the engine stopped. If the pilot had noticed the error and had immediately brought the lever of the magnetos back up (contacts on) the engine would have restarted and would have arrived on the airfield normally.[60]

October 1942 started with a massive clash on the 9th, lasting basically all day and involving dozens of planes, representing almost all the Allied and Axis forces involved in the theatre:

> At 09.00 on 9 October, 18 fighters of the 73ª and the 96ª Squadriglie, led respectively by *Tenente* Giulio Reiner and *Tenente* Emanuele Annoni (CO of the 96ª Squadriglia), took off to escort some Ju87s. The weather was cloudy and at 09.15, at 5,500 m over the El Quteifiya area (the Italian name of the airfield base of the Stab and II/JG 27 in the Daba area), they spotted eighteen Bostons escorted by 20 P40s and 20 Spitfires. The 73ª Squadriglia initially attacked the Bostons, but was chased by the P40s, while the 96ª Squadriglia engaged the Spitfires. After a hard and long combat, the fighters disengaged low on ammunition.[61]

The Allied formations were made up of sixty-seven Kittyhawks of Nos 112, 250, 450, 3 RAAF, 2 SAAF, and 4 SAAF Squadrons plus an unknown number of Tomahawks of No. 5 SAAF Squadron, backed by P-40Fs of 66th US FS, 57th Fighter Group, sixteen Mk Vc Spitfires of No. 601 and 92 Squadrons, and Hurricanes, escorting a formation of eighteen Bostons and six Baltimores of No. 223 Squadron attacking Axis airfields trying to catch the enemy forces on the ground. *Regia Aeronautica* pilots claimed one Boston, three Spitfires individually and one shared, seven P-40s, one Spitfire and four more P-40 probables, suffering in return no losses, but the aircraft of *Tenente* Reiner, *Tenente* Oblach, *Sergente* Angelini, *Sergente* Martinoli, and three of the 96ª *Squadriglia* were damaged (one of them belly-landing). *Luftwaffe* Bf 109s from 5./JG27, 7./JG27, 8./JG27, Stab II/JG 27, and 7./JG53 also took part in the morning fighting and claimed nine fighters and one bomber for the loss of three fighters. The Allies in reality lost one Baltimore, two Kittyhawks, and two Tomahawks with two more Kittyhawks badly damaged—it is impossible to say who actually

Above: Mussolini and the *Quadrumviri* just after the March on Rome (Rome, 30 October 1922). (*Archivio Istituto Luce, Roma*)

Below: The Balbo seaplanes fly over New York during the ocean crossing (19 July 1933). (*AUSAM, Roma*)

Above: The Balbo seaplanes fly over New York during the ocean crossing (19 July 1933). (*AUSAM, Roma*)

Below: Italo Balbo meets Mussolini on his return from the Atlantic flight (Rome, 12 August 1933). (*AUSAM, Roma*)

Right: Italo Balbo with Adolf Hitler (Germany, August 1938). (*AUSAM, Roma*)

Below: The signing of the Pact of Steel (Berlin, 22 May 1939). (*Archivio Istituto Luce, Roma*)

James H. Dolittle and the plane in which he won the 1925 Schneider Trophy Race—a Curtiss R3C-2 Racer.

Macchi 39, 1925. (*AUSAM, Fondo De Bernardi*)

Above and below: Macchi 39, 1925. (*AUSAM, Fondo De Bernardi*)

Left and below:
Macchi 39 flying over Norfolk, 1925. (*AUSAM, Fondo De Bernardi*)

Above: Macchi 39 team, 1925. (*AUSAM, Fondo De Bernardi*)

Below: Macchi 39 team and Balbo welcomed by Mussolini. (*AUSAM, Fondo De Bernardi*)

Macchi 39 at the *Museo Aeronautico di Vigna di Valle*. (*Author*)

Sailors present the results of the competition, Venice 1927. (*AUSAM, Emeroteca, Cart. 17*)

Macchi 52, 1927. (*AUSAM, Emeroteca, Cart. 17*)

Supermarine S.5B, Venice 1927.

Above and below: Macchi M.C.72019. (*AUSAM, Fondo Cometti, B. 27, F. 44*)

Above: The Macchi 72 at the *Museo Aeronautico di Vigna di Valle*. (*Author*)

Below: Macchi M.C.72019. (*AUSAM, Fondo Cometti, B. 27, F. 44*)

Macchi M.C.72019. (*AUSAM, Fondo Cometti, B. 27, F. 44*)

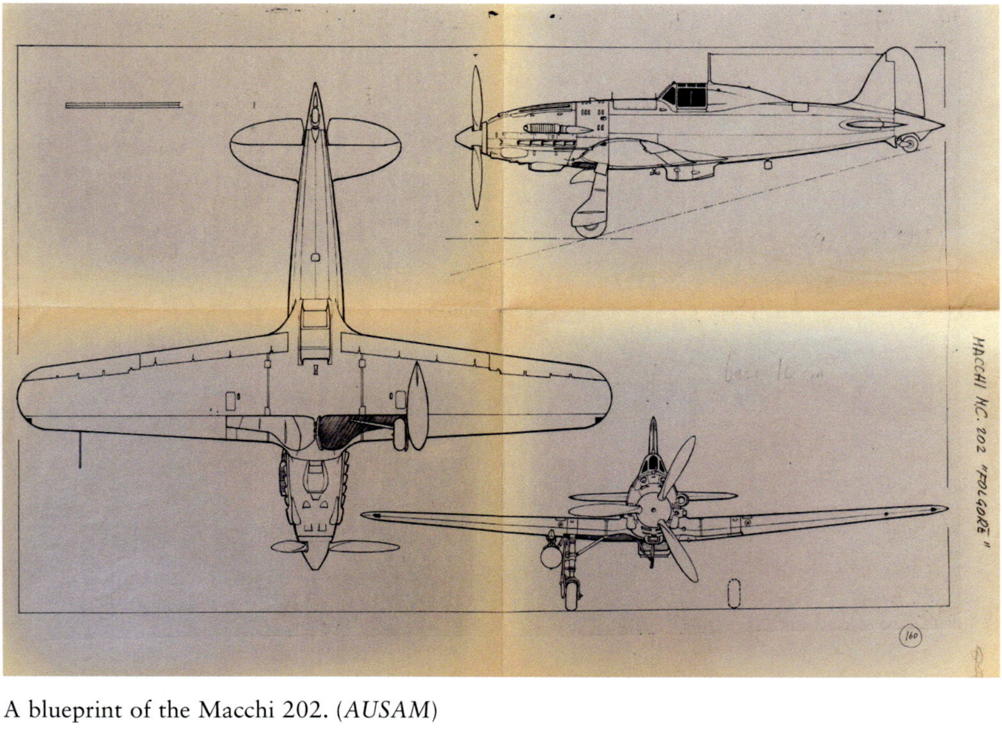

A blueprint of the Macchi 202. (*AUSAM*)

Some well-known personalities paying a visit to the Macchi factory. *From left to right*: the fourth is Castoldi, General Piccio, Balbo, De Bernardi, then with the stick the engineer Macchi. (*AUSAM, Fondo De Bernardi*)

Castoldi speaking with Carestiato before a test flight. (*Archivio Leonardo, Milano*)

Above and below: Macchi M.C.200, 1938. (*AUSAM, Fondo Cometti, B. 27, F. 51*)

Above and below: Macchi M.C.200, 1938. (*AUSAM, Fondo Cometti, B. 27, F. 51*)

Macchi M.C.200, 1938. (*AUSAM, Fondo Cometti, B. 27, F. 51*)

Macchi M.C.200, Castoldi standing close to the Saetta before take-off. (*Archivio Leonardo, Milano*)

Macchi M.C.200, flying over Sicily.

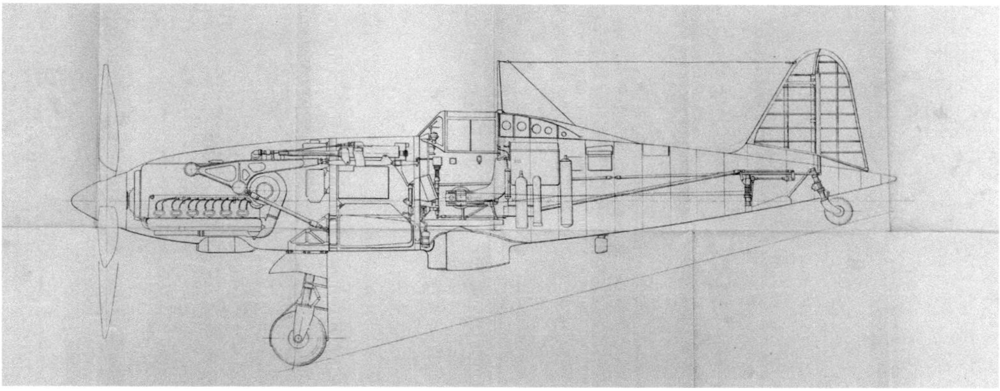

Above: Macchi M.C.202, technical profile plan. (*AUSAM*)

Below: Macchi M.C.202 MM7762, series III, produced by AerMacchi. The new dark olive green 'continental' camouflage scheme was introduced in the summer of 1941, and the yellow noseband on the propeller in the summer of 1941 but discontinued in October 1941, which suggests that this plane was produced in September–October 1941. Probably just off the AerMacchi assembly line at Lonate Pozzolo, this Folgore lacks the model designator on the tailplane, and the coloured band at the tip of the nosecone identifying the *Squadriglia*, to which presumably it had not yet been assigned (though it most likely ended up serving in the 17° *Gruppo*, 1° *Stormo* CT). The plane still lacks the sand filter, *presa d'aria dinamica antisabbia Corbetta*, fitted to the supercharger air intake, which was installed in the planes of this series before they headed to the theatre of operations in Libya. (*Archivio Leonardo, Milano*)

Above: The DB601A-1 direct fuel injection variant of the liquid-cooled, inverted V12 Daimler-Benz DB601 in-line engine, powered the prototype and initial production models of the M.C.202.

Below: The structural complexity of the M.C.202 made it ill-suited to industrial mass production, and it required a substantial amount of man hours to complete each fighter. This image well illustrates the high level of craftsmanship required to assemble the Folgore. It is also significant that there are a substantial number of women among the factory workforce. The '*anelli di fumo*' (smoke rings) camouflage and the predisposition for Breda-SAFAT 7.7-mm wing-mounted machine guns, which can be seen in another photo of this same set, characterised the AerMacchi planes of the Series VII, IX, and XIII, so this photo was probably taken in the period April 1942 to August 1943. (*Archivio Leonardo, Milano*)

The Alfa Romeo RA 1000 RC.41 was the Italian licensed copy of the DB601 in-line engine, powering the M.C.202s from *Serie* VII onwards. (*Museo nazionale della scienza e della tecnologia Leonardo da Vinci, Milano*)

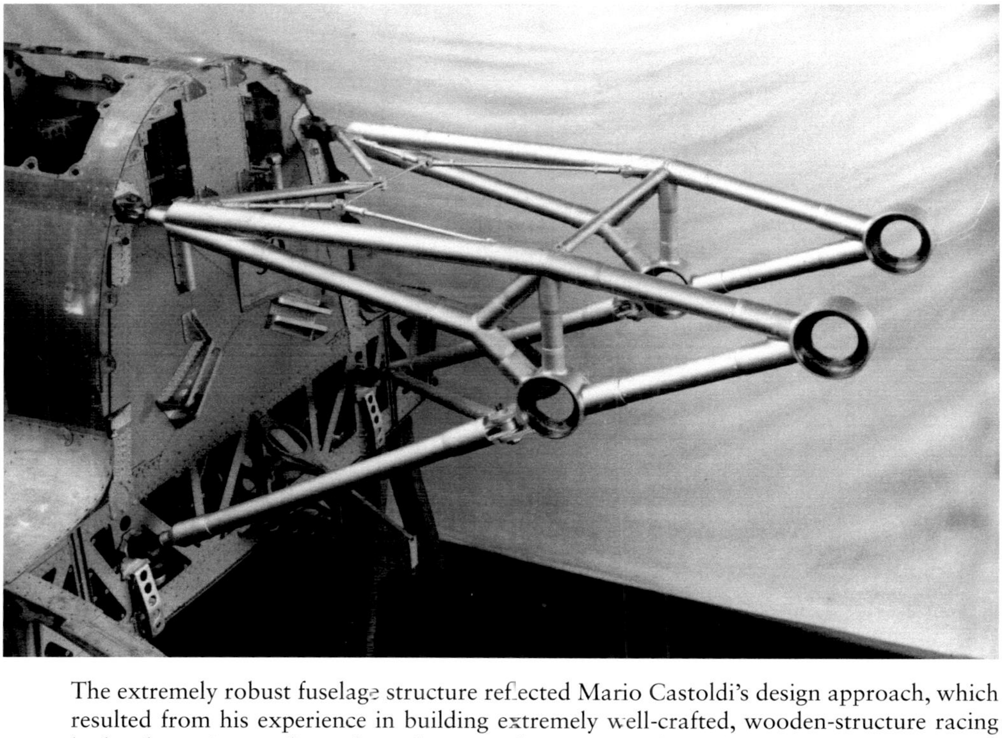

The extremely robust fuselage structure reflected Mario Castoldi's design approach, which resulted from his experience in building extremely well-crafted, wooden-structure racing hydroplanes, in very limited numbers. (*Archivio Leonardo, Milano*)

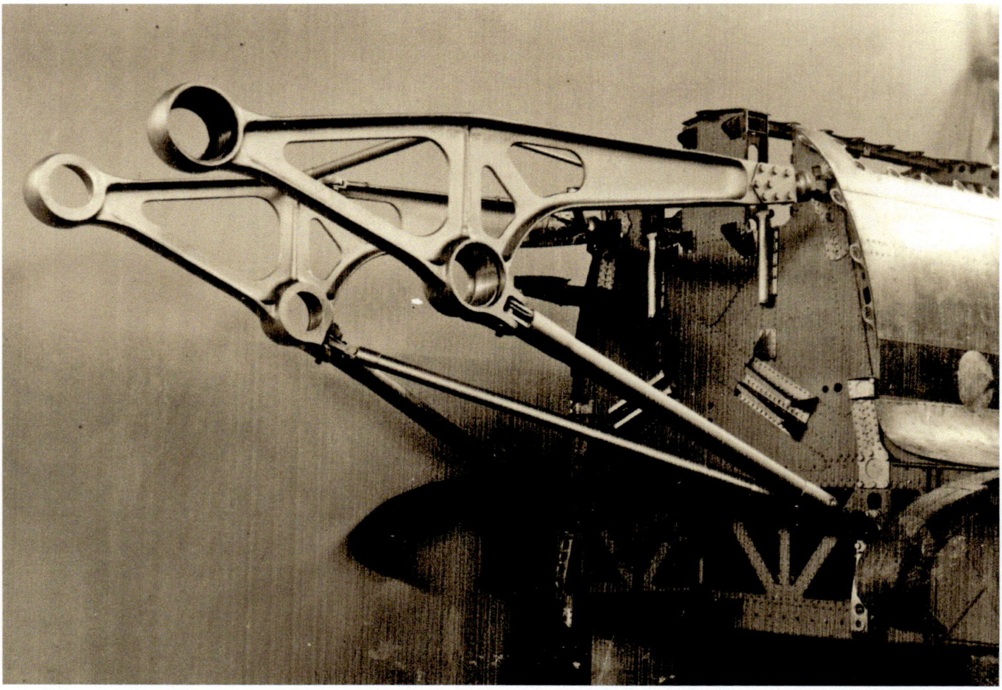

Above and below: The engine bearers of the Macchi prototype and series I to III were made of steel tubing; later series had them replaced by two forged elements of light alloy. (*Archivio Leonardo, Milano*)

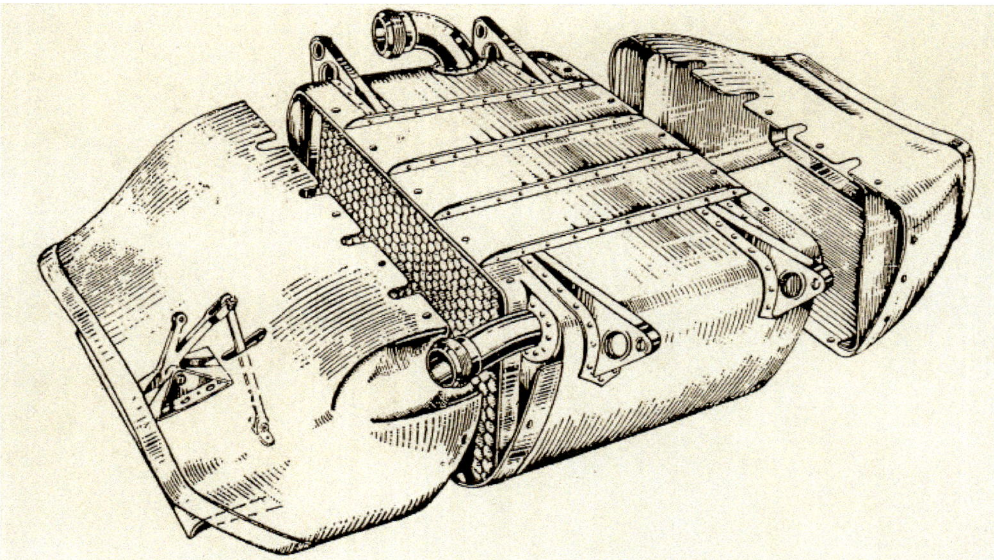

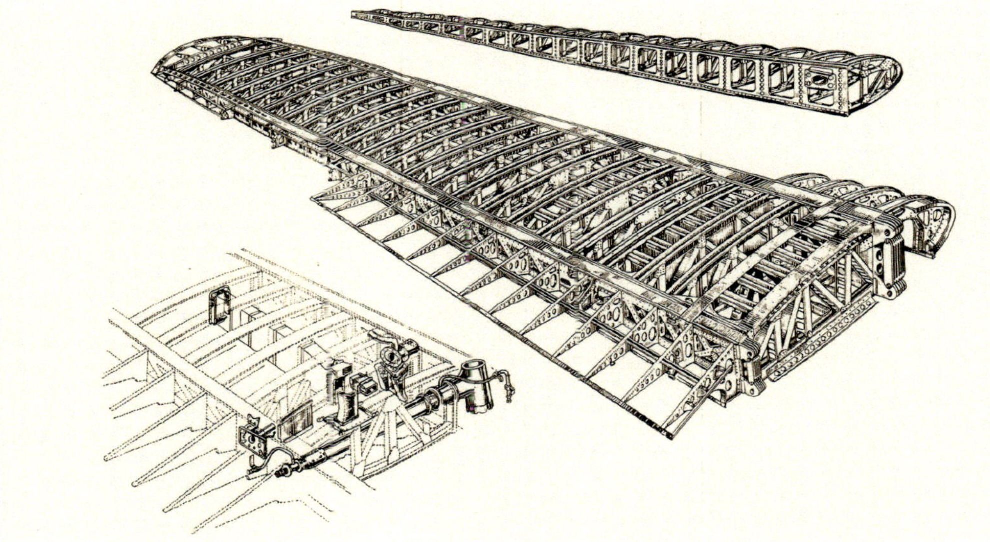

The M.C.202 oil radiator. (*'Società Ernesto Breda, Istruzioni e norme per il montaggio, la regolazione, l'impiego e la manutenzione del velivolo da caccia AER. MACCHI C. 202 con motore R.A. 1000 R.C. 41 I, I.a Serie BREDA, II.a Serie MACCHI, III.a Serie MACCHI. Roma: Ministero dell' Aeronautica, Direzione Generale delle Costruzioni e degli Approvvigionamenti, 1942'*, AUSAM, Roma)

The wing structure, showing the undercarriage pivot axis and main strut pivot, and the wing machine-gun housing with the side magazine for 500 rounds and the muzzle cooling chamber below the leading longeron. (*'Società Ernesto Breda, Istruzioni e norme per il montaggio, la regolazione, l'impiego e la manutenzione del velivolo da caccia AER. MACCHI C. 202 con motore R.A. 1000 R.C. 41 I, I.a Serie BREDA, II.a Serie MACCHI, III.a Serie MACCHI. Roma: Ministero dell' Aeronautica, Direzione Generale delle Costruzioni e degli Approvvigionamenti, 1942'*, AUSAM, Roma)

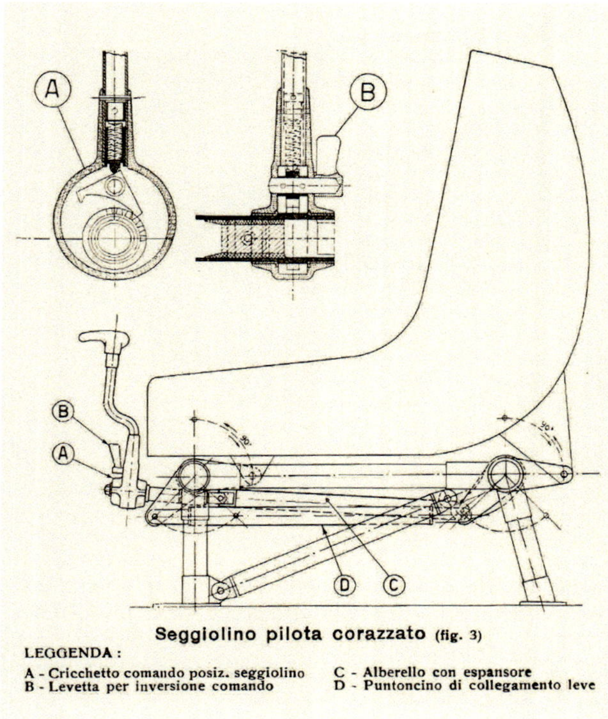

Left: This photo of a M.C.202 of the 1° *Stormo* (maybe 71ª or 72ª *Squadriglia*) is undated, but most likely of late autumn 1941, judging by the lack of the sand filter and the apparent dark olive green camouflage. It shows clearly the cockpit's tilting canopy, hinged on the right side, and the cockpit fairing, which contained a roll bar protecting the pilot in the event of overturning on landing, but it considerably limited rear visibility. (*ACS, Roma*)

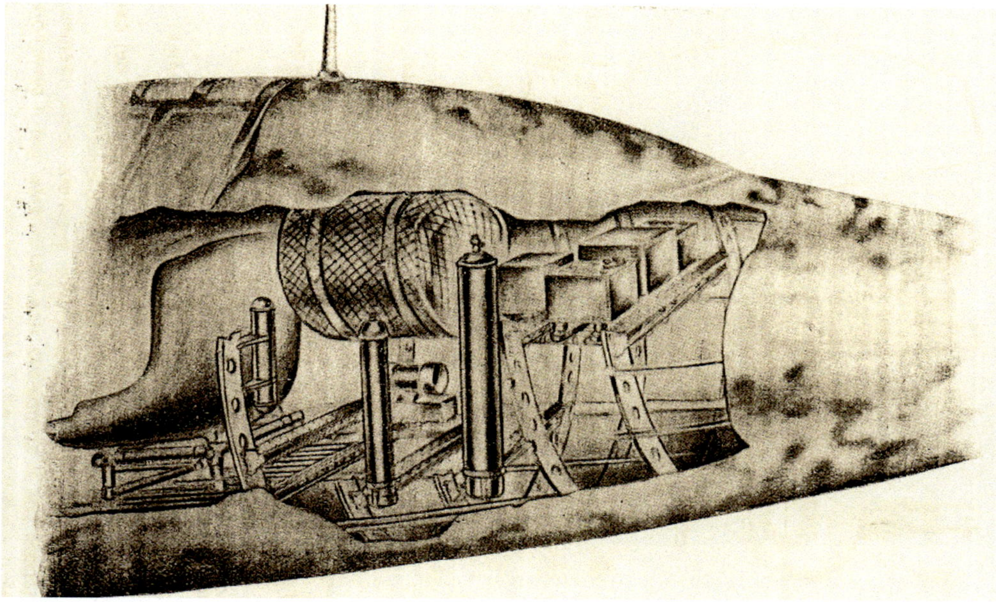

The armoured pilot seat position. (*'Società Ernesto Breda, lstruzioni e norme per il montaggio, la regolazione, l'impiego e la manutenzione del velivolo da caccia AER. MACCHI C. 202 con motore R.A. 1000 R.C. 41 I, l.a Serie BREDA, Il.a Serie MACCHI, III.a Serie MACCHI. Roma: Ministero dell' Aeronautica, Direzione Generale delle Costruzioni e degli Approvvigionamenti, 1942', AUSAM, Roma*)

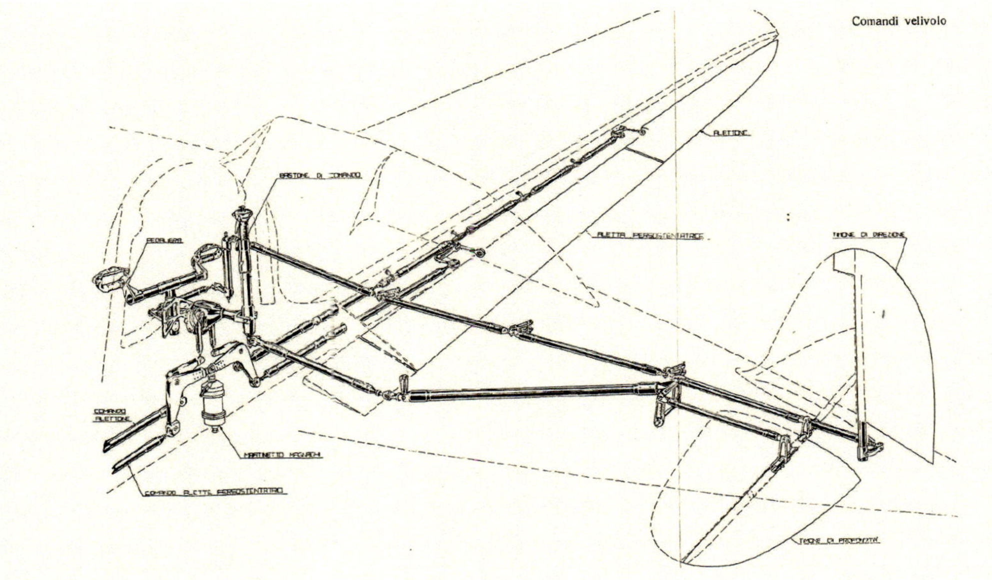

The setup of the rear fuselage of the M.C.202. (*'Società Ernesto Breda, lstruzioni e norme per il montaggio, la regolazione, l'impiego e la manutenzione del velivolo da caccia AER. MACCHI C. 202 con motore R.A. 1000 R.C. 41 I, l.a Serie BREDA, Il.a Serie MACCHI, III.a Serie MACCHI. Roma: Ministero dell' Aeronautica, Direzione Generale delle Costruzioni e degli Approvvigionamenti, 1942'*, AUSAM, Roma)

The aircraft controls, the stick, and the pedal bar were actuated via push-pull rods connected by ball bearings. (*'Società Ernesto Breda, lstruzioni e norme per il montaggio, la regolazione, l'impiego e la manutenzione del velivolo da caccia AER. MACCHI C. 202 con motore R.A. 1000 R.C. 41 I, l.a Serie BREDA, Il.a Serie MACCHI, III.a Serie MACCHI. Roma: Ministero dell' Aeronautica, Direzione Generale delle Costruzioni e degli Approvvigionamenti, 1942'*, AUSAM, Roma)

The layout of the instrumentation in the cockpit. This M.C.202 at the AerMacchi factory in Lonate Pozzolo is a *Serie* VII or later, as it has the distinctive *blindovetro* on the front panel of the cockpit canopy. In evidence is also the reflector gun sight *San Giorgio* type B. (*Archivio Leonardo, Milano*)

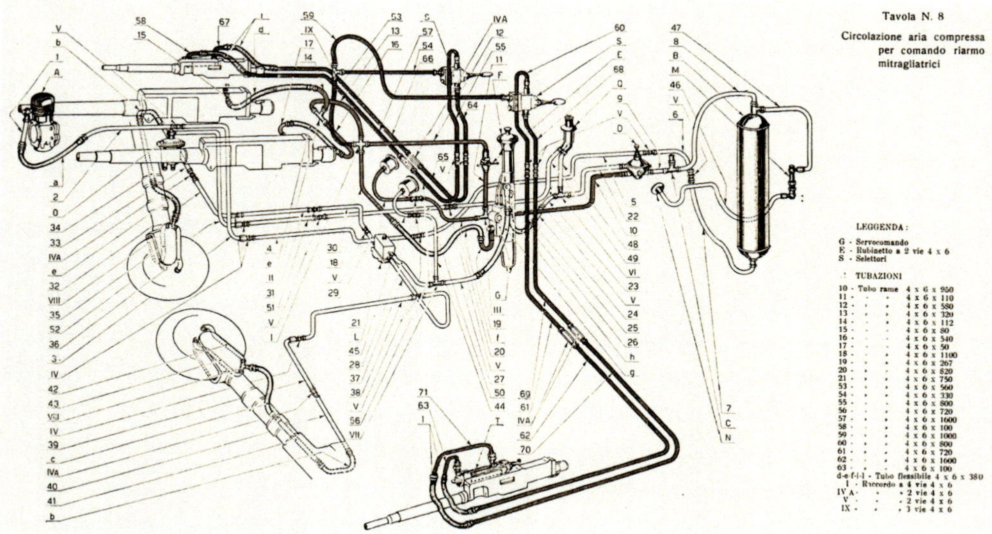

The engine and landing gear control levers on the left side of the cockpit. (*'Società Ernesto Breda, lstruzioni e norme per il montaggio, la regolazione, l'impiego e la manutenzione del velivolo da caccia AER. MACCHI C. 202 con motore R.A. 1000 R.C. 41 I, I.a Serie BREDA, II.a Serie MACCHI, III.a Serie MACCHI. Roma: Ministero dell' Aeronautica, Direzione Generale delle Costruzioni e degli Approvvigionamenti, 1942'*, AUSAM, *Roma*)

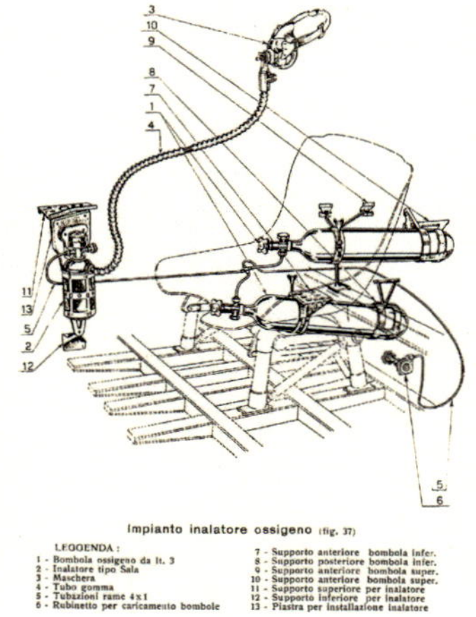

Above left: The pneumatic system of the Macchi M.C.202. In blue, the pneumatic arming, reloading, and unjamming system. (*'Società Ernesto Breda, lstruzioni e norme per il montaggio, la regolazione, l'impiego e la manutenzione del velivolo da caccia AER. MACCHI C. 202 con motore R.A. 1000 R.C. 41 I, l.a Serie BREDA, II.a Serie MACCHI, III.a Serie MACCHI. Roma: Ministero dell' Aeronautica, Direzione Generale delle Costruzioni e degli Approvvigionamenti, 1942'*, AUSAM, Roma)

Above right: The FM-62 OMI Nistri *fotomitragliatrice*. (*'Società Ernesto Breda, lstruzioni e norme per il montaggio, la regolazione, l'impiego e la manutenzione del velivolo da caccia AER. MACCHI C. 202 con motore R.A. 1000 R.C. 41 I, l.a Serie BREDA, II.a Serie MACCHI, III.a Serie MACCHI. Roma: Ministero dell' Aeronautica, Direzione Generale delle Costruzioni e degli Approvvigionamenti, 1942'*, AUSAM, Roma)

Below: The cockpit oxygen distribution system, with the Sala inhaler. This turned out to be problematic and caused losses among Folgore pilots. It was replaced in the course of the Malta campaign by a German Draeger system. (*'Società Ernesto Breda, lstruzioni e norme per il montaggio, la regolazione, l'impiego e la manutenzione del velivolo da caccia AER. MACCHI C. 202 con motore R.A. 1000 R.C. 41 I, l.a Serie BREDA, II.a Serie MACCHI, III.a Serie MACCHI. Roma: Ministero dell' Aeronautica, Direzione Generale delle Costruzioni e degli Approvvigionamenti, 1942'*, AUSAM, Roma)

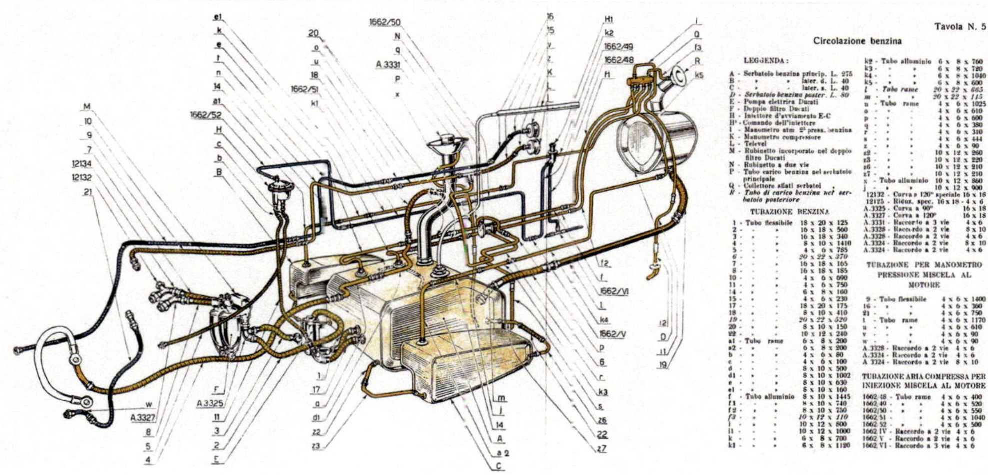

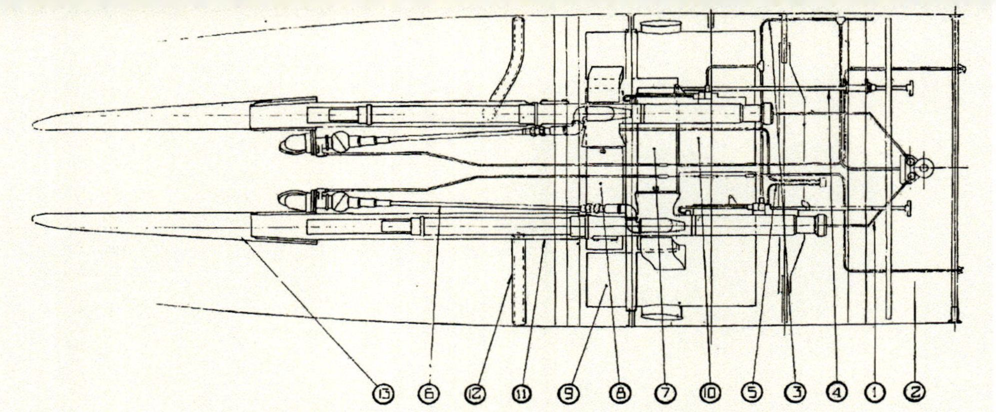

Schema disposizione armamento - vista in pianta (fig. 16)

LEGGENDA:

1 - Comando sparo.
2 - Comando sincronizzazione.
3 - Comando riarmo ad aria compressa.
4 - Manette comando carrello d'armamento.
5 - Comando contacolpi.
6 - Trasmissione per sincronizzazione armi.
7 - Cassetta porta nastro per arma sinistra.
8 - Cassetta porta nastro per arma destra.
9 - Cassetta raccogli maglioni e bossoli per arma sinistra.
10 - Cassetta raccogli maglioni e bossoli per arma destra.
11 - Camera d'aria per arma.
12 - Tubo scarico aria calda.
13 - Nicchia per arma sulla capottatura anteriore.

Above: The fuel circulation system and the four fuel tanks, with a total capacity of 430 litres. (*'Società Ernesto Breda, lstruzioni e norme per il montaggio, la regolazione, l'impiego e la manutenzione del velivolo da caccia AER. MACCHI C. 202 con motore R.A. 1000 R.C. 41 I, l.a Serie BREDA, II.a Serie MACCHI, III.a Serie MACCHI. Roma: Ministero dell' Aeronautica, Direzione Generale delle Costruzioni e degli Approvvigionamenti, 1942', AUSAM, Roma*)

Below: The setup of the two Breda SAFAT 12.7-mm machine guns on the fuselage, seen from above. (*'Società Ernesto Breda, lstruzioni e norme per il montaggio, la regolazione, l'impiego e la manutenzione del velivolo da caccia AER. MACCHI C. 202 con motore R.A. 1000 R.C. 41 I, l.a Serie BREDA, II.a Serie MACCHI, III.a Serie MACCHI. Roma: Ministero dell' Aeronautica, Direzione Generale delle Costruzioni e degli Approvvigionamenti, 1942', AUSAM, Roma*)

Guido Carestiato standing next to the M.C.202 prototype, MM445. The picture probably dates from the autumn of 1940, when the prototype, undergoing tests at the *Centro Sperimentale* of Guidonia, received the typical '*uova in camicia*' (poached egg) camouflage already in use on the M.C.200s.

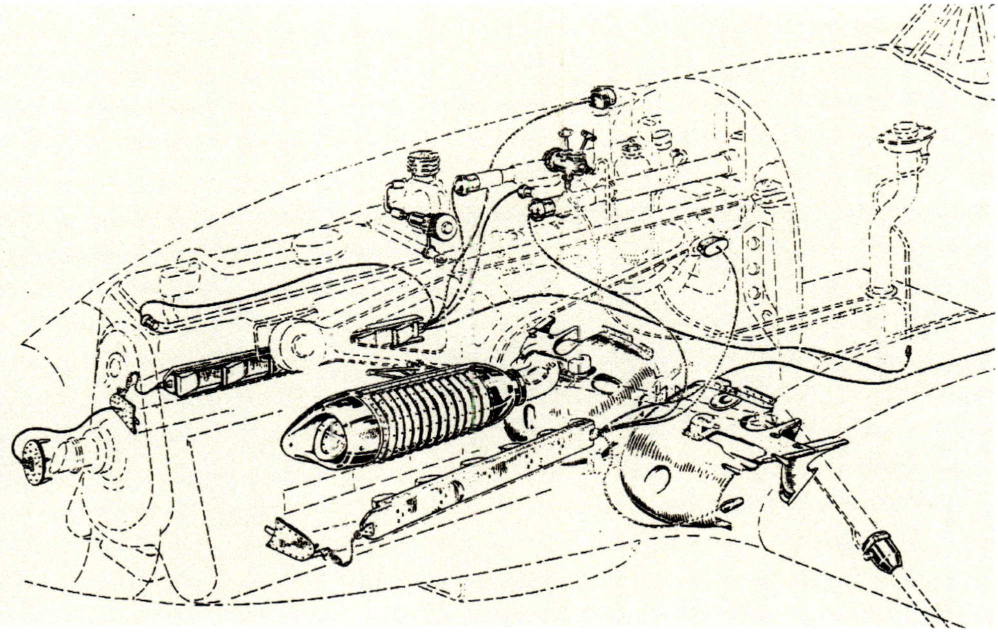

The housing and the control system of the rarely installed Breda SAFAT 7.7-mm wing-mounted machine guns. Owing to its limited firepower and additional weight, *Regia Aeronautica* pilots usually preferred to rely only on the main fuselage armament. (*'Aeronautica Macchi, Istruzioni e norme per il montaggio, la regolazione, l'impiego e la manutenzione del velivolo da caccia Aer.Macchi C. 202 con motore R. A. 1000 R. C. 41 I dalla IXa alla XIa Serie. Roma: Ministero dell'Aeronautica, Direzione Generale delle Costruzioni e degli Approvvigionamenti, 1942', AUSAM, Roma*)

Above: An AerMacchi Series III Folgore, MM7806, equipped with the Corbetta sand filter to the supercharger air intake. All the Folgore that underwent tropicalisation acquired the suffix AS (*Africa Settentrionale*), to indicate their capacity to operate in that theatre. This specific plane, lacking any unit insignia, might have just rolled off of the assembly line and not yet been taken up by a *Squadriglia*. (*AUSAM, Archivio Cometti, Roma*)

Below: The tropicalisation fittings of the M.C.202, converting it into a M.C.202AS (including the *presa d'aria dinamica antisabbia Corbetta*, fitted to the supercharger air intake). (*'Aeronautica Macchi, Istruzioni e norme per il montaggio, la regolazione, l'impiego e la manutenzione del velivolo da caccia Aer.Macchi C. 202 con motore R. A. 1000 R. C. 41 I dalla IXa alla Xla Serie. Roma: Ministero dell'Aeronautica, Direzione Generale delle Costruzioni e degli Approvvigionamenti, 1942', AUSAM, Roma*)

Above: Late 1941: MM7768, fitted experimentally with a coolant radiator under the engine. The experiment was a failure and the modification discontinued. (*Archivio Leonardo, Milano*)

Below: Italian Air Defence Organisation, 1943. (*Author*)

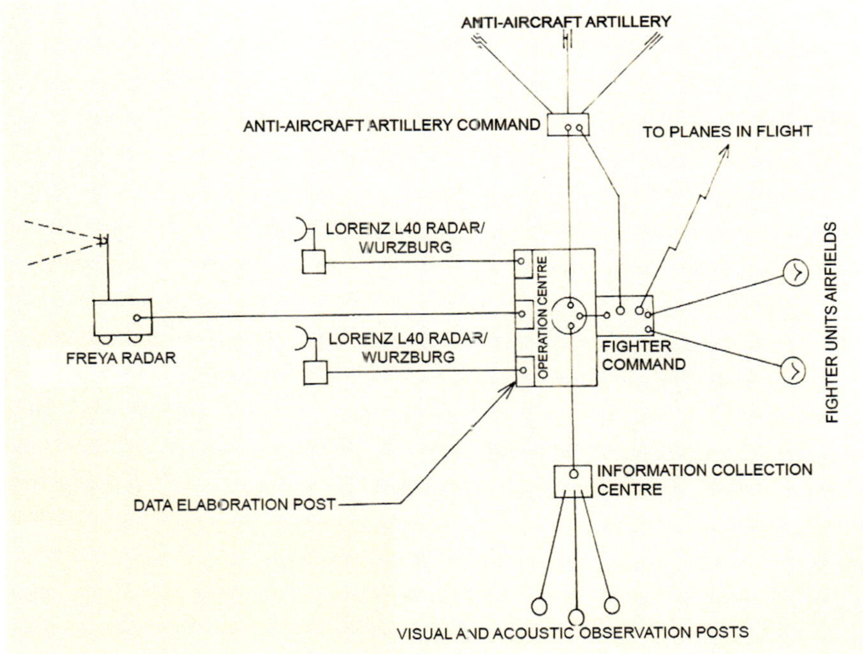

One of the five Breda-produced M.C.202ECs, fitted with two underwing gondolas for 20-mm Mauser MG 151/20 aircraft guns with 200 rounds per weapon, in order to increase the interceptor capacities of the Folgore. The modification was a failure as the additional weight and drag of the weapon installation degraded unacceptably the performance of the plane. (*Archivio Leonardo, Milano*)

Generale Pricolo and *Tenente Colonnello* Bruno Brambilla, commander of the 17° *Gruppo*, probably in October–November 1941 at Ciampino Sud, shortly before the departure of the *Gruppo* for Libya. The M.C.202s still sport the '*continentale*' camouflage but have their yellow nosebands already painted over, preserving just the tip of the propeller cone painted in the *Squadriglia* colours. The Folgores are still lacking the sand filter. (*Troupe Azzurra, Roma*)

Above: M.C.202 90-12 MM7792 of 90ª *Squadriglia*, 10° *Gruppo*, 4° *Stormo*, shot down by the South African Air Force at El Alamein. (*Troupe Azzurra, Roma*)

Below left: Macchi of the 84ª *Squadriglia*, 10° *Gruppo*, 4° *Stormo*, at Campoformido, undated but probably January or February 1942. The 10° *Gruppo* reunited with the 9° in January 1942 at Campoformido and they both re-equipped with *Serie* III AS Folgores. In spring, both *Gruppi* returned to Africa. The white star and the blue band on the propeller cone tip are the symbols of the 84ª *Squadriglia*. (*Archivio Leonardo, Milano*)

Below right: Four of the twelve Folgores, all brand-new Breda *Serie* VIII, which were sent to Russia, attached to the 21° *Gruppo* CT. The aircraft sport the typical markings seen in this theatre of operations, yellow nosebands, and wingtips, following German practice, and white triangles on the wings. (*Troupe Azzurra, Roma*)

Macchi M.C.202s in a SRAM hangar at Lecce airfield. The SRAM (*Squadra Riparazioni Aerei e Motori*/Aircraft and Engine Repair Team) was the fulcrum of all maintenance, overhaul, and repair activities of the *Regia Aeronautica*'s aircraft. The post-armistice *Regia Aeronautica* faced a daunting task in keeping the M.C.202s flying as spares were lacking and the aeronautical industries were in enemy territory in Northern Italy. Nonetheless, it managed to put together seventy-seven Macchi, mostly by painstakingly assembling the relatively compatible parts of M.C.200s, 202s, and 205Vs with the purpose of salvaging the largest number of aircraft possible. (*Troupe Azzurra, Roma*)

This rather rundown Macchi, probably belonging to the 4° *Stormo* CT, is the result of the cannibalisation of other planes, as is clearly shown by the engine cowling sporting a different camouflage pattern from the rest of the plane. Nonetheless, by the summer of 1944, even by obtaining spares from decommissioned planes, it was becoming hard to keep a sufficient number of Folgores in the air. Thanks to Allied support, the Italian fighter units started transitioning to US or British planes, such as the P-39 seen here next to the M.C.202. (*Troupe Azzurra, Roma*)

shot down what—and claimed nine victories in the morning, of the actual four achieved. At 12.15 p.m., Annoni scrambled again with eight M.C.202s, finding another five Folgores of the 70ª and 75ª *Squadriglia* of the 23° *Gruppo* already in the air, and they engaged enemy fighters and fighter-bombers. Shortly after, another three M.C.202s from the 91ª *Squadriglia* of the 10° *Gruppo*, 4° *Stormo*, led by *Sergente Maggiore* Leonardo Ferrulli, joined the Macchis of the 23° *Gruppo* and engaged yet another enemy formation (of No. 250 and No. 92 Squadrons) along with some Bf 109Fs of II/JG27. In those two combats, which merged into one, the *Regia Aeronautica* pilots claimed one Boston damaged, two P-40Fs, one Kittyhawk III, and one Mk V Spitfire shot down; one Kittyhawk III probable; and another six fighters damaged. In reality, British losses were one Kittyhawk III and one Mk V Spitfire, and two Kittyhawk III damaged.

In the afternoon of October 9, combat continued unabated, involving also dozens of Bf 109Fs of III/JG53, and again the Macchis of the 4° *Stormo*, which entered combat in several patrols scrambling at intervals, to engage the above-mentioned Allied units operating in the El Daba area. This day of combat was known by the British as *Daba Prang* (from the name of the area of operations, El Daba, and the RAF slang for a bombing raid), and was characterised by heavy overclaiming, with at least twenty-eight victories claimed by the *Luftwaffe* and twenty victories claimed by the *Regia Aeronautica* (nineteen by the 4° *Stormo* and one by the 23° *Gruppo* of the 3° *Stormo*); in reality, sixteen RAF planes were lost.[62] The Desert Air Force claimed ten victories during the day and at least fifty aircraft destroyed on the ground.

An equally large attack on Axis airfields took place on 20 October, when a formation of Baltimores and B-25s, escorted by P-40Fs of No. 450 Squadron, Tomahawks of 66th Fighter Group, and Kittyhawks of No. 3 RAAF and (perhaps) No. 2 SAAF attacked Fuka airfield:

> The high number of aircraft flying in the area during these days caused such confusion that the German Freya radar personnel had trouble identifying friend or foe aircraft. So, the alarm was delayed, and … the bombers were releasingtheir cargo over the airfield when the 73ª *Squadriglia* (*Tenente* Giuseppe Oblach, *Tenente* Vittorio Squarcia, *Sergente* Armando Angelini and *Sergente* Leonardo Rinaldi), 84ª *Squadriglia* (*Capitano* Lucchini, *Tenente* Alessandro Mettimano and *Sergente Maggiore* Piero Buttazzi), 91ª *Squadriglia* (*Capitano* Carlo Maurizio Ruspoli di Poggio Suasa, *Sergente Maggiore* Leonardo Ferrulli and *Sergente Maggiore* Alessandro Bladelli), and 97ª *Squadriglia* (*Tenente* Jacopo Frigerio, *Sottotenente* Giovanni Barcaro, *Sottotenente* Leo Boselli and *Maresciallo* Giovanni Bianchelli) scrambled to attack them.[63]

Some M.C.202s were damaged on the ground and two destroyed while attempting to take off.[64] Seven other Macchis, from the 23° *Gruppo* at Abu Aggag, led by *Capitano* Claudio Solaro, also took part in this combat, losing the plane of *Tenente* Giorgio Santamaria, who was killed in action. About an hour later, another Allied formation of fighter-bombers attacked LG21 of El Daba, and in the resulting combat, the intervening 10° *Gruppo* of the 4° *Stormo* claimed three enemy fighters shot down (of which in fact only one appears to have been damaged by a M.C.202). About two hours later, the 4° *Stormo* scrambled again to confront a mixed formation of bombers and fighters.

In the course of the day, the 23° *Gruppo* scrambled another eight times until early afternoon, not always managing to intercept enemy aircraft, while the 4° *Stormo* took off for the last time that day at about 4 p.m. to attack some British bombers with their usual fighter escort. In total, the 4° *Stormo* claimed twenty-four enemy aircraft shot down during the day, but of the fifty-seven fighters (forty-three of which were combat-ready) available in the morning, only eleven were serviceable in the evening.[65]

The 18° *Gruppo* of the 3° *Stormo* lost thirteen M.C.200s in the 21 October bombing, and the 23° *Gruppo* some M.C.202s, too (the daily serviceability of this *Gruppo* being of fourteen or fifteen fighters per day, or about 40 per cent). Those were replaced by twelve old M.C.202s of the 10° and ten of the 9° *Gruppo* assigned to the 18°, and twelve to the 23° *Gruppo*, delivered on 27 October at Abu Smeit.[66]

The 9° and 10° *Gruppo* of 4° *Stormo* received in exchange brand-new fighters at Martuba, flown in from Italy on 5 November by pilots of the 1° *Stormo* (28 to the 9° and an undetermined quantity to the 10° *Gruppo*), and flew them to the front just in time to cover the retreat of the Axis forces.[67]

The Desert Air Force relentlessly pounded the airfields at Fuka, Abu Nimeir, and Abu Aggag also on 22 October, and the following days air combat was equally unremitting, especially with the start of the second battle of El Alamein on 23 October, the sign that the command of the air was passing inexorably to the Allies with their great numerical superiority and resources. Large and confused air battles took place on all the frontline over the last days of October, seeing also what is probably the first Macchi shot down by an USAAF P-40F, the M.C.202 of *Sergente* Amleto Monterumici (perhaps), heavily damaged (in practical terms a total write-off) by 1Lt Roy E. Whittaker of 65th Fighter Squadron.[68]

As the Axis front collapsed in a retreat in the very first days of November, the *Regia Aeronautica* units started to be redeployed on airfields to the rear; the 4° *Stormo* at Martuba Airfield, after having left their few last flyable planes to the 3° *Stormo*. On 5 November, the 3° *Stormo* moved to Abar

Nimeir, and later in the day to Bu Amud. The 150° *Gruppo Autonomo* left its bases at the rear of the frontline on 10 November, returning to Italy to refit (at Ciampino Sud Airport), and the day after, the 13° *Gruppo* of the 2° *Stormo*, which at this point had eighteen M.C.202s, retreated to El Nofilia.[69] The 9° *Gruppo*, having received the new M.C.202s, deployed at Ara Fileni, and the 10° transferred on 16 November to Tauorga, where the 23° *Gruppo* of the 3° *Stormo* had moved coming from El Nofilia.[70]

The retreat continued in December 1942, as the 8th Army pushed ahead. The command of the 4° *Stormo* with its 9° *Gruppo* fell back on 6 December from Ara Fileni to Misurata, and shortly after to Castelbenito (Tripoli). Likewise, the command of the 2° *Stormo* with its 13° *Gruppo* redeployed at Villaggio Crispi (Misurata Sud), with a few M.C.200s and only two M.C.202s. This retreat left the 3° *Stormo* as the only frontline unit available, and it concentrated all its *Gruppi* at Taourga, and later, towards the end of December, at Castelbenito.

The 5ª *Squadra Aerea* pushed for the retreat to Italy of the most depleted units, while only a trickle of reinforcements still reached Libya as the retreat went on. So the 4° *Stormo*, exhausted by the cycle of operation, was sent back to Italy, to Campoformido; the 10° *Gruppo*, at the end of December, handed its aircraft to the 9° *Gruppo*, and the 9° *Gruppo*, on 17 January 1943, handed its aircraft to the 3° *Stormo* at Castelbenito.[71] The 18° *Gruppo* had also received some M.C.202s from the 13° *Gruppo* on 31 December.

The 202s suffered from lack of fuel, spares, and replacements, and by January 1943, when German and Italian troops under *Generalfeldmarschall* Erwin Rommel reached Tunisia, only a handful remained, serving with the 3° *Stormo* and a squadron of the 13° *Gruppo*. While the *Regia Aeronautica* fighter units were depleted, their pilots overburdened, and the strategic situation under threat, they still showed determination and abnegation, as in the case of the attack by the 13° *Gruppo* on British airfields in the Wadi Tamet on 11 January 1943:

> MC200s from the 13° *Gruppo* attacked the area. These fighter-bombers were escorted by MC202 from the 18° *Gruppo*. Acting as close escort on this mission were four aircraft from the 95ª *Squadriglia* under the command of *Capitano* Solaroli. A little bit higher up were *Maggiore* Gustavo Garetto with six aircraft. As top cover at 6,000 to 7,000 metres were six MC202s from the 23° *Gruppo* under the command of *Capitano* Mario Rigatti and above these were six more under the command of *Tenente Colonello* Tito Falconi. The Italian aircraft were attacked by the RAF and the 18° *Gruppo* managed with difficulty to defend the fighter-bombers. During the combat *Sottotenente* Telleschi and *Maggiore*

> Garetto were shot down together with a MC200 from the 13° *Gruppo*. It is probable that Telleschi and Garetto were claimed by the British ace Flying Officer Neville Duke of 92 Squadron in Spitfire MK.Vb EP338 'QJ-S' (victory 8 and 9). The Italian attack was, however, a success and a fuel depot, a transport aircraft, which was surprised while taxiing, and several parked aircraft were destroyed on the British airfield. Also six British Spitfires were claimed in the combat. One of them was claimed by Solaroli, one by *Sergente* Luigi Gorrini (who also claimed one damaged) and a third by *Maresciallo* Felice Longhi, who returned with his aircraft damaged by enemy fire in several places. The Italians also claimed hits on 9 additional enemy aircraft.[72]

From January to December 1942, the Italian fighter units performed a total of 23,555 sorties, about 30 per cent of which must be attributed to the M.C.202s. The M.C.202s were more than a match for the enemy aircraft of all types, usually maintaining superiority in one-to-one combat until Mk V (trop.) Spitfires appeared. Nonetheless, their relatively small numbers and, more importantly, the huge supply difficulties and lack of spares threatened their operational impact. This was not only the result of the poor production rate of M.C.202s and the long supply lines from Italy to Libya, but also the effect of the specific effort of the Desert Air Forces in hitting the lifeline of the Axis armies in Africa.[73]

As the Axis forces were retreating hurriedly westward through Libya, the Allies landed in French North Africa (in Morocco and in Algeria), thus opening up a new, broad front. The first response of the *Regia Aeronautica* to the landings was to deploy units in Tunisia as soon as possible, and to Sardinia to escort strikes on the Algerian coast, at Bône and Bougie. The 155° *Gruppo* of the 51° *Stormo* had received its M.C.202s in March 1942 and had operated from Sicily against Malta. On 10 November, twenty-one M.C.202s of the 351ª *Squadriglia* and 378ª *Squadriglia* of this *Gruppo* were led by *Tenente Colonnello* Aldo Remondino from Gela to El Aouina, some of which suffered some slight damage from a British Beaufighter raid the very same day.[74]

The following night, the airport, still short of any significant flak for lack of fuel and supplies, was raided again, this time destroying on the ground three Macchis (MM8361 code 351-8, MM8366 code 351-11, and MM7788 code 378-7) and damaging seven, and yet again on 14 November, with the destruction of one Macchi, and the damaging of another (MM9095), and the injurying of *Capitano* Carlo Miani of the 360ª *Squadriglia* of the 155° *Gruppo*, and of *Tenente* Emilio Marchi of the 80ª *Squadriglia* of 17° *Gruppo*, who happened to have landed at El Aouina with engine trouble after a strafing attack on Bône.[75] In its short stay at El

Aouina, the 155° *Gruppo* was reduced to four combat-effective Macchis out of the original twenty-one. Two had been destroyed on the ground, four were damaged but reparable at unit level, five were sent back to the factory for overhauling, and ten were in flyable condition but unfit for combat.[76,77]

The 153° *Gruppo* of the 53° *Stormo*, made up of the 372ª, 373ª, and 374ª *Squadriglia* deployed to Sardinia with twenty-four M.C.202s between 7 and 20 November, coming from Sciacca and joined there the 17° *Gruppo* of the 1° *Stormo* led by *Colonnello* Alfredo Reglieri. The 17° *Gruppo* had arrived in Decimomannu on 7 November, with thirty-four M.C.202s, and was deployed for the first time shortly afterwards, on 14 November.[78,79,80] That day, ten M.C.202s led by *Capitano* Pericle Baruffi strafed Bône Airfield (according to Allied reports, to no avail), suffering damage to the M.C.202 of *Tenente* Pietro Maurichi, and one plane, that of *Tenente* Emilio Marchi, forced to land because of engine trouble.[81] On 14 November, the 88ª *Squadriglia*, 6° *Gruppo* of the 1° *Stormo*, also arrived in Decimomannu.[82,83] The 80ª, 88ª, and 71ª *Squadriglia*, 1° *Stormo*, attacked Bône again on 16 November, with twelve Macchis led by *Capitano* Dante Ocarso, CO of the 88ª *Squadriglia*; the fighters strafed the airport in two line-abreast formations, and suffered three losses by AA and British fighters (MM9391 of *Tenente* Mario Galli, MIA; MM9394 of *Sottotenente* Alfredo Civetta, POW; MM9518 of *Tenente* Glauco Vatta, MIA); and one damaged which crash-landed (*Tenente* Pietro Maurichi). Later that day, the 17° *Gruppo* was in action again as escort for a formation of S.84 and Cant Z.1007bis, bombing troop concentrations along the Bizerta–Tabarca road.[84]

The other *Gruppo* of the 1° *Stormo*, the 6°, moved its headquarters to Decimomannu, leaving the 79ª *Squadriglia* at Ciampino to protect the capital, on 17 November. The 155° *Gruppo* of the 51° *Stormo* was bombed again at El Aouina on the 18th, leaving five M.C.202s damaged.

During the same days, the first encounters between M.C.202s and USAAF units took place; for instance, on 19 November 1942, perhaps the first clash between M.C.202s and USAAF B17s and P-38s: a lone Folgore of *Sottotenente* Francesco Fagiolo, 155° *Gruppo*, intercepted a formation of bombers and fighters, albeit causing no losses to them but being damaged in return. A couple of days later, a second encounter with USAAF bombers took place, when twelve USAAF B-17s of the 97th Bomber Group escorted by P-38s of the 48th Fighter Squadron, 14th Fighter Group were intercepted by four M.C.202s of the 360ª *Squadriglia*, 155° *Gruppo*, who claimed heavy damage to five bombers and one P-38—in fact, only the P-38 was damaged and forced to crash-land at base.

Both the units in Sardinia and at El Aouina operated continuously for the rest of the month, mostly as escort for fighter-bombers or ground-attack planes.

By December 1942, the Allies had managed to firmly establish their air units in the new theatre of operations. The *Regia Aeronautica* kept only the 155° *Gruppo* in Tunisia, in the exposed position of El Aouina which got bombed regularly, causing losses to the *Gruppo* (e.g. on 1 December by A-20 Havocs escorted by P-38s, with the loss of M.C.202 MM8354, code 360-3, of *Tenente* Romano Biasiol, which belly-landed and was then destroyed on the ground, and of the *Folgore* of *Tenente* Agostino Cigala Fulgosi, damaged).[85] On 11 December, the depleted 155° *Gruppo* was transferred back to Italy, being deployed at Gela in Sicily, while the 71ª and 72ª *Squadriglie* of the 17° *Gruppo*, 1° *Stormo*, which were transferred from Sardinia to Pantelleria on 6 December, were joined by the 80ª *Squadriglia* on 13 December, thus reuniting the 17° *Gruppo* on the island.

The 155° *Gruppo* was replaced by the 6° *Gruppo*, 1° *Stormo*, initially moving the ten M.C.202s of the 81ª *Squadriglia* from Pantelleria to Sfax on 11 January, and subsequently the balance of the *Gruppo*, but keeping the 79ª *Squadriglia* in Pantelleria.[86] Its main mission was escorting the sea and air traffic between Sicily and Tunisia.[87] It was in the course of one such missions, on 21 January 1942, that some M.C.202s of the 79ª *Squadriglia*, 6° *Gruppo*, and the 80ª *Squadriglia*, 17° *Gruppo*, while escorting two S.84s in reconnaissance, stumbled upon a group of USAAF B-26 of 319th Bomber Group escorted by P-38s of the 82nd Fighter Group; in the ensuing combat, both the S.84s were lost, along with M.C.202s MM9093 of *Maresciallo* Mario Tozzi (79ª *Squadriglia*) and MM9516 of *Sergente* Dario Cereda (80ª *Squadriglia*), and the USAAF lost two P-38s.[88]

As Rommel's *Afrika Korps* retreated westward towards the Mareth line in January 1943, the Folgores of the 3° *Stormo*, which had covered the retreat across Tripolitania, were transferred to Medenine, Tunisia. On 19 January, the 74ª and 75ª *Squadriglie* from the 23° *Gruppo* and the 85ª and 95ª *Squadriglie* from the 18° *Gruppo,* and on 20 January the 83ª *Squadriglia* of the 18° *Gruppo* along with the 70ª *Squadriglia* from the 23° *Gruppo* were the last Italian air units to leave Libya.[89] On 26 January, the 95ª *Squadriglia* was detached to Gabès, to pick up more M.C.202s from the 13° *Gruppo*, then rejoining their parent unit at El Hamma on 8 February. The number of M.C.200s of the 18° *Gruppo* dwindled rapidly in Tunisia, being replaced by M.C.202s. By 16 February, thirteen M.C.202s out of twenty-nine were still serviceable. At the end of March, the unit withdrew to Italy, having no aircraft left.

The 6° *Gruppo*, 1° *Stormo*, continued to operate from Sfax until the end of January, scrambling regularly to intercept bombers and their escorts, most often P-38s (e.g. on 28 and 31 January and 2 February) and flying patrols both over land and on sea routes (e.g. on 30 January).[90, 91, 92] By now, the first Mk IX Spitfires had begun arriving on the Tunisian front with No. 81 Squadron, tipping further the qualitative balance to the disadvantage of the M.C.202s.[93]

In February, the 79ª *Squadriglia* was in Sfax and the 81ª *Squadriglia* in Aichichina (Al Hushayshinah).[94] On 15 February 1943, the *Regia Aeronautica* disbanded the *Aeronautica della Tunisia* and reorganised the command under the 5ª *Squadra Aerea*, the *Settore Nord*, comprising all of Tunisia roughly north of the 35th parallel, under *Colonnello* Augusto Bacchiani, and *Settore Sud*, south of the 35th parallel, under the command of *Colonnello* Carlo Drago. By then, there were fifty-five M.C.202s in Tunisia, distributed between the 6° *Gruppo* (under the *Settore Nord*), while in the *Settore Sud* there were the nineteen M.C.202s of the 18° and 23° *Gruppi* of the 3° *Stormo* at El Hamma, and the 16° *Gruppo* deployed with Folgores on Landing Grounds K41, then K34, and eventually on 24 February at Medenine.[95, 96]

On 21 February, the *Regia Aeronautica* further reinforced its units already present in Tunisia, the 6° *Gruppo* and the 3° *Stormo* with the 88ª *Squadriglia* of the 6° *Gruppo* arriving at Gammarth from Pantelleria, with nine M.C.202s (building up to a total of fifty-five M.C.202s).[97] Another ten Folgores arrived at Landing Ground K41 from Sicily with the 169ª *Squadriglia* of the 16° *Gruppo*, and twenty more with the 167ª and 168ª *Squadriglie* of the same *Gruppo*, between 23 and 26 February.[98] On 2 March, the 368ª *Squadriglia* of 151° *Gruppo*, 53° *Stormo*, left Sfax for Pantelleria, relinquishing its G50 to re-equip with M.C.202s.[99] By 22 March, it would be back in the fray, with five Folgores engaging P-38s of the No. 82 Fighter Group off Bizerte and losing one aircraft, MM9693 with *Tenente* Vittorio de Martinis, KIA.[100] The same unit would lose another M.C.202 (MM9634), that of *Sergente* Umberto dal Pozzo, KIA, off Cap el Karon to a Spitfire IX, a definitely superior quality aircraft.

In this period, several combats occurred with the pilots of the USAAF 12th Air Force, the Folgores encountering on many occasions P-38s of the 1st and 14th Fighter Groups, the P-39 Airacobras of the 81st and 350th Fighter Groups, Mk V Spitfires of the 31st and 52nd Fighter Groups, and heavy bombers. The M.C.202 was somewhat superior to the P-38, in manoeuvrability and climb rate, while not a match in terms of armament. The Airacobras were likewise better armed, but otherwise underperforming as compared to the Macchis, and were usually relegated to ground-attack duties. Clashes with B-17s such as that of 10 March 1943 over Tunis involving the 80ª and 71ª *Squadriglie* of the 17° *Gruppo* demonstated how difficult it was for the M.C.202 to engage heavily armed and robust aircraft such as the USAAF heavies with the lack of punch of the two 12.7-mm Breda SAFAT, and resulted in two Folgores being seriously damaged (and two M.C.202s of the 88ª

Squadriglia of the 6° *Gruppo* destroyed on the ground), with no loss to the bombers.[101]

On 6 and 7 March, *Regia Aeronautica* units, including the M.C.202s, were engaged in an Italian-German counteroffensive (the Battle of Medenine), which stemmed temporarily the momentum of the Allied offensive. In that month, the C.202 supported twenty-one fights, during which they managed to down nineteen Spitfires, one P-40, and one P-38. The 16° *Gruppo* took part in the battle, seventeen M.C.202s claiming on 7 March nine Spitfires and a P-38 for the loss of two of their own. Nine new M.C.202s were received at K41 Landing Grounds on 20 March to replace those lost to Allied bombing in the previous days.[102] The 6° *Gruppo* also detached six Macchis from Sfax to Gabès for armed reconnaissance duties during the battle, on 6 March.

From 16 to 31 March 1943, the two operations Pugilist and Supercharge II battered and then pierced the Mareth Line, resulting in the retreat of the Axis forces.

Reinforcements were sent to the *Regia Aeronautica* on 25 March in the shape of the thirty-five Folgores of the 7° *Gruppo*, which deployed at El Hamma with the 76ª, 86ª, and 98 ª*Squadriglie*, with detachments at K34 and K41 Landing Grounds.[103] On 30 March, it joined the 16° *Gruppo* in the reformed 54° *Stormo*.[104] The 88ª *Squadriglia* of the 6° *Gruppo* left for Pantelleria on 30 March. *Regia Aeronautica* airfields were regularly bombed, receiving particularly heavy incursions on 29 March, at Achichina where the 3° *Stormo* and the 6° *Gruppo* were based, with the destruction of five M.C.202s and another twelve damaged; on 30 March at Sfax, and again on the 31st, when the attack hit the Folgores as they were scrambling, with five aircraft and another ten damaged. Between February and March, twenty Macchis were lost and forty-seven were damaged to varying degrees. The balance of air superiority was shifting as the well-experienced and battle-hardened Axis air units were by then clashing with Allied pilots who were becoming more competent (a substantial quantity of them being in their second cycle of operations in Africa), better supplied, and flying superior machines, such as the Mk IX Spitfire.

Massive and constant bombing raids also contributed to the whittling down of the *Regia Aeronautica*; after being pummelled at Sfax and K41, by 4 April, the 16° *Gruppo* had four M.C.202s serviceable. The same day, the last elements of the 3° *Stormo* abandoned Africa for Sciacca, Sicily, leaving their planes to the 54° *Stormo*.[105] The Allies, enjoying by now a significant numerical superiority, kept up the pressure on the enemy airports with continuous strikes, and started hitting, with Operation Flax, the air transport ensuring the lifeline between Italy and the beleaguered Axis troops in Tunisia, so that M.C.202s frequently acted as transport escorts.[106] The battle of Wadi Akarit on 6–7 April opened up the Gabès Gap, allowing the Allies to pursue the retreating enemy troops towards Tunis. The battle heavily involved the 54° *Stormo*, flying protection patrols over the Italian lines and intercepting bomber formations, flying multiple sorties per day. A pilot of the 86ª *Squadriglia*, 7° *Gruppo*, *Sergente* Arnaldo Mauri, was a member of the alert crew at La Fauconnerie on that day, together with *Sergente Maggiore* Filippo Guarnaccia and *Sottotenente* Mario Caliani of the 98ª *Squadriglia* of the same *Gruppo*:

> It was hot and the *Sottotenente* was a little sleepy because of the great tiredness brought on by uninterrupted flying. Quite suddenly we saw an escorted formation of twin-engine aircraft approaching the airfield, we immediately called Caliani while we jumped into the aircraft, taking off immediately. Some German Me. 109s were also scrambling from a nearby airfield. We began to gain altitude quickly, trying to attack from below and by surprise the bombers and fighters, about six Spitfires who followed the twin-engined planes closely [in fact they were Kittyhawks of No. 3 RAAF Squadron]. The manoeuvre was succeeding and by then we saw distinctly a dozen Bostons and Marauders, I can't remember exactly, when a Spit noticed our arrival and began to flap its wings, strangely though, without communicating the sighting via radio. Perhaps his radio was damaged, otherwise it would not have been necessary for that pilot to overtake all the formation, flapping his wings and firing warning bursts. The signal was immediately well understood, so that the fighters immediately broke formation to avoid the threat. The aircraft that had performed this manoeuvre had to recall, since it was flying at only 1500–2000 m, and I found it perfectly framed in my collimator. The burst of fire did not miss and, turning upside down, it began to smoke, quickly falling to the ground, where it crashed.... In the fight we did not see *Tenente* Caliani and unfortunately we learned that, having taken off immediately after us, his 202 was mistaken by German Me.109s for an isolated enemy fighter and downed.[107, 108]

The next day, the same pilot took part in a patrol to protect troops on the ground and clashed with Spitfires, most likely from USAAF 308th FS of 31 FG:

> The enemy took a hard hit and started to smoke while pieces of metal peeling from the wings were flying, fluttering, towards me, almost brushing me. We lost altitude quickly when, unexpectedly, a barrage of machine gun fire struck me full on, making the roof fly off and riddling my instument panel, which fell apart. I realized that, in my turn, I had

> been tailed by another Spit and was receiving my full ration of bullets. We were almost in a chandelle and the speed well exceeded the maximum of 650 km/h allowed for my Folgore. The cloche vibrated violently and the smoke increased, clouding the air and making it unbreathable. I could not eject because of the high speed and, on the other hand, I was not able to recall the plane because my opponent did not give up and continued to fire precise bursts. The yellowish surface of the ground came nearer and nearer in a few moments. I started to make out the features of the stony desert interspersed with splashes of marshland. At this point the pilot of the Spit realized that there was no escape for me and so recalled, letting go of his prey.[109, 100]

Mauri crash-landed and made his way back to the lines by foot.

On 8 April, ten Folgores from 7° *Gruppo* led by *Capitano* Bruno Politi engaged a group of Mk V Spitfires, against which the M.C.202s could still be a credible match, if the conditions were right. In this case they were: height advantage and the sun behind. *Capitano* Adriano Visconti shot down the formation leader and hit another Spitfire. *Sergente* Giuseppe Marconcini brought down the left wingman, and *Sergente* Domenico Laiolo attacked another Spitfire, shooting it down. For Visconti, it was the fourth victory.[111]

During March and April, the M.C.202s of the 151° *Gruppo*, 53° *Stormo*, based in Sicily, were also busy protecting the shipping lanes to Africa, but losing a constant trickle of planes both to enemy action and, as on 31 March and 1 April, to bad weather.[112]

By mid-April, only the 54° *Stormo* remained in Tunisia: the other units, without aircraft and with decimated personnel, had left Africa definitively. On 15 April, the 5ª *Squadra Aerea* was disbanded and the *Aereonautica della Tunisia* re-established.[113]

The attacks on air transports, usually both German Ju 52s and Italian SM.82s, increased steadily from mid-April, regular combats involving the M.C.202s of the escorts, until 18 April, Palm Sunday, when a huge formation of ninety Ju 53/3ms escorted both by Bf 109s and M.C.202s was intercepted by several Allied formations, with thirty-seven transports shot down and several more damaged, though no M.C.202s apparently lost.[114]

The last major clash involving the Folgores before the surrender in Tunisia took place on 29 April, when thirteen Macchi 202s of the 7° *Gruppo*, protecting a naval convoy sailing between Cap Bon and the island of Zembra, engaged sixty Spitfires and P-40s about to attack the ships; the *Regia Aeronautica* pilots claimed five shot down, one by *Capitano* Adriano Visconti, and five probables, for the loss of one plane—

that of *Capitano* Ugo Diappi of the 86ª *Squadriglia*—and three more damaged.

The last combat action of the 54° *Stormo* in Tunisia took place on 6 May, with fourteen Macchis that had taken off from Soliman engaging som P-40s in combat near Cap Bon. On 7 May 1943, the 7° *Gruppo* was in Soliman with nineteen M.C.202s. The next day, as the Soliman base was too exposed to enemy bombardment, the unit, under the command of *Maggiore* Molinari, joined the 16° *Gruppo* in Korba. This concentration of units did not go unnoticed by the enemy, so on 9 May, Korba was the object of five waves of bombing, between 11 a.m. and 7 p.m. Of the nineteen aircraft of the 7° *Gruppo*, only four were salvaged. On the same day, those four aircraft, with eight pilots on board, took off from Tunisia passing through Sicily. A fifth plane was able to take off after some repairs.

On the evening of 9 May, therefore, they made a stopover in Pantelleria, reaching the Sciacca base in Sicily on 10 May 1943 together with the 16° *Gruppo*, the M.C.202s abandoning Africa until it reappeared again in 1948 with Egyptian insignia. With the return to Sicily on 18 May, the 7° *Gruppo* remained without aircraft and crews and was disbanded on 27 May, together with the 54° *Stormo*.

Malta, 1941–42

After the departure of the X *Fliegerkorps* in May 1941, it was up to *Generale di Divisione Aerea* Renato Mazzucco's *Aeronautica della Sicilia* to eliminate Malta's British offensive potential and to protect the sea lines of communication to Africa in the Strait of Sicily. This mission was to be achieved with an insufficient number of bombers, and with the core of the fighter arm of the *Regia Aeronautica* being equipped with aircraft manifestly inferior to those based on Malta. Moreover, the RAF in Malta had been substantially reinforced in May–June, and the aerial defence network improved. The main fighter type on Malta by then was the Hurricane of the newer Mk II type, equipped with a 1,480-hp Rolls-Royce Merlin XX engine with a top speed of 340 mph and an increased armament of twelve .303 machine guns (Hurricane Mk IIB) or four 20-mm Hispano Mk II cannons (Hurricane Mk IIC). The Mk II Hurricanes were more than a match for the *Regia Aeronautica*'s M.C.200s and completely outclassed its CR.42s.

The Italian strategy consisted of a limited amount of daylight bomber raids, and a more substantial amount of high-altitude area bombing at night, with fairly light ordnance—the strategy being also determined by the materials available. *Aeronautica della Sicilia*, having more fighters available, made an attempt to lure the RAF into a campaign of attrition in the hope of restoring air superiority, and fighters were used in strafing sweeps on Malta's airports.

By the end of the summer of 1941, it had become clear that the M.C.200s were not up to the task of establishing air superiority, when facing the Mk II Hurricanes, whose superior armament and speed, combined with boom and zoom energy tactics that were the result of the lessons learnt in the battle of Britain, prevailed over the greater manoeuvrability of the M.C.200s. Moreover, the *Saetta*'s armament of only two Breda SAFAT 12.7-mm MGs made it a poor choice as an improvised fighter-bomber for ground-strafing roles. By October 1941, around twenty M.C.200s had been lost in combat over Malta since June, while the defenders lost less than half that number of Hurricanes.[115] On 29 September, however, the first Macchi M.C.202s started arriving in theatre, with the 9° *Gruppo*, 4° *Stormo*; the *Gruppo* had transitioned to the Folgore in Gorizia, and was transferred to Comiso, with the plan to reach the North African front. The day after the arrival of the *Gruppo*, the Macchi M.C.202 received its baptism of fire while operating out of Comiso, when *Sottotenente* Jacopo Frigerio of the 97ª *Squadriglia*, 9° *Gruppo*, shot down a Hurricane from the RAF No. 185 Squadron, based in Malta.[116, 117]

The appearance of the M.C.202s put considerable pressure on the defenders of Malta, as eventually also the *Regia Aeronautica* was equipped with a fighter clearly superior to Malta's Mk II Hurricanes, being faster and more manoeuvrable (though still underarmed compared to the latter). The first M.C.202 combat over the island proper took place on 1 October when seven of the 73ª *Squadriglia*, 9° *Gruppo*, led by *Capitano* Mario Pluda (other pilots being *Capitano* Carlo Ivaldi, *Tenente* Pietro Bonfatti, *Sottotenente* Giuseppe Oblach, *Sergente Maggiore* Enrico Dallari, *Sergente* Santo Gino, and *Sottotenente* Alvaro Querci, the latter being forced to return due to problems with the infamously unreliable oxygen supply of the M.C.202), conducted a fighter sweep over the island. The Folgores bounced eight Hurricanes from No. 185 Squadron scrambling after the incoming 'bandits', at about 7,000 metres, 50 km north-east of the island, and Sqn Ldr Peter Mould (Z5265/GL-T) was shot down. During the skirmish, three of the 73ª *Squadriglia* pilots, *Capitano* Ivaldi, *Tenente* Pietro Bonfatti, and *Sergente Maggiore* Enrico Dallari, jointly claimed two Hurricanes shot down and two probables in the first pass, although Ivaldi's aircraft (MM7723) was hit in its main fuel tank (by Sgt Ernie Knight) and was obliged to force-land on a beach near Pozzallo on the Sicilian coast.[118] Macchis performed strafing runs, bomber escorts, and armed reconnaissance over the island, as for instance on 14 October, when six low-flying M.C.202s of the 9° *Gruppo* strafed Luqa. They attacked in two pairs of three and it seems that they did not inflict any damage on the airfield or its aircraft, a result of the inadequacy of M.C.202's armament for the role of fighter-bomber. Five MNFU Hurricanes took off to intercept, led by Flt Lt Cassidy. Three each from No. 185 and No. 249 Squadrons followed them. Plt Off. David Barnwell (Hurricane Z3512) of the MNFU claimed on radio one enemy fighter shot down, which was probably that of *Sottotenente* Emanuele Annoni, who despite having sustained two cannon shell strikes in the fuselage, was able to make it back to Comiso:

> Left with a jammed weapon, while I fumbled to unjam it, a Hurricane attacked me. A 20 mm round that penetrated the side at the height of the white band pierced the rudder depth control rod, which remained in one piece but by an inch, and pulverized the battery, making a 40 cm hole on the opposite side of the fuselage. Another round of 20 mm got me at the base of the tail, blocking the movement of the handwheel and limiting the excursion of the bar. Paolazzi then took my opponent off my tail.[119]

Barnwell then failed to return, and he was proabably shot down by either *Sottotenente* Bruno Paolazzi, *Maresciallo* Manlio Olivetti, or jointly by *Sergente Maggiore* Luigi Taroni and *Sergente* Gustavo Minelli.[120] From the arrival of the 9° *Gruppo* in Sicily at the end of September to the end of November, the M.C.202s' tally was of eight Hurricanes and one Fulmar over Malta. The satisfaction of the *Stato Maggiore dell'Aeronautica* was extremely high, and in October, Pricolo wrote to Mussolini about the first results of the M.C.202:

> Exceptional performance of the new machine, with brilliant flight characteristics, very well made [this was not the case, because as of then it had problems of filter crystallisation, of oxygen distribution in cockpit and of radio communication, to mention but a few] ready to receive two other weapons in the distinguished itself immediately in combat with victorious results.[121]

The fight was not wholly one-sided, as four Folgores were lost in the same period, the first M.C.202 being shot down on 25 October, the pilot killed in action being the CO of 4° *Stormo*, *Tenente Colonnello* Eugenio Leotta.[122, 123, 124]

While the Macchi showed its worth over this period, it had failed to help the *Aeronautica della Sicilia* in its strategic objectives, the strength of Malta's defences and air assets actually increasing between June and November. Radar would play a vital role in this, as the British were able to vector intercepting fighters onto approaching bomber formations at the correct altitude. While the *Luftwaffe* had started installing its radar system, the lack of coordination between the two Axis partners prevented the *Regia Aeronautica* from benefitting from it. To compensate somewhat for this disadvantage, the Italians developed a highly advanced radio interception apparatus that allowed communications between RAF aircraft and their ground bases to be intercepted and monitored, thus providing information to the *guida-caccia* stations at airfields throughout Sicily, which in turn would guide the fighters. Such a laborious system, though, was no match for the British radar and fighter control.[125, 126, 127]

On 25 November, the 96ª and 97ª *Squadriglie* of the 9° *Gruppo* transferred to Libya (with their sand filters missing and without tropicalisation, a choice not conductive to a lengthy lifespan of the engines), while the 73ª *Squadriglia* remained in Sicily, being also tasked with photoreconnaissance with some Macchis being equipped with the *macchina fotoplanimetrica* AGR90. At least one M.C.202RF of this *Squadriglia* has been positively identified, MM7727 (code 73-10); Macchis of this version kept their armament and were regularly involved in combat.[128] The refusal of the *Capo di Stato Maggiore* of the *Regia Aeronautica*, Pricolo, to send the Macchis to Libya without proper tropicalisation (in particular engine sand filters), regardless of the *Duce*'s pressing requests to that effect, was the last straw in a tug-of-war within the Italian supreme command, which saw *Capo di Stato Maggiore Generale* Ugo Cavallero pushing for the dismissal of his *Regia Aeronautica* colleague, under the pretext that he had failed to ensure the protection of Axis convoys to Africa and the development of an adequate anti-shipping capability. Pricolo was dismissed on 14 November and the next *Capo di Stato Maggiore* was Rino Corso Fougier, the former commander of the *Corpo Aereo Italiano* (CAI) in Belgium. Fougier prioritised the production of the new series of fighters with the DB601A-1 engine, the Reggiane Re.2001 and particularly the M.C.202, and saw the need to reorganise the bomber arm, both processes being rather time-consuming, so that in fact the operational tempo of the *Aeronautica della Sicilia* (that Fougier put under the command of *Generale* Silvio Scaroni, a First World War ace) actually decreased from December 1941 to March 1942. *Regia Aeronautica* units were in fact transferred out of Sicily to make room for the arriving II *Fliegerkorps* who would take over the offensive.

The M.C.202s of the 73ª *Squadriglia*, in this second cycle of operations starting in December 1941, would operate alongside *Luftwaffe* units, often as escorts for the continuous and heavy II *Fliegerkorps* raids on the island (such as for instance on 20 December).[129] The significantly larger and qualitatively better aircraft of the *Luftwaffe* rapidly regained air superiority over Malta, and by the end of January, thirty-one RAF planes had been destroyed on the ground, and eight in the air; by the end of February, a further fifty-one on the ground and twenty-two in the air.

By March, the RAF had been reduced to twenty-one Hurricanes left on the island, and the conditions for the invasion of the island, *Operazione C3*, seemed to be present. In preparation for this, *Capo di Stato Maggiore* Fougier ordered more reinforcements to Sicily on 18 March, but these did not arrive until April and May as units were in the course of transitioning to M.C.202s and Re.2001s. The 96ª and 97ª *Squadriglie* of the 9° *Gruppo*, having returned to Campoformido to receive new M.C.202s with sand filters, and the 10° *Gruppo*, which had received the new M.C.202s from December, arrived back in Sicily, at Castelvetrano, on 2 April with twenty-six new Folgores, to take part in the renewed offensive against Malta.[130] In total, the 9° and 10° *Gruppi* would deploy fifty-two Macchis for the forthcoming battle. On 19 April, pilots from the 10° *Gruppo* undertook their first acclimatisation flight and suffered their first loss when *Sergente* Elio Trevisan of the 90ª *Squadriglia* experienced a problem with his oxygen supply and was forced to bale out. He was subsequently picked up safely. The problem of oxygen distribution in the cabin would not be solved until the replacement of the apparatus by a German one.

Meanwhile, on 7 March, the RAF started reinforcing its presence on the island with fifteen Mk Vc (trop.) Spitfires. The Mk V possessed a top speed of 362 mph and an armament of four .303 in machine guns and two 20-mm cannon, and was a match for the M.C.202 in all respects, being superior in armament. The Spitfires were transported on the decks of the aircraft carrier HMS *Argus*, taking off at some distance from Malta and landing on one of the various airports. A further nine Mk Vs arrived on 21 March, transported on the aircraft carrier HMS *Eagle*, and nine more on 29 March. With the help of the US Navy, forty-six more Spitfires reached Malta on 19 April, carried by USS *Wasp* (Operation Calendar). Such an injection of reinforcements on the island called for heavy bombing raids: the *Regia Aeronautica* and the *Luftwaffe* responded that same day by hitting Malta's three airfields—Takali, Luqa, and Hal Far with 272 bomber sorties.

The Italian contribution to the raid consisted of nineteen M.C.202s from the 10° *Gruppo*. Unfortunately, just thirty minutes into the flight, two Folgores collided, killing the formation leader and forcing his wingman to bale out into the sea off Porto Empedocle. The mission was immediately aborted.[131] During this mission, the pilots of the *Gruppo* complained about the severe problems with the oxygen distribution apparatus in the cockpit. To solve them, 'it was necessary to request supply from Germany of the Draeger type inhaler, obtained through the personal intervention of Marshal Kesserling.'[132]

On 27 April, twenty-seven M.C.202s of the 4° *Stormo* escorted thirty-five JU88s, twenty-one JU87s and five Z1007bis in raids on Luqa, Takali and the Grand Harbour, meeting no air opposition from the battered RAF. The 4° *Stormo* kept up an intense operational tempo with daily missions of various types: on 1 May, the 9° *Gruppo* escorted Cant Z.1007s on a bombing mission on a dispersal area in Micabba. On 2 May, they escorted German Ju 88As on bombing fuel depots in Micabba; on 3 May, CANT Z.1007s were escorted on Ta Venezia, and on 4 May 1942, five Cant Z.1007bis from the 211ª *Squadriglia* were escorted to bomb the Grand Harbour, and *Sottotenente* Alvaro Querci and *Sergente* Martinoli of the 73ª *Squadriglia* claimed one Spitfire each, which might have been that of Sgt J. N. McConnell's BR187/O, of No. 601 Squadron, which crash-landed at Luqa.[133]

Nonetheless, Malta continued to be reinforced via aircraft carriers, and subsequently pummelled by Axis forces, such as on 9 May 1942, in response to the arrival of sixty-one Spitfires transported by carriers USS *Wasp* and HMS *Eagle* (Operation Bowery). In the course of one of the numerous bombing raids to catch the Spitfires on the ground, the day after, the first confirmed M.C.202 loss took place when fifteen M.C.202s of the 9° *Gruppo* and five of the 10° *Gruppo*, along with Re.2001s of 2° *Gruppo*, escorting five Z.1007bis of the 50° *Gruppo* B.T., were intercepted by a large number of Spitfires; in the subsequent combat, a Z.1007bis and the M.C.202 of *Capitano* Roberto Dagasso, CO of the 97ª *Squadriglia*, were lost, the latter falling victim to New Zealander Plt Off. Wally Caldwell (flying BR344/4-H) of No. 601 Sqn.[134, 135]

From that day onward, the intensity of air combat slowly decreased and the presence of the *Regia Aeronautica* units was more apparent than that of the *Luftwaffe*, a clear sign of disengagement on the German side as most of the units of *Luftflotte* 2 departed Sicily for service in other areas. In fact, between the competing demands of the *Operazione C3* and Rommel's *Operazione Venezia* aiming at reconquering Tobruk, Hitler had opted on 30 April for the latter. As Rommel's offensive in Africa pushed towards Egypt, by the end of June 1942, all serious Axis planning for an invasion of Malta ceased abruptly, and thus ended the Axis campaign of aerial denial over Malta. On 21 and 24 May, the 4° *Stormo* from Sicily returned to Africa for its third operational cycle with its 9° and subsequently 10° *Gruppo*. The RAF took advantage of the decreased aerial activity in June and heavily reinforced the island with Spitfires; soon fighter-bombers and bombers returned to Malta's airfields to resume attacks on Axis convoys. Heavy combat over Malta did not cease until the end of October, but from then on, the aim of the Axis was to protect its own supply lines from Italy to Africa.[136]

By the beginning of the summer, the *Regia Aeronautica*, now called upon to maintain the balance of the effort against Malta, reinforced its fighter arm by sending to Sicily its available Folgore-equipped units. The 20° *Gruppo* (151ª, 352ª, and 353ª *Squadriglia*), which had returned from Africa at the end of December 1941 and had received its Macchi M.C.202s in March, moved in June 1942 to Chinisia and then Gela as part of the newly reformed 51° *Stormo*.[137] The other *Gruppo* of the same *Stormo*, the 155° *Gruppo* (351ª, 360ª, and 378ª *Squadriglia*), having received its M.C.202s in March, arrived on 18 May in Gela, led by *Maggiore* Duilio Fanali. For much of June, the main activity of the M.C.202s was fighter sweeps, but on 14 June, the 155° *Gruppo* moved to Chinisia in order to escort Ju 87s during the attacks on the Malta-bound Harpoon supply convoy:

> At 11:00 hours on 15th June, 25 MC202s from the 155° *Gruppo* CT (6 from the 351ª *Squadriglia*, 10 from the 360ª *Squadriglia* and 9 from the 378ª *Squadriglia*), led by *Maggiore* Fanali, took off to escort 10 Italian Ju 87s of the 102° *Gruppo* (led by *Capitano* Giuseppe Cenni), which set out to attack the 'Harpoon' convoy bound for Malta. They found the convoy 70km south of Pantelleria. At 12:10 hours, while the Junkers were diving with their 500kg bombs, escorting Spitfires from 601 Squadron attacked them. The 360ª *Squadriglia* attacked the British fighters, and *Capitano* Carlo Miani (CO of the 360ª *Squadriglia*), *Tenente* Tullio Martinelli, *Sottotenente* Francesco Fagiolo and *Maresciallo* Pasquale Bartolucci claimed a Spitfire each, while *Sottotenente* Romano Biasiol, *Tenente* Giambattista Caracciolo, *Sottotenente* Nicola Longano and *Sergente Maggiore* Mario Varacca claimed a shared Hurricane.... None of the escorting MC202s were damaged.[138]

In July, yet another *Regia Aeronautica* offensive started over Malta, the *Luftwaffe* sending some combat-proven units to support their allies. On 6 July, twenty-four M.C.202s of the 20° *Gruppo* and fourteen Re.2001s of the 2° *Gruppo* escorting three Z.1007bis, were intercepted by eleven Spitfires from No. 249 Squadron. Other Folgores, led by *Capitano* Furio Niclot Doglio of the 151ª *Squadriglia*, 20° *Gruppo* (Niclot Doglio was an ace with seven kills, and a very experienced pilot, holding several flight records from pre-war times), were also over the island flying a sweep ahead of the bombers. FS George 'Screwball' Beurling, who was to become Malta's top-scoring ace, in Spitfire Mk V BR323/S (code UF-S) met the incoming bombers head on, firing as he flew past them; he then engaged the escorts:

> As the bombers turned to run I saw a Macchi 202 boring up on 'Smitty's' [Flg Off John Smith] tail. I did a quick climbing turn and bored in on the 'Eyetie', catching him unawares. A one-second burst smacked him in the engine and glycol tank. He burst into flames and went down like a plummet.[139]

Beurling's victim was *Sergente Maggiore* Francesco Pecchiari of the 352ª *Squadriglia*, 20° *Gruppo*, who survived (Beurling would be made an ace that same day, shooting down another two enemy planes). On 7 July, Niclot Doglio and seven other Macchi pilots, escorting the Ju 88A-4 of *Kampfgeschwader* 77, clashed over Luqa with seven Spitfires, Niclot and his wingman, Ennio Tarantola, shot down the Spitfire (AB500) of FS D. Ferraby from No. 249 Squadron. The same day, twenty-three Folgores of the 155° *Gruppo* (seven from the 351ª *Squadriglia*, nine from the 360ª *Squadriglia* and seven from the 378ª *Squadriglia*) and twelve from the 20° *Gruppo*, led by Duilio Fanali (both from the 51° *Stormo*), and twelve Re.2001s from the 2° *Gruppo*, escorted nine Cant Z.1007bis of the 9° *Stormo* to attack Luqa. Twenty-two Mk V Spitfires of No. 126 and No. 185 Squadrons scrambled to intercept, and in the ensuing fight, two Spitfires of No. 185 Squadron were shot down and their pilots killed. One of the Spitfires was claimed as shared by pilots of the 20° *Gruppo*, who also claimed to have damaged five Spitfires; two of them by *Capitano* Miani (CO of the 360ª *Squadriglia*) and *Sottotenente* Romano Biasiol (360ª *Squadriglia*). In return, the M.C.202 (MM9033) of *Tenente* Fabrizio Cherubini (353ª *Squadriglia*, 20° *Gruppo*) was shot down by FS J. W. Yarra (BR387 'W') of No. 185 Squadron, who claimed one more fighter as a Re.2001. Three Cant Z.1007s were also damaged.[140]

By mid-July, the Italian offensive against Malta had run out of steam. *Regia Aeronautica* bombers reduced their raids over the island, while the fighter units were struggling to keep sufficient aircraft serviceable to sustain a heightened tempo of operations. The lack of incisiveness of the Italian offensive gave rise to complaints on the part of the *Luftwaffe*. In the course of a meeting with Fougier and Scaroni, on 23 July, Bruno Loerzer, the commander of the II *Fliegerkorps*, who was responsible for German operations in the Mediterranean and Malta, accused the *Regia Aeronautica* of not doing enough, picking out the fighter arm in particular as underperforming. The *Regia Aeronautica* was at this point unable, for organisational and industrial reasons, to keep more than 30–50 per cent of any unit's aircraft serviceable, and Fougier could only admit the bitter truth to the Germans.[141]

On 27 July 1942, thirteen Folgores (eleven from the 20° *Gruppo* and two from the 155° *Gruppo*) were assigned as indirect escort for nine Ju

88s. Niclot Doglio leading three other Macchis, including that of his wingman Ennio Tarantola and that of Faliero Gelli, saw six Spitfires of No. 126 Squadron attacking head-on, but he failed to notice eight other Spitfires of the No. 249 Squadron coming from the left. As he was preparing to counterattack the Spitfires of 126 Sqn, his wingman, *Sergente* Ennio Tarantola, tried to warn his commander by waggling his wings (as Italian radios typically worked badly) of the Spitfires diving at them from the left, but Niclot understood that Tarantola was warning him about the Spitfires he had already spotted. FS George 'Screwball' Beurling, from 249 Sqn, recalled:

> I spotted four Macchis running in line astern and took No 4. They saw me coming and pulled into a climbing turn to the right. As they did so, I came up on my man's starboard quarter and let him have a burst. It was a straight deflection shot which went into his engine and radiator. He flicked into a spin, but managed to pull out and crash-landed on Gozo, able to walk away from the mess.[142]

The Macchi was *Sergente* Faliero Gelli's, who described the action from his point of view:

> I saw one Spitfire firing at me but felt no hits. I took violent evasive action and, when I disengaged, noticed that the engine temperature was mounting rapidly. I turned north in an effort to reach my base but soon realised I could not do this as my oil tank was hit as well as my radiator. I turned back and force-landed on Gozo, getting away with a few bruises.[143]

Just after Beurling shot down Niclot Doglio's MM9042. 'The poor devil simply blew to pieces in the air', commented Beurling. Niclot Doglio was his fourteenth 'kill'. The death of Doglio was a bad blow for the morale of the *Regia Aeronautica*, as his squadron mate Ronaldo Scaroni recounted: 'When he died, some of the fighting spirit of the *Regia Aeronautica* died with him. There was a feeling that if Furio Doglio Niclot couldn't survive, none of us could. For the first time we began to doubt that Malta could be taken'.[144]

The M.C.202 was involved again in aeronaval battles in mid-August, in the course of Operation Pedestal (3–15 August), the British operation to resupply the island of Malta especially with crucial aviation fuel. On 11 August, in Sicily and Pantelleria there was one M.C.202 from the 76ª *Squadriglia*, 7° *Gruppo*, six Folgores from the 20° *Gruppo*, and twenty-one from the 155° *Gruppo*. In Reggio Calabria, there were three M.C.202s from a *Sezione Fotografica*.[145, 146] M.C.202s and Re.2001s based in Sicily escorted the Ju 87s and the SM.79s attacking the Allied ships.

On 12 August, seventeen M.C.202s from the 351ª, 360ª, and 378ª *Squadriglie* of the 155° *Gruppo* took off from Pantelleria, led by Duilio Fanali, to escort fourteen SM.79 torpedo-bombers of the 132° *Gruppo*, attacking the Pedestal convoy.[147] After the SM.79s had released their torpedoes, the escorting fighters clashed with six to eight Sea Hurricanes. The 155° *Gruppo* claimed four enemy planes shot down and one probable; the 20° *Gruppo*, led by the 51° *Stormo* CO, *Tenente Colonello* Aldo Remondino on M.C.202 MM9029 code 378-1, also took part in the operation and claimed three additional Hurricanes destroyed. The Fleet Air Arm in fact lost a Fulmar and a Sea Hurricane heavily damaged and total write-offs.

The Operation Pedestal convoy was also the objective of the 153° *Gruppo* (372ª, 373ª, and 374ª *Squadriglie*) of the 53° *Stormo*, who had been deployed on the Decimomannu airfield in Sardinia on 11 August with twenty-one M.C.202s. The following morning, fourteen Macchis led by *Maggiore* Andrea Favini set off to escort Italian bombers and torpedo bombers towards the convoy. The Macchis engaged Fleet Air Arm Sea Hurricanes, shooting down Sub-Lt John Lucas's V7659 from No. 800 Naval Air Squadron, and damaging Lt Brian Patterson's Hurricane of No. 885 Naval Air Squadron.

Three days later, on 15 August, the 153° *Gruppo* returned to Torino Caselle, but in preparation for the renewed Axis air offensive on Malta, planned for October, it was deployed in September to San Pietro di Caltagirone in Sicily, along with the HQ of the 53° *Stormo*, with a total force of fifty-three M.C.202s.[148]

In September 1942, with the failure of the Alam el Halfa offensive and the expectation of an imminent British counteroffensive, the issue of the the neutralisation of Malta became once more imperative. Rommel, the commander of the *Afrika Korps*, declared that it was necessary to ensure a regular flow of supplies to the Axis armour operating on the El Alamein front, so that, after a victorious defence, it could possibly go on the offensive, while at the same time fending off any further British attempt to send convoys to Malta. On 24 September, *Generalfeldmarschall* Kesselring met with *Sottocapo di Stato Maggiore* of the *Regia Aeronautica* Giuseppe Santoro and with the *Capo di Stato Maggiore* Fougier, to find a common implementation strategy. In the course of the meeting, some concerns were raised about the involvement of the M.C.202s in the renewed offensive, as it had become clear in combat over Malta that the performance of the Folgore deteriorated considerably above 7,000 metres, and was no match for the Mk V Spitfire at that height.

As the Bf 109G2, a fast climber and excellent performer at high altitude, had just entered service with *Luftwaffe* units in Sicily, the Italians sought to establish some form of cooperation that ensured high-altitude protection to the M.C.202s and prevented them from being jumped from above, so that their great manoeuvrability could be better used at lower heights. *Colonello* Angelo Tessore, the head of the *Comando Aviazione Caccia* in Sicily, and *Hauptmann* Heinz Bär, commander of I/JG.77 were tasked with ensuring that the agreement would be implemented by the *Luftwaffe* Fighter Command.[149,150]

October saw a renewed effort by both the *Regia Aeronautica* and the *Luftwaffe* to neutralise Malta, the so-called 'October Blitz', which commenced on 11 October and would end one week later. The Italians mustered ninety-four M.C.202s among the 51° and 53° *Stormi* for the operation, of which sixty-six were serviceable.[151] In the nine days of the offensive, the 153° *Gruppo* did engage the enemy regularly, but notwithstanding the target-rich environment they only managed to claim three Spitfires destroyed, five probables, and some more damaged. In return, they suffered the loss of *Tenente* Giuliano De Marchi of the 372ª *Squadriglia*, who was forced to bale out because of engine trouble on 11 October and was posted MIA.

On 12 October, eight Ju 88s escorted by ten M.C.202s from the 155° *Gruppo* and twenty Bf 109s were engaged halfway to Malta, by eight Spitfires from No. 249 Squadron, seven from No. 229 Squadron, and six from No. 1435. The 155° *Gruppo* claimed two shot down and three damaged Spitfires. One was claimed by *Sottotenente* Plinio Sironi (MM9087) from the 378ª *Squadriglia* while the second was claimed as a share between *Maggiore* Fanali and several other pilots of the 351ª, 360ª, and 378ª *Squadriglie*. The RAF in fact lost only one Spitfire, Sgt W. B. Knox-Williams's EN978 'O' of No. 1435.

On the same day, four M.C.202s of the 360ª *Squadriglia*, five of the 378ª *Squadriglia*, and two of the 20° *Gruppo*, led by *Maggiore* Fanali on MM9065 code 155, escorted five Ju 88A-4s of KG54, together with Bf 109s in another attack. They were engaged by sixteen Spitfires of No. 229 and No. 1435 Squadrons, and the *Regia Aeronautica* pilots claimed two destroyed and two damaged off Malta coast, to no loss of their own. In fact one of them, it is unclear who, might have managed to shoot down Flt Lt Art Roscoe's Spitfire BR464 of No. 229 Squadron, who crash-landed his plane at Takali.[152]

The attacks on Malta continued the next day, 13 October, with four major raids against the island. In the afternoon *Maggiore* Fanali led five M.C.202s of the 360ª *Squadriglia* and four of the 378ª *Squadriglia*, together with five of the 20° *Gruppo*, fifteen of the 153° *Gruppo*, and forty-two Bf

109s, escorting eight Ju 88A-4s to bomb Hal Far. They were intercepted by Spitfires 20 miles north of Gozo. In the ensuing combat, two of the 153° *Gruppo*'s M.C.202s were lost—that of *Capitano* Enzo Radini, CO of the 373ª *Squadriglia*, and his wingman *Tenente* Felice Mezzetti. *Capitano* Radini was rescued at sea south-east of Delimara by rescue launch HSL 128, badly burned and became a POW while *Tenente* Felice Mezzetti was posted missing. In return, the RAF suffered two Spitfires crash-landed, and one damaged.[153]

The October Blitz ended after nine days, during which the *Regia Aeronautica* and the *Luftwaffe* mounted approximately 2,400 sorties, mostly by fighters, but failed to obtain appreciable results. For the rest of the month, the Axis reverted to fighter sweeps and small-scale fighter-bomber raids, *de facto* nuisance actions that had little strategic impact. The last M.C.202 raid of any significance occurred on 27 October when six Jabos escorted by about sixty C.202s and Bf 109s attacked Luqa airfield. Spitfires scrambled to engage the enemy aircraft but no interception was made.

By the end of October 1942, the siege of Malta was all but over, thanks to the Allied victory at El Alamein, the occupation of Libya, and the start of Operation Torch. The 53° *Stormo* departed Sicily in early November to initiate operations over Tunisia, while the 20° *Gruppo*, 51° *Stormo* (151ª, 352ª, and 353ª *Squadriglia*), at Castelvetrano left in December for Ciampino (it would return to Sicily in May 1943, at Chinisia). The 6° *Gruppo*, 1° *Stormo* (79ª, 81ª, and 88ª *Squadriglia*), arrived at Pantelleria in December.

The 153° *Gruppo* of the 51° *Stormo* returned from Decimomannu to Sciacca at the end of November 1942, continuing to operate on shipping routes to Africa, and clashing often with the Spitfires based on Malta.[154]

Russia, 1942–43

In September 1942, to supplement the small Italian Air Force that operated in the Russian theatre from late summer of 1941, some M.C.202s were sent to the Soviet Union. The heavy demands of the war both in the Western Desert and Malta allowed the despatch of only twelve Folgores, which were attached to the 21° *Gruppo* CT (356ª, 361ª, 382ª, and 386ª *Squadriglia*), which was equipped mainly with M.C.200s.

The Folgores were distributed equally among the squadrons of the groups. It is quite clear that distributing such a trivial number of modern planes to an army-sized expeditionary corps was nothing more than a propaganda operation, as confirmed by the fact that only two Macchis were sent that had been modified with a fairing on each wing's attack edge to accommodate two AVIA film cameras, with the purpose of filming combat scenes for newsreel.[155] The *Gruppo* units participated in the offensive of the VIII Armata towards the Don River and subsequently occupied the airfields at Voroscilovgrad, Millerovo, and Kantemirovka. The Russian counteroffensive, Operation Little Saturn, found three *Squadriglie* at Voroscilovgrad, while one of them would be deployed at Kantemirovka in turn. Kantemirovka was abandoned on 18 December 1942 in the face of the Soviet advance, and Voroscilovgrad was left on 17 January; the last strafing sortie was performed on 17 January 1943 by twenty-five aircraft in the Millerovo area, helping some surrounded German troops. On 21 January, the contingent retreated to Stalino, and then to Saporoshje. In the course of its stay in Russia, M.C.202s only managed seventeen sorties with no losses or claims, most of them being escorts for M.C.200s acting as fighter-bombers, and sometimes strafing runs.[156] On 13 February, the *Gruppo* started to reach Odessa, from where it would leave the theatre of operations. After a stop in Zagabria, by 15 May, the *Gruppo* was back in Italy, at Firenze Peretola.

The Aegean, 1943

On 26 February 1943, the 154° *Gruppo Autonomo* CT (395ª and 396ª *Squadriglie*) of the *Aeronautica dell'Egeo* received its first M.C.202s at Rodi-Gadurrà; they were seven Folgores surrendered by other units, therefore quite worn-out aircraft. Initially, the Macchis were distributed among the *Squadriglie*, but subsequently they were concentrated in the 396ª *Squadriglia* led by *Capitano* Fernando Giocondi. The activities of the 154° *Gruppo* consisted mostly of convoy escort and torpedo bomber escort, but with no significant air combat. Only on 30 July 1943 did the M.C.202s have their chance to engage five Beaufighters of No. 227 Squadron based on Cyprus, over the islet of Alimnia. Despite the claims of the pilots of the *Regia Aeronautica*, only one enemy plane was damaged, in return for two Folgores damaged.[157]

Sicily and Italy, 1942–43

Italy had been hit for the first time on 4 December 1942 by twenty B-24s of the 9th Air Force, now in reach from their North African bases, with a raid on Naples.[158] Southern Italy was especially exposed, Naples being a primary objective as the starting point of the supply lines to Africa, but it was not the only one. On 7 February, the 12th Air Force entered the fray as well, its B-17s bombing Cagliari-Elmas. From then on, Italy would be subject to an ever-increasing and relentless bombing campaign. The M.C.202s were part of the air assets of the *Regia Aeronatica* devoted to protecting Italian cities and lines of communication. These assets included the 22° *Gruppo* at Capodichino, the 164ª *Squadriglia* in Reggio Calabria, led by *Capitano* Adriano Porcu and equipped with a mix of M.C.202s and M.C.200s, that protected the Messina area, or the 377ª *Squadriglia Autonoma*, which was assigned to protect Palermo.[159, 160, 161]

Clashes in Africa with the USAAF heavies, the B-17s and B-24s, had already shown the inadequacy of the M.C.202s (and of most of the Italian fighters, in fact) to challenge those heavily armed and extremely robust bombers.

The first shooting down of US heavies by M.C.202s took place on 11 January in the skies above Naples, when a flight of four B-24s of the 376th Bomber Group was intercepted by two patrols of 371ª and 369ª *Squadriglia*, 22° *Gruppo*, for a total of eight Folgores.[162] Of those, only one managed to get to the height of the bombers to intercept—that of *Capitano* Monaco of the 369ª *Squadriglia*. Incredibly, he managed to shoot down two B-24s, but only because the weapons of virtually all the bombers jammed (the oil in the Browning MGs had frozen), therefore opening a gap in the all-round defence of the aircraft and allowing the competent (and very fortunate) *Regia Aeronautica* pilot to strike from up close the Tail-end Charlie of the four, shooting it down:

> The fighter closed in on our tail, and when he got no return fire, he just sat there and raked the whole aircraft. I was in the nose with my bombardier [Lt. E. C. Matheny]. We helped each other put on our chutes because it was obvious that we were going down with the engines on fire.[163]

Once the formation was broken, *Capitano* Monaco could close in to the lead plane of the diamond-shaped formation, exploiting the lack of return fire:

> I looked out of my plexi-glass window and on my left at about 5 o'clock sat this jerry ME109 [the USAAF crew misidentified the M.C.202 for a Bf 109] just keeping pace with us. I swung my guns on him and he must have spotted this movement because he banked to his left and went underneath us. I had attempted to fire but to no avail. Then all hell broke loose. A 20 mm hit my plexi-glass window (3 ¾″ thick) dead center and it was smashed. I could not see anymore.... The plane was staggering

> badly by now.... I checked my chute straps—opened the door and bailed out. Bob followed. On the way down the jerry pilot flew by me and for what I could make out, saluted me. I saluted back.[164]

While those were exceptional circumstances, attacking the heavies was no mean feat, requiring daring and sound tactics. With the help of the Germans, who already had some experience with those bombers (but had fighters that were altogether better armed), some basic attack tactics were defined by *Superaereo* on 12 February 1943, for interceptors such as the M.C.202:

> Frontal attack intended to break up the opposing formation, carried out by successive patrols of four aircraft in line abreast, which at a useful firing distance widen out so that the two central aircraft can concentrate their fire on the leading enemy plane, while the two side guns strafe two other enemy planes. Subsequently, once the formation has been broken up, the attacking planes concentrate their fire two by two against single attacking planes, returning towards them by tight turns. Regarding the frontal attack it is necessary to bear in mind that, given the great speed attained by modern aircraft, this tactic is only possible when firing from very far away, that is when the fighters are equipped with weapons of a calibre greater than 12.7. It can be very profitable as well as against formations, even against isolated aircraft, especially if one can open fire at the end of a dive to immediately recall the aircraft and return to the attack position again. Another system tested with good results is the following: attack from above in the aft sectors of the enemy formation. Each fighter aims at a single target. Passage at the tail end or through the enemy formation at high speed. Exploitation of the speed attained in the dive to then perform a surge allowing the attack from the bottom upwards, concentrating the fire of two or three fighters belonging to the same formation, slightly staggered over time, against a single enemy bomber (formation or section leader). The attack from below can often produce excellent results, especially when it is the terminal phase of a dive from above, so as to have a considerable reserve of speed.[165]

The suggestion was also made of hitting the cockpit to kill the pilots, and in the event of escort fighters being present (usually placed higher and slightly behind the bomber boxes), it was suggested to attack frontally from below, disengaging immediately. Each *Squadriglia* though, on the basis of the pilots' experience, had developed its own methods, or came to the same conclusions as *Superaereo*, as demonstrated by the interception of eighteen B-24s of the 98th and 376th Bomb Groups over Naples by a combination of M.C.202s (led by *Tenente* Lanfranco Baschiera) and M.C.200s (led by *Tenente* Orazio Ferlin) of the 22° *Gruppo*, when *Maresciallo* Antonino Lo Schiavo fired at the cockpit: 'I came out of a cloud and found myself traversing the right wing of an enemy aircraft a few metres away. I fired instantly and saw the pilots collapsing over the controls'.[166, 167] The capture of a couple of B-24s, which had landed by accident on Italian territory, allowed for a through study of the weaknesses and strengths of the USAAF heavy bombers, too.[168] The 4° *Stormo* devised its own approach, as described by *Capitano* Giulio Reiner, of the 73ª *Squadriglia*, 9° *Gruppo*:

> We positioned ourselves to the side, higher and in the same direction as the enemy, then with a half overturn, swooping and speeding, we set ourselves on a collision course towards the nose of the four-engine bomber, crosswise. Due to the high relative speed that was attained, in the collimator the outline of the large bomber grew rapidly and became clearly delineated in all its details. At close range we tried to hit the cockpit, fired and, when contact seemed inevitable, we deliberately threw ourselves into a chandelle, recalling almost immediately and coming out sideways with respect to the direction of the enemy formation, we regained altitude and repeated the attack. In this way the Macchi fire was directed towards the most delicate parts of the enemy aircraft, the cockpit, the engines, the tanks, and the number of weapons that could answer back was smaller, while this fire was also less precise because of the increased relative speed of the attacker. The four-engine pilots saw the Macchi open fire against them and this placed them in a psychological situation different from that of an attack on the tail, which led to the formation widening out or breaking up, with greater possibilities for the Macchi to isolate some aircraft and bring them down.[169]

Regardless of the tactics, though, the other outstanding problem was the inadequacy of the M.C.202s' armament. *Sergente* Arnaldo Mauri of 86ª *Squadriglia*, 7° *Gruppo* of 54° *Stormo*, was surprised by the limited punch packed by the two 12.7-mm Breda SAFAT of the M.C.202s:

> The calibre and range were fine for light fighters and twin-engined bombers, but against the four-engine bombers one felt the need to have three times the number of machine guns or rather to be able to rely on a cannon with more effective shooting possibilities. I myself noticed this when I attacked a Liberator formation over Messina; I took quite a beating, I was injured and I only succeeded in getting the engine to smoke on one of those beasts.[170]

Adriano Monti, *Generale di Divisione Aerea* commanding the *Aeronautica della Sicilia*, wrote in a report to *Superaereo* about combat with USAAF Bombers:

> The continual engagements that the MC202 aircraft has had in the skies over the island with the four-engine enemy bombers over the last two months, have once again highlighted the serious insufficiency of the calibre of the current armament. It is now well known and indeed become habitual that the pilots, while managing to intercept, follow and catch up with (thanks to the still excellent characteristics of the MC202) this type of day bomber and being able easily to hit it with all the ammunition available, often they see the enemy get away without apparent damage. And without obtaining, apart from any other consideration, that visible result that enhances and compensates for the audacious effort of the attacker ... what is particularly felt by the pilots is the need to have armoured windscreen glass. Few aeroplanes are equipped with it whereas, instead, apart from being a not inconsiderable protection, it has an important effect on morale in the crucial point in the action, that is when the pilot, from a very short distance, aims precisely towards that target from which he sees violent frontal fire being released.[171]

As a consequence of this situation, consideration was given to rearming the M.C.202s with the same Mauser MG 151/20A 20-mm cannons that were being installed on the M.C.205s. In the spring of 1943, Castoldi built a modified M.C.202 with the cannons in wing pods; the experiment was unsuccessful, though, as the weight and turbulence created by this installation reduced the performance of the fighter. While the DB601 engine had the space between the banks for a coaxial gun, placing it on a compact fighter like the M.C.202s would have required an unrealistic major reengineering of the whole frontal part of the plane. Macchi 202 pilots, therefore, continued to face the USAAF bombers with what was available, trying to remedy the lack of punch by their tactics.

On 1 March 1943, twenty B-24s from the 98th and nine from the 376th Bomb Groups successfully attacked Naples harbour, but were intercepted by twenty-four fighters of the 22° *Gruppo*. Among those, there was the *Regia Aeronautica*'s *Tenente* Riccardo Monaco on M.C.202 MM9055.[172]

> I had heard some talk about the attack technique from above, the side or the front. Climbing as high as possible, I dived on an enemy formation of six, but the fire against me was deadly. I didn't pull up after the attack, but I kept diving. I managed to fire only a few rounds, while the

> dark outlines of the fuselages of the enemy bombers passed quickly by below me. While turning to regain contact, I could see on the left, lower down, another formation of six, the one that had come from Caserta and crossed my route. I dived on this second formation and then did a chandelle under them. In order not to crash into them, I had to cut the engine and give the pedals a kick. At the same time I was firing at the plane above me and in front of the nose. As I fired, I saw white smoke this time, pouring from the stricken plane. But as I kicked the pedals hard and went down I couldn't see anything anymore. My fighter had been riddled with bullets.[173]

Pier Paolo Paravicini, of 360ª *Squadriglia*, 155° *Gruppo*, 51° *Stormo*, was one of the *Regia Aeronautica* pilots whose task was to intercept USAAF bombers over Naples:

> We did not have a standardized technique for attacking American four-engine aircraft. According to our German allies, the best method was the three-quarter frontal attack. But what was right for them was absolutely impossible for us because of the light armament of our Macchi. Considering the 1,000 km/h relative speed of approach to the target and the 200-250 metres of useful range of our SAFAT 12.7 mm, we would have had less than a minute of fire at our disposal. Too little to get any results with the two weapons of the Macchi MC202. Therefore the only practical form of attack for us was from above, in a dive, provided that our take-off preceded the arrival of the bombers by seven or eight minutes and that in that short time we had climbed to at least 8,000 metres. Only then would we have had the opportunity to perform the dive attack. Sometimes we found the bombers higher, so we also had to exceed 9,000 metres, a height at which our Macchis lost much of their manoeuvrability. However, we had no other choice. We usually started off in patrols of two or three aircraft. As soon as we reached the right altitude we began to circle between the sun and the direction of the oncoming bombers. We attacked them in a dive aiming carefully at a point between the fuselage and the engines. Given our low volume of fire, we could not waste rounds, so it was essential to know how to use the reflection collimator with maximum precision. Unfortunately not all the pilots were able to do this with due skill, owing to their lack of training and experience. Once the attack had been carried out, we would make a wing turn and avoid passing on the tail of the bombers. It was hell. If all went well, after having invariably lost altitude for two or three thousand metres, we would give full throttle and go back out to bring us back in front of the bombers, at the right height to repeat the attack.

> This manoeuvre took five or six minutes, so it was not possible to repeat it more than once, because the bombers had already outdistanced us.[174]

It is quite clear that a successful interception depended on sufficient warning about incoming bomber formations by the radar network, giving sufficient time for the interceptors to gain height. There are ample testimonies, though, that this was not always the case. On 10 April, Paravicini scrambled with his comrades to confront one of the many bombing raids on Naples, this time by B-24s of 98th BG:

> The skies above Naples, eight thousand metres. Dodo is in front, me and Monconi behind. The radio crackles, altitude eight thousand, they are about to arrive. There are about thirty of them, we are about eight hundred metres above them. They make no impression on me, they seem small and funny, yellow-coloured toys, whilst in reality we find ourselves in the midst of tracers that give me the impression of fireworks. Instinctively I follow Dodo, who attacks very badly, almost in the tail. Monconi abandons us. Another 202 appears in our midst, thankfully. We are at least three. I am right on the tail of a Liberator, a flurry of tracers hits me. I fire a volley and pull away. I suddenly become aware of those terrible tracers. A second attack from the side, this time Dodo performs it very well. In front of me a 202 leaves a trail of white smoke. I don't think about it because I'm in range and I'm collimating ... I fire for a long time, I turn over, I can't see the formation anymore. I return to the attack by gaining altitude. I attack from below badly, fortunately the lower turret fires badly too, I can see all the rounds high up and behind me, this time it went well. That 202 was Sergeant Bocchi [Enrico Luigi Bocchi, on a MM9707], after being hit he parachuted out and was found dead in the gulf.[175]

The raid of 10 April saw also the first operational use of a new weapon of uncertain effectiveness, the so-called *Bomba Greca* CV, a *de facto* time-fused fragmentation bomblet, which was introduced on the correct assumption that breaking up bomber formations made the stragglers easier to attack. One of the M.C.202 pilots testing those weapons, *Sergente* Marcello Vannucci, recalled:

> On 10 April I was flying with a MC202 fitted with a housing on the wings carrying five 15 kg bombs each, held by a chain and designed to explode after a certain number of seconds from launch. I was with two other MC202s, and the formation was commanded by *Tenente* Moresi. We left as soon as the alarm sounded and climbed up to 7,500

> metres, over a formation of four-engine enemy aircraft. We dropped our bomb and saw the formation break up, but no enemy aircraft was shot down.[176]

The next day, Paravicini, in the course of another similar high-altitude combat with B-24s, had to break off his attack as the oxygen distribution system typically failed.[177, 178]

After the end of fighting in Africa, and in preparation for the invasion of Sicily, the Allied air effort concentrated on four main objectives: the subduing and capture of the fortress island of Pantelleria; the elimination of the airport complexes, of the harbours, and lines of communication in Sicily; the disruption of communication and supply routes in mainland Italy; and the protection of the concentration points and routes that the Allied convoys would follow for the forthcoming invasion.

Over the island of Pantelleria, most of the clashes involved the M.C.202s and 205s of the 1° *Stormo*, as for instance in the clash, lionised by the Italian press, that took place on 20 April 1943, with the Italian pilots claiming fourteen enemy fighters, of which in fact none was lost, in exchange for two Macchis shot down, and two damaged.[179] Pantelleria's fundamental role as an early warning position was threatened by the removal of the surviving Freya radar on 21 May. After that, it made no sense to keep the section of four M.C.202s on the island and so they were withdrawn to Sicily on 3 June.[180] From then until its fall, the protection of the island was delegated to occasional patrols of Axis units over the island, of which only a small percentage resulted in interceptions of the numerous enemy raids, as there was no efficient fighter guidance system left.

The protection of the concentration points and invasion sea lines to Sicily implied the elimination of the Axis airfields in Sardinia, which were heavily bombed on an almost daily basis by the Strategic Air Force in May 1943. Among the defenders of the island were the 24° *Gruppo Autonomo* CT, with the 354ª, 355ª, and 370ª *Squadriglia*, which had moved to Venafiorita from Elmas by 14 May. The *Gruppo* received a few M.C.205Vs, but given the scarcity in numbers of the new fighter, it was mostly equipped with M.C.202s.[181] While still in training on the new machine, pilots of the 355ª *Squadriglia* intercepted B-25 Mitchells escorted by P-38s of the 82nd and 1st Fighter Group; two of the planes of the latter group were shot down by *Sottotenente* Evasio Cavalli, while one M.C.202, that of *Maggiore* Bruno Ricco, was damaged, probably by one of the 82nd FG P-38s.[182]

Substantial reinforcements were sent to Sardinia: the 51° *Stormo* had been refitted in December 1942 with more M.C.202s at Ciampino Sud, after its *Gruppi* returned from Sicily (20° *Gruppo*) and Tunisia (155° *Gruppo*); on 16 May, led by *Maggiore* Gino Callieri, the 20° *Gruppo*, with the 151ª, 352ª, and 353ª *Squadriglie* arrived in Capoterra, and the 378ª *Squadriglia*, led by *Capitano* Manlio Biccolini, arrived at Monserrato. They were in action shortly afterwards, on 19 May, when twenty-seven M.C.202s of the 20° *Gruppo* and ten of the 378ª *Squadriglia* intercepted bombers escorted by P-38s, and claimed one by *Sergente* Ferruccio Serafini on MM9704 and one jointly by *Tenente* Giovanni Franchini and *Sergente* Umberto Moriconi, although the USAAF in fact suffered no losses.[183] A few days later, another bomber intercept involved the pilots of the 51° *Stormo*, on 20 May.

A mixed formation of five M.C.202s and two M.C.205s of the 352ª *Squadriglia*, led by *Capitano* Angelo Fanello, and eleven M.C.202s from the 353ª *Squadriglia*, both of the 20° *Gruppo*, engaged the bombers, thought to be B-24s but in fact being B-25s, and claimed a Liberator shot down, though that was not the case. Two Macchis were lost, that of *Tenente* Corrado Corradi and that of *Tenente* Bernardo Crucioli.[184] The 24° *Gruppo* was also heavily involved in bomber interceptions in this period, as in the large raid by one hundred and two B-17s escorted by twenty-nine P-38s on 24 May over Olbia and Maddalena, involving five M.C.202s of the 354ª and 370ª *Squadriglie*, and subsequently in the raid on Olbia on 1 June.[185]

Sardinia was not the only target of the Allied strikes. The same day, forty-two B-24s of the 98th and 376th Bomber Groups attacked Villa San Giovanni and Reggio Calabria, being intercepted by fourteen M.C.202s and a D.520 of the 161° *Gruppo Autonomo*, which had been deployed in mid-May to Reggio Calabria, where it had received M.C.202s and seven D.520s.[186]

On 25 May, the USAAF bombers attacked Messina with a P-38 escort. In the ensuing combat, which involved fifteen M.C.202s of the 161° *Gruppo Autonomo* from Reggio Calabria, and later some of the 153° *Gruppo* of 53° *Stormo* from Sicily (and some Bf 109s from II/JG27) the *Regia Aeronautica* pilots claimed several B-17s, of which one was in effect shot down, though it is unclear by whom, and one of the six P-38s was effectively shot down (by *Sottotenente* Dino Saglio), in return for a M.C.202 lost in combat, and eighteen more destroyed on the ground at Palermo (perhaps from the 151° *Gruppo*).[187]

On 28 May, USAAF bombers raided heavily the Sicilian airfields, Sciacca, Castelvetrano, Chinisia, Trapani-Milo, and Pantelleria. In the case of Chinisia and Pantelleria, M.C.202s of the 153° *Gruppo*, along with several other units of the *Regia Aeronautica* and *Luftwaffe*, scrambled to intercept.[188] By now, Southern Italy was in easy reach for both medium and heavy bombers, taking off from their North African airfields in overwhelming numbers, though at least the *Regia Aeronautica* in Sicily benefitted from a better developed radar network by now, mostly of German origin and under German control.

Naples was raided massively on 30 May by 111 B-17 heavies in a bombing that had doubtlessly as much a political as a strategic purpose. The harbour, the marshalling yards, the airports of Capodichino and Pomigliano, and the Alfa Romeo factory of Pomigliano (where the RA1000 RC41-I Monsone engines for the M.C.202s were produced) were hit. Fifteen M.C.202s of the 22° *Gruppo* engaged the bombers, claiming three shot down and two probables, for the damaging of one Folgore which crash-landed.[189] Capodichino was bombed again on 1 June with the loss of three M.C.202s. This campaign of attrition not only wore down the machines of the *Regia Aeronautica*, but also the pilots themselves:

> In the spring of 1943 our unit consisted of three *squadriglie*, none of which had a full complement, as they had been formed exclusively from experienced pilots, who at that time were already in short supply. They didn't have a moment's respite. Almost not even time to wash our faces. In the pre-alarm phase we had to sit inside our fighters, fully equipped with flying suits and shoes for the high altitude, a parachute, a lifebuoy, a rescue boat, signal flares, a Very pistol and other accessories. The wait sometimes lasted for hours, with the only comfort being some sandwiches. Normally the bomber formations arrived in the late afternoon, between 16.00 and 18.00. We took off as soon as the German radar stations positioned on the Amalfi Coast confirmed the arrival and direction of the bombers. Returning from the fight, we had to go to report, write a technical report, then we were taken to our lodgings at the Royal Palace of Caserta where we had a meal around 9.00 pm. The next day, wake up at 6, and start again.[190]

The 22° *Gruppo* was again intercepting USAAF bombers on 31 May, over Foggia, losing one plane which crash-landed, while in Sardinia the 20° *Gruppo* of the 51° *Stormo* scrambled to engage another raid on Cagliari.

While the Folgores of the 153°, 20°, 161°, and 22° *Gruppi* (with their comrades of the 1° *Stormo* on M.C.205s) scrambled almost daily to intercept USAAF bombers and fighters hitting Sicily, Sardinia, and Calabria, Operation Corkscrew, the air campaign against Pantelleria, increased its tempo. On 8, 9, and 10 June, M.C.202s of various *Gruppi* (151° and 153° *Gruppi* of the 53° *Stormo* on 8 and 9 June, together with the 161° *Gruppo Autonomo* on 10 June), along with the M.C.205s of the 6° *Gruppo*, 1° *Stormo*, and/or Bf 109s of the 150° *Gruppo*, intercepted USAAF heavies and medium bombers, P-38s, P-40s, and Spitfire fighters in what was the culminating effort of the ten-day air bombardment of the second phase of Corkscrew, and the attempt by the *Regia Aeronautica* to wrestle back air superiority over the island.[191] In the evening of 10 June, a formation of thirty *Regia Aeronautica* fighters (six Bf 109Gs from the 150° *Gruppo*, eight M.C.202s from the 151° *Gruppo*, ten M.C.202s from the 153° *Gruppo*, and six M.C.202s from the 161° *Gruppo Autonomo*) engaged medium and heavy bombers escorted by fighters (Spitfires from the 31st FG and P-40s of the 85th and 87th FSs of the 79th FG).

The Italians lost four M.C.202s from the 53° *Stormo*—three from the 151° *Gruppo*, including its CO, *Capitano* Domenico Bevilacqua, *Sergente* Rino Nava of the 366ª *Squadriglia*, and *Tenente* Giancarlo Celle of the 367ª *Squadriglia*, and Maresciallo Paolo Franchi of the 373ª *Squadriglia*, 153° *Gruppo*—and three from the 161° *Gruppo Autonomo*. Three M.C.202s were lost by the 161° *Gruppo* pilots (*Tenente* Giuseppe Marazio and *Maresciallo* Giuseppe Ravasio of the 164ª *Squadriglia* and *Sottotenente* Iolando Soprani of the 159ª *Squadriglia*). The 53° *Stormo* pilots reported shooting down a B-24, a Boston, and two Spitfires, as well as damaging five Bostons and one P-38, though in fact no Spitfires, B-26s, or B24s were lost but three P-40s and one B-26 were damaged.[192] Pantelleria surrendered the day after, the first conquest of an enemy naval and air base by the use of virtually only airpower.

The Allied efforts could now be concentrated on Sicily, and by 14 June, the Desert Air Force also started its first operations against the island. USAAF bombers continued hitting the airfields on the island, on 15 June, Chinisia, Trapani-Milo, Palermo, and Castelvetrano, the defending nineteen M.C.202s from the 151° and 153° *Gruppi* shot down a P-40 (misidentified as a Spitfire, by *Sergente* Giuseppe Saracino) and two bombers, most likely two B-26s, in return for two M.C.202s damaged. Comiso and Biscari were bombed on 17 June, despite the interception efforts of the pilots of the 161° *Gruppo*, and Messina on 18 June, though this time the 161° *Gruppo* managed to damage one B-17F of 97th Bomber Group. For the rest of the month of May, raids continued unabated also on Naples and Sardinia, dragging the Italian fighter arm into a war of attrition it could not win, with the dwindling numbers of M.C.202s not replaced by a sufficient intake of new planes. On 28 June, the 155° *Gruppo*, 51° *Stormo*, engaged a group of P-40s going towards Elmas; Pier Paolo Paravicini, of the 360ª *Squadriglia*, was one of the *Regia Aeronautica* pilots taking part in the clash:

> Scramble on alarm, altitude four thousand. *Maresciallo* Bartolucci is my wingman. Since the radio silence is absolute, he begins to make broad gestures to indicate to me that American patrols of P40s are crossing below. Having seen some P38 Lightnings below me, I decide to keep

> my altitude a little longer, but Bartolucci is impatient and turns around and I lose sight of him. I notice that over Elmas a merry-go-round of aeroplanes has formed and one of our fighters is in a bad shape. I head in that direction and at that very moment I see a P40 in front of me. I take aim and fire, I can see that I've hit him. Pieces of his wing come off and spin down towards the ground. I climb and turn around. I hear shots hitting my aeroplane. I dive hard and I perform two rounds of controlled spin. I recall and draw breath. No, it's not over, I hear two or three more shots. I roll over again. I have time to see a huge blaze on the ground. I think it's the P40 I hit. Now I'm very low, I feel a beastly heat. The one behind, which struck me, I've lost it.[193]

Paravicini had shot down P-40L 42-111102 flown by 2Lt Roman Mierzejewski, who baled out but died after crashing into a rock on landing. His M.C.202, hit in the radiator, crash-landed at Villacidro.

On the eve of Operation Husky, the invasion of Sicily, on 9 July 1943, M.C.202s equipped the following units.[194]

UNIT	AIRFIELD	ASSIGNED AIRCRAFT	SERVICEABLE AIRCRAFT
2° *Stormo* CT (13° *Gruppo*)	Lonate Pozzolo	15	11
3° *Stormo* CT (18° *Gruppo*, 23° *Gruppo*)	Cerveteri	18	4
22° *Gruppo Autonomo* CT	Capodichino	16	9
151° *Gruppo* CT	Monserrato	23	21
24° *Gruppo Autonomo* CT	Venafiorita	19	10
4° *Stormo* CT (9° *Gruppo*, 10° *Gruppo*)	Finocchiara, Sigonella, San Salvatore	38 (+10 M.C.205s)	12 (+1 M.C.205s)
161° *Gruppo Autonomo* CT	Reggio Calabria	18 (+2 CR.42s, 13 D.520s, 4 M.C.200s)	11 (+2 CR.42s, 4 D.520s, 0 M.C.200s)
21° *Gruppo Autonomo* CT	Chinisia	21	0
153° *Gruppo* CT	Palermo	7	3
154° *Gruppo Autonomo* CT	Rhodes	9	6

In preparation for the landing, the Allied forces continued their round-the-clock bombing raids on airports, accompanied by fighter sweeps and strafing runs on strategic facilities, such as radar stations; M.C.202s along with other available fighters regularly rose to intercept, usually in small numbers due to limited serviceability rates that put the *Regia Aeronautica* under extreme pressure. On 5 July, the 4° *Stormo* CT made ninety-five sorties from Gerbini and Catania, intercepting heavy bombers, and in the earliest one Franco Lucchini, one of the top-scoring Italian aces with twenty-two kills, was shot down:

> At 10:25, 27 MC202s and MC205s of the 4° Stormo scrambled to intercept 52 bombers escorted by about 20 Spitfires, that were heading to bomb the airfields around Catania. The 9° *Gruppo* was led by *Capitano* Giulio Reiner, while *Capitano* Lucchini was leading the 10° *Gruppo* [on MM6582]. The 10° *Gruppo* consisted of the 84ª *Squadriglia* (*Capitano* Lucchini, *Sottotenente* Francesco Palma, *Sottotenente* Enzo Dall'Asta and *Capitano* Luigi Giannella [CO of the 84ª *Squadriglia*] flying MC202s and *Tenente* Alessandro Mettimano, *Sergente Maggiore* Piero Buttazzi and *Sergente* Livio Barbera flying MC205s), the 90ª *Squadriglia* (*Tenente* Luigi Cima, *Maresciallo* Massimo Salvatore and *Sergente Maggiore* Giambattista Ceoletta flying MC202s) and the 91ª *Squadriglia* (*Tenente* Mario Mecatti [CO], *Sottotenente* Giovanni Silvestri and *Sottotenente* Elio Miotto).... The Italian fighters made a frontal attack over Gerbini, ignoring the escorting Spitfires. Two B-17s were claimed by Salvatore and *Tenente* Vittorio Squarcia (73ª *Squadriglia*) together with some BF109s. Lucchini claimed a Spitfire while Reiner, Salvatore and Mecatti claimed a probable bomber each. Three bombers were claimed damaged by Lucchini, Giannella, Mettimano, Dall'Asta and Buttazzi. Additional damaged bombers were claimed by Reiner, Salvatore, Mecatti (who also claimed a damaged Spitfire), *Sergente* Ettore Chimeri (73ª *Squadriglia*), *Sergente* Bruno Biagini (96ª *Squadriglia*), Cima and Ceoletta. When the Italian fighters landed again at 11:55, Lucchini was missing. He had been seen by Dall'Asta attacking the bombers against heavy defensive fire and then diving into the ground east of Catania. During the alarm, some of the ground crew also reported to have seen a MC202 falling with the canopy closed, some kilometres east of the airfield. A car from the unit tried to reach the place, but it couldn't go on due to the bombing of the area. Lucchini's body wasn't found until two days later.[195]

After Lucchini's death, command of the 10° *Gruppo* was given to *Capitano* Ranieri Piccolomini, who retained command until the Armistice on 8 September 1943. It seems that the Macchis had been intercepting B-17s from 99th Bomber Group, which were out to attack Gerbini, escorted by Spitfires from No. 72 and No. 243 Squadrons. Three B-17s from the 99th BG (42-29486 and 42-29483 of the 348th BS and 42-29492) were lost that day.

Another four M.C.202s were lost by the unit that day, three shot down and one (that of *Sergente Maggiore* Mario Veronesi) made a gear-up emergency landing near Comiso after receiving hits in the engine and in the water cooler. Of those shot down, MM9479 belonged to *Sottotenente* Leonardo Ferrulli of the 91ª *Squadriglia*, who had scrambled in the early afternoon with *Tenente* Bertolaso and *Sergente* Giulio Fornalé to intercept B-17s with a close escort of P-38s and Spitfires from No. 126 and No. 1435 Squadrons on top cover:

> In the combat Leonardo Ferrulli was seen to shoot down one of the bombers, from which three men baled out, along with an escorting P38 before he was in turn jumped by a flight of Spitfires that had been patrolling over the B-17s. Ferrulli baled out of his damaged MC202 but was too low, his parachute failing to deploy before he hit the ground near Scordia and killing him.[196]

Ferrulli, another ace of the *Stormo*, at the moment of his death had twenty-two kills.

The intensity of the combat proved that the invasion was imminent, and on 9 July, the *Regia Aeronautica*, which had 133 fighters of all types on the island, of which only forty-nine were serviceable, sent eight M.C.202s from the 3° *Stormo* from Cerveteri and ten M.C.205s of the 51° *Stormo* from Sardinia.[197] The next day, Sicily was invaded.

The M.C.202s were employed in responding to enemy bombing raids, fighter sweeps, and strafing enemy troops, as on 11 July when four Folgores and Veltros from the 84ª *Squadriglia*, 9° *Gruppo*, and the 96ª *Squadriglia*, 10° *Gruppo*, strafed lorries on the Floridia–Siracusa road. They were intercepted by P-40s and Spitfires, losing one M.C.202 of *Tenente* Enzo dell'Asta, and one 205, of *Tenente* Otello Gensini, who described the action:

> In front of us we begin to see the southern coast strewn with landing craft. How many? I had other things to look at. Above, below, behind. Especially behind. It was the job of the other pair to watch the backs of the formation.... Suddenly I saw them. Not behind, but ahead and above us, from the right. They were turning left. They had probably already seen us. I warned the commander and he motioned for me to look to the left and above. Another formation was bearing down on us. Annoni

climbed slowly, then more decisively, veering towards the planes that were coming at us.... In that situation, staying together is important, but anyone who has found themselves in that situation knows that doing it is quite another matter.... A few hundred metres ahead of me, a Spitfire coming from the right into a left turn cut across me, too far, but he hadn't seen me and I started following him, tightening my turn to get closer. At 4,000 metres the MC202 had excellent manoeuvrability; from time to time I glanced around very quickly. For the collimator we had it was still too far away. Tightening still, he was finally in the collimator at the right distance. Did something move on my instrument panel, an animal? Some instruments were gone. I quickly turned my head back to the left and, beyond the white wake from the water of my engine, I saw the red nose of another enemy plane, very close. I carried out a sharp and extreme turn, reducing the engine to the minimum and going to the left. I found myself immediately below him, out of the range of his weapons. I continued in the violent turn up to the vertical, then I began the recall and gave full engine throttle heading for Catania. The Spit was still behind me but far enough away. After a while I didn't see him again. The next day I knew that my wingman, *Serg. Magg*. Fomalé had caught up with him and persuaded him to leave. The engine was beginning to show unmistakable signs. The trail was no longer white but dark, the flames began to come out over the left side. The running of the engine had become irregular. I reduced power, but to maintain a safe lift speed I lost altitude. At 300 metres I increased the power but the engine didn't respond. It only remained for me to leave the plane. I pulled open the roof of the cockpit, hooked the parachute clip and undid the belts. I climbed onto the seat. The racing wind crushing me against the back prevented me from jumping. I thought of sitting back, then the right idea: a kick to the cloche. I was immediately flung into the void and as I rolled around in the air the extractor, followed by the white streak of the parachute silk, passed from the left in front of me. Finally the tug to open it and then silence.[198]

By 12 July, many of the Axis airfields in Sicily were lost: Sigonella, Palermo, Catania, and Castelvetrano were barely usable; Gerbini, Sciacca, and Gela were unusable; and Comiso and San Pietro had been captured by the enemy. The 4° *Stormo* and the 21° *Gruppo* were depleted, with about twenty Macchis left between them. By 14 July, the Allies had control of six airfields and started transferring units there, while the number of Axis fighters had further shrunk, and it became less frequent to encounter larger formations in the air, such as the twelve M.C.202s bounced by Mk IX Spitfires (which were starting to appear in theatre in significant numbers and were a superior aircraft to the Folgore) on the afternoon of that day.

The *Regia Aeronautica* abandoned the airfield of Trapani-Milo and Sciacca on 17 July, redeploying to Chinisia and Castelvetrano. By 20 July, the only M.C.202s left on the island were those of the 20° and of the 155° *Gruppi*of the 51° *Stormo*, which received orders to leave the island on 18 July, and had completed their retreat by 27 July 1943.[199]

The attempt to disrupt communication, infrastructures, and supply routes in mainland Italy brought the Allied bombers to many northern targets in the country, which they could now reach with ease from their North African air bases. On 19 July, Rome was attacked in a massive air raid, which included 150 B-17s, 125 B-24s, several B-25s and B-26s, and P-38 escorts, for a total of 500 planes. The *Regia Aeronautica* responded with its available assets, including the M.C.202s of the 18° *Gruppo* and 23° *Gruppo* of the 3° *Stormo*, and of the 153° *Gruppo*, but inflicted trivial damage on the attackers.[200] The bombing of Rome caused shock in Italy and had important military and political consequences, destroying the credibility of the the fascist regime and accelerating the fall of Benito Mussolini, which took place on 25 July.

Meanwhile, the war in the air continued, the bombing and strafing of targets in Italy taking place during the days that followed, such as on 26 July in Southern Sardinia, 27 July on Capua Airfield and Foggia, all of which were intercepted by Macchis of the 20°, 155°, and 22° *Gruppi*.[201]

Sicily was the operational swansong of the M.C.202, its numbers dwindling and it being replaced, whenever possible, by the more competitive M.C.205. For all of August, the M.C.202s provided interceptions against a veritable onslaught of Allied bombers, which were paving the way for the next operation, the invasion of mainland Italy, Operation Baytown.

Just before the Allied landings, the *Regia Aeronautica* had a substantial part of its forces concentrated in central and Northern Italy, either refitting or involved in the defence of the main cities, especially Rome and Naples. Within the 4ª *Squadra Aerea*, there were only a few M.C.202s left within the 21° *Gruppo* (Gioia del Colle).[202] As the landings took place on 3 September, the following day, the *Regia Aereonautica* organised a large ground-attack operation, involving seven M.C.202s of the 21° *Gruppo*, along with M.C.205s and Re.2001s.[203]

The final combat mission of the M.C.202 was flown on 8 September by a few Folgores of the 3° *Stormo*, joined by the test pilot Adriano Mantelli (who had been assigned to lead one of the *Stormo*'s groups, and who happened to pass by Foligno) that scrambled to intercept 131 B-17s that had raided Frascati to attack Kesserling's HQ:

On the morning of 8 September, 130 B.24 are reported to be heading towards the suburbs of Rome. In Foligno there is a pilot captain who has just obtained the command of one of the groups of the 51° Stormo, and is therefore waiting to move to Monserrato (Cagliari), where the pilots and planes of the department are located. The fate of this pilot is unique: throughout the war, he repeatedly applied to be assigned to an operational unit, but his request, which had always been turned down, was only now accepted. When the warning of the raid comes, he asks for and obtains permission to take off on a C.202. It's a long time since he flew this plane, or, rather, a long time has passed since he had the opportunity to test the prototype. On board everything has changed and he uses the few moments he has available to find what he needs and go over the essentials. Before sighting the bombers, he sees the earth bubbling on the slopes of the Alban hills, in Frascati. The objective of the aircraft will turn out to be the Kesserling Headquarters, or the Command of the German forces in Italy. Over the radio, our pilot hears many orders from the *guida-caccia*, given that other aircraft of the 3° Stormo, under the command of *Tenente* Solaroli, are heading to oppose the B.24. The C.202 gains the right height and the pilot then makes a first pass; he returns shortly after and finishes discharging his weapons. He therefore disengages from the opposing formation, without however being able to ascertain any damage caused. The C.202 lands again in Foligno and the pilot, Adriano Mantelli, still has a few hours in front of him before hearing the announcement of the armistice and discovering that this was his last flight for the *Regia Aeronautica*.[204, 205]

Italy, 1943–45

Italian industry made a great effort to make good the losses caused by the last battles in Italy; but by the Armistice, only 122 Folgores were dispersed around the country from the South to the Alps, and of these machines, only fifty-three were serviceable. Some reached the Allied-held sectors and were incorporated into the Co-Belligerent Air Force. However, most of M.C.202s were in Northern Italy, and so where the production lines were for those which were about to be completed. Some Macchis also reached Northern Italy from the bases where they were deployed. Some of those aircraft were absorbed by units of the RSI *Aeronautica Nazionale Repubblicana*, but due to the availability of M.C.205s and Fiat G.55s (and later of Bf 109Gs), and probably the fact that the Alfa Romeo factory producing the engines lay in ruins in enemy territory, the M.C.202s saw limited use, until lack of spares or the termination of engine life decommissioned them.

The *Regia Aeronautica*, 1943–45

After the armistice of 8 September 1943, about twenty-nine M.C.202s were to be found in Southern Italy, belonging to the 21° *Gruppo*, based at Brindisi and Manduria airfields, to the 155° *Gruppo* at Milis and Casa Zeppera, to the 82ª *Squadriglia* of the 13° *Gruppo* at Olbia Venafiorita, and six Macchis that had reached Allied-controlled territory from Northern Italy.[206] From this rather modest start, the *Regia Aeronautica* managed to put together seventy-seven Macchis over the course of its existence, mostly by painstakingly assembling the relatively compatible parts of M.C.200s, 202s, and 205Vs with the purpose of salvaging the largest number of aircraft possible.

The industrial infrastructure of Southern Italy was in ruins, including the factory in Pomigliano d'Arco producing the *Monsone* engines for the M.C.202.[207] Therefore, the *Regia Aeronautica Cobelligerante* had to entrust the reconstruction to the *Servizio Tecnico Caccia* and *Aeronautica Sannita* of Benevento, which refitted several M.C.202s and before the end of 1943 had transformed at least twenty-seven cells of Folgore, bringing them up to the Veltro standard.

Reorganisation of the *Regia Aeronautica* forces on Southern Italian bases began on 15 September 1943, with the first contacts between *Generale* Sandalli, *Capo di Stato Maggiore* of the *Regia Aeronautica* chief of staff, and Air Commodore Forster, chief of the Allied Control Commission's Aeronautical Division. In agreement with the Mediterranean Allied Air Force (MAAF), it was decided to establish the *Regia Aeronautica* as a fully autonomous force from the logistical and operational point of view.

On 21 September 1943, new Italian national markings were adopted, the three-colour cockade, and the theatre of operation was designated as the Adriatic and the Balkans, in order to support Italian troops operating together with local partisans in that area. The reorganisation was finalised on 15 October 1943. Operational units were subdivided into three specialised groups (fighters, bombers/transports, and seaplanes), controlled by the *Comando Unità Aerea*, which was controlled by *Superaereo*, which in turn was under the command of the MAAF.[208, 209] The Macchi M.C.202s were grouped together with the other available fighters units in the *Raggruppamento Caccia*, and were deployed to Campobasso-Campomarino airfield and occasionally to Lissa. Subsequently, they were transferred to Puglia, at Leverano and Galatina.

Although Italy officially declared war on Germany only on 13 October 1943, military operations against the Germans began immediately after the armistice was announced.

By 15 October 1943, M.C.202s were in the following *Raggruppamento Caccia* units:

Unit			Aircraft	Airfield
4° *Stormo* CT	9° *Gruppo*	96ª *Squadriglia*	M.C.202, M.C.205	Brindisi
		97ª *Squadriglia*	M.C.202, M.C.205	Brindisi
	10° *Gruppo*	84ª *Squadriglia*	M.C.202, M.C.205	Lecce
		90ª *Squadriglia*	M.C.202, M.C.205	Lecce
		91ª *Squadriglia*	M.C.202, M.C.205	Lecce
	21° *Gruppo*	356ª *Squadriglia*	M.C.202	Brindisi
		361ª *Squadriglia*	M.C.202	Brindisi
		386ª *Squadriglia*	M.C.202	Brindisi

The first action of the Folgores, with improvised new national roundels, took place the day after the armistice, when four M.C.202s from the *Aeronautica della Sardegna*, probably from the 82ª *Squadriglia* of the *13° Gruppo*, escorted the Italian fleet that, following the armistice agreements, was transferring from La Spezia to Malta. Macchis of the 155° *Gruppo* carried out some reconnaissance flights in September and early October, meeting no aerial opposition.

On 18 September, operations started over the island of Corfu, where the local Italian garrison refused to surrender to the Germans, in order to regain aerial superiority and attack German landing forces. The 4° *Stormo*'s M.C.202s and 205 were tasked with escort duties for the Re.2002 fighter-bombers. After the island fell, the 4° *Stormo* and the 21° *Gruppo* continued to fly reconnaissance missions over Albania and Dalmatia.

The priority of the Italian high command in the Adriatic theatre was to re-establish contact with its troops in the Balkans and to respond to the desperate requests for supplies. M.C.202s would fly missions to counter the *Luftwaffe*, and to escort supply missions. On 16 October, ten Re.2002s of the 5° *Stormo Tuffatori*, escorted by six Macchi M.C.202s and six M.C.205s of the 4° *Stormo* and the 21° *Gruppo Autonomo* attacked Scutari Airfield, where a substantial *Luftwaffe* force (twenty-five Ju 88s, Bf 110s, and Bf 109s) had been reported. On 1 November, twenty M.C.202s and M.C.205Vs attacked the Podgoritza airfield, paving the way for a supply air drop by two S.82s, escorted by twelve P-38s in the Plievlja area.[210]

In mid-November, Macchis of the 4° *Stormo* and 21° *Gruppo Autonomo* also flew escorts to 5° *Stormo* dive bombers against enemy shipping, and on 31 December 1943, twenty-four Macchis took off to simultaneously neutralise Scutari and Podgoritza airfields, in conjunction with an Italian air drop in the area.

By the summer of 1944, M.C.202s were in the following *Raggruppamento Caccia* units:

Unit			Aircraft	Airfield
4° *Stormo* CT	9° *Gruppo*	96ª *Squadriglia*	M.C.202, M.C.205, P-39	Nuova-Termoli
		97ª *Squadriglia*	M.C.202, M.C.205, P-39	Nuova-Termoli
	10° *Gruppo*	84ª *Squadriglia*	M.C.202, M.C.205, P-39	Nuova-Termoli
		90ª *Squadriglia*	M.C.202, M.C.205, P-39	Nuova-Termoli
	12° *Gruppo*	73ª *Squadriglia*	M.C.202, M.C.205, P-39	Nuova-Termoli
		91ª *Squadriglia*	M.C.202, M.C.205, P-39	Nuova-Termoli
	21° *Gruppo*	351ª *Squadriglia*	M.C.202	Lecce
		386ª *Squadriglia*	M.C.202, M.C.205	Lecce
	155° *Gruppo*	361ª *Squadriglia*	M.C.202, M.C.205	Lecce
		378ª *Squadriglia*	M.C.202	Lecce
5° *Stormo* Tuff. (subsequently, CT)	8° *Gruppo*	92ª *Squadriglia*	C.200, CR.42, M.C.202	Leverano
		93ª *Squadriglia*	C.200, CR.42, M.C.202	Leverano
	101° *Gruppo*	208ª *Squadriglia*	M.C.202, Re.2001	Lecce
		238ª *Squadriglia*	M.C.202, Re.2001	Lecce
	102° *Gruppo*	209ª *Squadriglia*	M.C.202, Re.2002	Nuova-Termoli
		239ª *Squadriglia*	M.C.202, Re.2002	Nuova-Termoli

In the first half of June, the 5° *Stormo Tuffatori* was transformed into the 5° *Stormo* CT, relinquishing its Re.2002s; it started receiving instead the former 4° *Stormo*'s Macchi C.202s while the 4° *Stormo* transitioned to Aircobras.

The spares situation had by now become critical, which quickly reduced the efficiency of the available M.C.202s, so that the 5° *Stormo* was forced to operate with just the 102° *Gruppo* until January 1945.[211] By early 1945, the retreating enemy was outside the range of Italian-based M.C.202s, so that those aircraft, replaced by Spitfires, P-39s, and C.205/Ss, were mostly retired and used infrequently or for training purposes.[212]

The *Aeronautica Nazionale Repubblicana*, 1943–45

In Northern Italy, the *Aeronautica Nazionale Repubblicana* managed to deploy thirty-six Folgores (including those in the completion stage, damaged at Breda by bombing on 30 April 1944). The process was started on 22 October 1943 when *Capitano* Fernando Malvezzi was tasked by Ernesto Botto, *sottosegretario* of the *Aeronautica Nazionale Repubblicana*, to concentrate at the *Scuola Caccia* of Castiglione del Lago all the available planes, mainly M.C.202s. Those planes were transferred to Fossano in March, and subsequently to Cervere, where the 3° *Gruppo Caccia* was set up as a fighter training school and three *Squadriglie* (7ª, 8ª, and 9ª). On 21 June, the airfield was heavily attacked by P-47s of the *Armée de l'Air* with the loss of several of its aircraft. The rest of the M.C.202s were kept in the flight line until August 1944. More modern planes were available though in Northern Italy, and the M.C.202s were soon phased out and assigned to training and liaison roles, also as a consequence of the *Luftwaffe*'s attempt to absorb the ANR on 19 August.

Luftwaffe, 1943–45

As the Germans took over Italy after the armistice, they collected as much military materiel as possible, and the *Rüstung und Kriegsproduktion Stab* took over control of Italian industrial production, encouraging factories to keep rolling out the war materiel that was not deemed obsolete. Therefore, M.C.202s were also produced after the armistice; the Breda Factory, which had to deliver eighty-two M.C.202s of XII and XV *Serie*, was taken over by the Germans on 15 September, along with five M.C.202s ready for delivery, and before the bombardment of 30 April 1944, which put the factory out of commission, sixty-one (or sixty-two) M.C.202s seem to have been completed. Neither the AerMacchi, which was supposed to deliver fourteen *Serie* XIII, nor SAI Ambrosini, which had thirty-three *Serie* V on order seem to have delivered any M.C.202s. Many captured Italian aircraft, in particular fighters, went to German *Flugzeugführerschulen* and the *Schuljagdgeschwader*, and the M.C.202s were no exception. Some M.C.202s were certainly available at the *Jagdlehrerüberprüfungsgruppe*, in Guyancourt, already in late November 1943 and until June 1944.[213, 214] Several were serviceable at the *Jagdlehrschule* (advanced fighter pilots training unit) JG103 (in Bad Voslau, then in Vienna, then in Mulhouse) where their presence is documented from December 1943 to June 1944, and at least another at JG110 in Streutz in July 1944.[215, 216] Between January and February 1944, fourteen M.C.202s *Serie* XII were transferred to Orange in Southern France, to be assigned to the local *Jagdlehrschule* JG100; apparently, some of those were then assigned to JG107 in Toul. By March 1944, the *Luftwaffe* had on its rolls thirty-three serviceable M.C.202s.

On 8 August 1944, the Germans destroyed what was left of the factory and semi-completed planes, three wrecks from the bombing of 30 April and another twelve stored at the airport of Milano-Bresso. On 25 November 1944, another eight disassembled M.C.202s *Serie* XII were sent to Germany by rail.

The German pilots testing the M.C.202s at a *Jagdlehrschule* had considerable difficulty in adapting to the different setup of the throttle control on Italian aircrafts. The full throttle was reached in an Italian aircraft by pushing the lever fully forward, whereas on German aircraft the throttle lever had to be pulled fully backwards. Trainee pilot Rudolf Braunburg recalled:

> In a week's time with *Schulungsjagdgeschwader* JG 101 in Bad Voslau we lost 6 planes with their pilots, always owing to the same cause.... Italian aircraft concealed a lethal trick: to get full throttle one had to pull the throttle lever fully forwards ... theoretically, we had been instructed about this basic difference. However, we were still too inexperienced and, in critical situations, also too shaken to be able to control our reactions. And scrambles often took place when our reactions were not under control.[217]

Thus Italian planes were modified to German standards, including the M.C.202, but some *Luftwaffe* pilots still found it a complex machine to handle. Karl-Heinz Gloer flew a modified M.C.202 in October–November 1944 as a trainee pilot at *Jagdgeschwader* 110's 6.*Staffel*, based on the island of Usedom:

> The C202 had not that control response we were accustomed to. During my stay, this was fatal to a pilot. Following a spin, he could not recover a sufficiently high altitude and then from a clockwise spin he fell into an anticlockwise one. So he unnecessarily lost too much altitude and crashed into the bay.[218]

Others were more enthusiastic, such as trainee pilot NCO Konrad Augner of JG100 *Jagdlehrschule* who flew the Folgore in February 1944:

> ... as to its flying qualities, the Macchi C202 was rather better than our BF109E concerning manoeuvrability and also speed. It had more sensitive controls, i.e. it required lighter effort on its control column. It was agreeable to fly and had no particular faults, such as sudden attitude changes when pushed into a very tight turn, nor had it any tendency to spin.... Landing was, however, a little more difficult than with a BF109E.

> It 'floated' much longer and when one wanted to stop it and the plane had still plenty of speed, it was still flying 5 to 8 m higher above the ground. Landing flaps were not as efficient as those on the BF109E.... As far as I know, my comrades were also as enthusiastic as I about the Macchi C202.[219]

The Air Force of the Independent State of Croatia, 1943–44

Twelve brand-new Macchi M.C.202s of the XII series, produced after the armistice, equipped the 3.*Staffel* of (Kro) JGr1 of the *Zrakoplovstvo Nezavisne Države Hrvatske* (Air Force of the Independent State of Croatia).[220] The unit, which was originally an operational training unit to supply 2.*Staffel* with combat-ready pilots, received them at the end of January–early February 1944, at the airport of Gorizia-Merna, where they were flown by ANR pilots.[221] In the meantime, operational training on CR.42s and G.50s started as a prelude to C.202 training, which started in March, with the help of ANR personnel.

On 1 April, the unit was redesignated I./*Jagdgruppe Kroatien*, just in time for the first combat, but the unit was strafed on 6 April by Mk IX Spitfires of the South African Air Force's No. 7 Wing, with the loss of one M.C.202 and one damaged, to add to another one that had previously crashed during a test flight. The first actual combat occurred on 23 April, as five M.C.202s, led by *Major* Ivan Cenic, scrambled from Lucko to intercept the Fifteenth Air Force bombers on their return flight after having raided Wiener Neustadt, Bad Vöslau, and Schwechat. The Macchis encountered their escort instead, the P-51 Mustangs of the 308th FS, 31st FG, near Bjelovar, and lost two aircraft shot down, including Cenic, though *Unteroffizier* Leopold Hrastovcan claimed the unit's first confirmed victory when shooting down a B-24. By early May, six pilots from I./JGrKro were also sent to Nis airfield to collect four M.C.202s and two C.200s, but one of the C.202s crash-landed during the ferry flight. The remaining three were incorporated into 2./JGrKro and the C.200s went to 3./JGrKro. The six remaining 2./JGrKro M.C.202s had been dispersed to Borovo airfield on 29 May.[222]

Croatian pilots did not have a positive opinion about the Macchi interceptor, because of its weak armament (a pair of 12.7-mm machine guns and a pair of 7.7-mm), ineffective against the USAAF heavy bombers. The commander of 2./JGrKro, *Major* Helebrant, considered the Macchi as 'old, tired and unusable' and described the morale of his men as 'low and the results of his unit equal to zero'.[223]

On 30 June, the unit intercepted heavy bombers of the USAAF raiding various targets in Hungary and Yugoslavia, with three M.C.205s and three M.C.202s, the former piloted by Eastern Front veterans *Major* Helebrant, *Oberleutnant* Bencetic, and *Feldwebel* Bartulovic. In the ensuing battle, only one M.C.205 survived, the other planes being lost with two pilots baling out and three crash-landing. They had been shot down by a combination of bombers' defensive fire and by attack by 5th FS, 52nd FG, Mustangs. After this combat, though, there are no longer documentary traces of the use of the Macchis by Croatian air forces.[224]

Royal Egyptian Air Force, 1948–50s

In 1947, the *Aeronautica Militare Italiana* returned to AerMacchi seventy M.C.202s and 205s, their cells and other components, for the firm to rebuild some composite aircraft to the Veltro standard. The purpose of the deal was, for the *Aeronautica Militare*, to obtain in exchange some MB308 trainers. For AerMacchi, this was the opportunity to strike a deal with Egypt for the sale of their planes. There had been, in fact, informal contacts in Rome between the Egyptian Ambassador *Generale* Eraldo Ilari (director-general of the Macchi) and Italian government representatives, and on 23 June 1948 a contract was signed for the delivery of twenty-four Veltro (of which in fact all but eight were reconditioned M.C.202s).[225] The first twenty-four Macchis (MM1201–1224) were accepted by the Royal Egyptian Air Force between 15 June 1948 and 17 February 1949. A second batch (MM1225-1242) was orderd on 23 February 1949 (three brand-new M.C.205s and fifteen former M.C.202s) and yet another in May 1949 (ten M.C.205s and ten upgraded M.C.202s) This last contract was not finalised and, given the end of the Israeli War of Independence, the fighters were delivered to the *Aeronautica Militare Italiana* between February 1950 and May 1951. The Veltros were fully equipped, while the Folgore conversions were armed with only two 12.7-mm Breda machine guns, the standard armament of the Second World War that already back then had revealed itself to be inadequate. The communications equipment was replaced by modern, US-produced radios. Fifteen of the Macchis were delivered to Egypt before the end of the 1948 Arab-Israeli War, and were assigned to No. 2 Squadron REAF. They saw brief combat against the Israeli Air Force, being also used as fighter-bombers, as they were equipped with underwing bomb racks. On 7 January 1949, a M.C.205 claimed an Israeli P-51D Mustang. In return, two or three Veltros had been lost to IAF fighters by the end of the war in July.

The last Veltros were delivered in 1951, serving mainly with No. 2 Sqn until the mid-1950s.

The *Aeronautica Militare Italiana*, 1945–51

After the end of the Second World War, the few surviving Folgores were concentrated in the *Scuola di Volo* of Lecce-Galatina—a total of about thirty planes. There, they continued to be used as advanced trainers until 1951, with the exception of some machines returned to AerMacchi to allow it to fulfil the contract with Egypt. The Folgore was struck off the register in 1948, with the exception of those M.C.202 airframes transformed into Veltros, which were retired in 1951.

Royal Air Force	***Luftwaffe***
Marshal of the RAF	*Generalfeldmarschall*
Air Chief Marshal	*Generaloberst*
Air Marshal	*General der Flieger* *General der Flieger* *General der Fallschirmtruppe* *General der Luftnachrichtentruppe* *General der Flakartillerie* *General der Luftwaffe*
Air Vice-Marshal	*Generalleutnant*
Air Commodore	*Generalmajor*
Group Captain	*Oberst*
Wing Commander	*Oberstleutnant*
Squadron Leader	*Major*
Flight Lieutenant	*Hauptmann*
Flying Officer	*Oberleutnant*
Pilot Officer	*Leutnant*
Warrant Officer	*Stabfeldwebel*
Acting Pilot Officer	*Oberfähnrich*
Flight Sergeant	*Oberfeldwebel*
Sergeant	*Feldwebel*
Officer Cadet	*Fähnrich*
Corporal	*Unterfeldwebel*
Officer Cadet	*Fahnenjunker*
Corporal	*Unteroffizier*
Senior Aircraftman	*Hauptgefreiter* until 1944 *Stabsgefreiter* from 1944
Leading Aircraftman	*Obergefreiter*
Aircraftman First Class	*Gefreiter*
Aircraftman Second Class	*Flieger*

	Italian *Regia Aeronautica*	**United States Army Air Force**
	Maresciallo dell'Aria	General of the Army *
	Generale di armata aerea	General
	Generale di squadra aerea	Lieutenant General
	Generale di divisione aerea	Major General
	Generale di brigata aerea	Brigadier General
	Colonnello	Colonel
	Tenente Colonnello	Lieutenant Colonel
	Maggiore	Major
	Capitano	Captain
	Tenente	First Lieutenant
	Sottotenente	Second Lieutenant
	Maresciallo di prima classe	Master Sergeant
	Maresciallo di seconda classe	Flight Cadet
	Maresciallo di terza classe	Technical Sergeant
	Sergente maggiore	Staff Sergeant
	N/A	Flight Cadet
	N/A	Sergeant
	Sergente	Flight Cadet
	N/A	Corporal
	Primo Aviere	Private First Class
	Aviere Scello	N/A
	N/A	N/A
	Aviere	Private

Epilogue

The Macchi 202 was a beautiful aircraft, with remarkable flight characteristics for the era in which it was introduced, but it was also a plane not fit for war. As we wrote in the preface, the number of working hours necessary to assemble an M.C.202 (21,000) was at least four times greater than the Bf 109, which also had the same engine. Likewise, many military historians agree that, in addition to the too many 'types' supplied to the *Regia Aeronautica*, an effect of the fascist policy of not wanting to displease the demands of aeronautical companies, the aircraft assembly and construction method was handcrafted in type.

Another absurdity was the use of precious materials for interior finishes, as well as the replacement of parts of the aircraft that had to be adapted from time to time to the vehicle itself. The design then was the result of the vision of Castoldi alone: in fact, there was no ideal and necessary *milieu* for the free contribution of a team of engineers, each tied to his own specialist sector. Among the many pilots who loved this fighter and certainly preferred it to the other types available in the *Regia*, many complained, however, of the poor firepower compared to the enemy fighter, equipped with cannons or with a superior firepower.

It was not until the end of the conflict, in the context of Hitler's Italian puppet state (the *Repubblica Sociale Italiana*), that Italy would equip itself with an aircraft equipped with cannons, although in such small numbers as not to influence the course of the war in any way. The country, unlike for example Japan, lacked the capacity for an important effort to make up for the shortcomings of the industry; after all, Italy did not want to fight a total war for the fascist regime, as had already been proven by previous conflicts. Particularly embarrassing for Mussolini must have been the comparison with the war effort made by the country in the First World War, at the time of the former liberal Italy.

Fascist Italy therefore showed that it had unquestionable capabilities in the aeronautical field but these were accompanied by political and industrial shortcomings that held back production that had any effective value in wartime. The history of this beautiful aircraft is therefore particularly bitter because it is symbolic of the inability of the country to function as a modern entity, being on the contrary tied to an anachronistic and backward-looking craft culture. And this story perhaps also says something about today's Italy.

Endnotes

Chapter 1

1 Montanari, M., *Politica e strategia in cento anni di guerre italiane. 3.1 Il periodo fascista. Le guerre degli anni Trenta* (Rome: General Staff Historical Archive, 2005), p. 83.
2 *Ibid.*, p. 84.
3 Minniti, F., 'La realtà di un mito', in P. Ferrari, ed., *L'aeronautica italiana. Una storia del Novecento* (Milan: Angeli, 2004), pp. 43-44.
4 Isnenghi, M., and Rochat, G., *La grande guerra, 1914–1918* (Bologna: Il Mulino, 2014), pp. 213-220.
5 Montanari, *op. cit.*, p. 84.
6 Rochat, G., *Le guerre italiane 1935–1943. Dall'Impero d'Etiopia alla disfatta* (Turin: Einaudi, 2005), p. 221.
7 *Ibid.*
8 On the ideological use of aviation, see Lehmann, E., *Le ali del potere. La propaganda aeronautica nell'Italia fascista* (Turin: UTET, 2010).
9 Rochat, *Le guerre italiane 1935–1943*, p. 222.
10 *Ibid.*, p. 223.
11 *Ibid.*, p. 224.
12 *Ibid.*, p. 225.
13 Montanari, *op. cit.*, p. 85.
14 See in this volume pp. 27-37.
15 *Ibid.*, p. 27-37.
16 Rochat, G., *Italo Balbo aviatore e ministro dell'aeronautica, 1926–1933* (Ferrara: Bovolenta, 1979), p. 134.
17 *Ibid.*, pp. 134-138.
18 Segrè, C. G., *Italo Balbo. Una vita fascista* (Bologna: Il Mulino, 1988), p. 189.

19 Rochat, *Italo Balbo aviatore e ministro dell'aeronautica*, pp. 125-126.
20 *Ibid.*
21 Montanari, *op. cit.*, p. 86.
22 Rochat, *Italo Balbo aviatore e ministro dell'aeronautica*, pp. 140-141.
23 *Ibid.*, p. 204.
24 *Ibid.*, p. 206.
25 *Ibid.*, pp. 206-207.
26 Segrè, *op. cit.*, p. 196.
27 Rochat, *Italo Balbo aviatore e ministro dell'aeronautica*, pp. 142-144.
28 Minniti, 'La realtà di un mito', pp. 49-50.
29 Segrè, *op. cit.*, pp. 196-197.
30 Rochat, *Le guerre italiane 1935–1943*, p. 230.
31 Giulio Douhet (1869–1930) was a prominent theoretician of aerial warfare. In works like *Il dominio dell'aria* (1921), he argued strongly for the strategical importance of bombing. On this figure, see Lehmann, E., *La guerra dell'aria. Giulio Douhet, stratega impolitico* (Bologna: Il Mulino, 2013).
32 Rochat, *Le guerre italiane 1935–1943*, p. 228.
33 Montanari, *op. cit.*, p. 88.
34 *Ibid.*
35 *Ibid.*
36 Segrè, *op. cit.*, p. 340.
37 *Ibid.*, pp. 337-340
38 Quoted in Rochat, *Le guerre italiane 1935–1943*, pp. 228-229.
39 Kershaw, I., *Hitler: 1936–1945: Nemesis* (London: Penguin, 2001), p. 26.
40 The Stresa Front was an anti-German agreement between French foreign minister Pierre Laval, British Prime Minister Ramsay MacDonald and Mussolini. The three statesmen met in the eponymous town on Lake Maggiore between 11 April and 14 April 1935.
41 Knox, M., *Mussolini Unleashed 1939–1941: Politics and Strategy in Fascist Italy's Last War* (Cambridge: Cambridge University Press, 1982).
42 Gooch, J., *Mussolini and His Generals: The Armed Forces and Fascist Foreign Policy, 1922–1940* (Cambridge: Cambridge University Press, 2007).
43 Rochat, *Le guerre italiane 1935–1943*, pp 44-47.
44 *Ibid.*, pp. 65-70.
45 Ceva, L., 'L'aeronautica nella guerra civile spagnola', in Ferrari, ed., *L'aeronautica italiana. Una storia del Novecento*, p. 351.
46 *Ibid.*
47 Minniti, F., 'La politica industriale del Ministero dell'aeronautica. Mercato, pianificazione, sviluppo, 1935–1943', in *Storia contemporanea*, vol. 12, no. 1-2, p. 29 (Bologna: Il Mulino, 1981).
48 Minniti, 'La realtà di un mito', p. 60.
49 Minniti, 'La politica industriale del Ministero dell'aeronautica', p. 22.
50 *Ibid.*, pp. 21-38.
51 Montanari, *op. cit.*, p. 768.
52 Rocca, G., *I disperati. La tragedia dell'Aeronautica italiana nella Seconda Guerra Mondiale* (Milan: Mondadori, 1991), pp. 61-67.

53 Minniti, 'La politica industriale del Ministero dell'aeronautica', pp. 43-51.
54 Maiolo, J., *Cry Havoc: The Arms Race and the Second World War, 1931–41* (London: John Murray, 2010), pp. 334-342.
55 Minniti, 'La realtà di un mito', p. 60.
56 Rochat, *Le guerre italiane 1935–1943*, p. 233, n. 34.
57 *Ibid.*, pp. 233-235.
58 Overy, R., *Why the Allies Won* (London: Pimlico, 2006), p. 270.
59 Just as clear is Overy's opinion concerning the Italian production: 'Over three years of Italian intervention in the war only 7,183 new aircraft were built, producing in a year what the British economy was producing in a month by 1943'. Overy, R., *The Air War 1939–1945* (Lincoln, Nebraska, USA: Potomac Books, 2004) p. 41.
60 Brian R. Sullivan came to the same conclusions in his 'Downfall of the Regia Aeronautica, 1933–1943', in R. Higham and S. J. Harris, *Why Air Forces Fail: The Anatomy of Defeat* (Lexington, Kentucky, USA: The University Press of Kentucky, 2006), pp. 135-176, especially on pp. 169-170: 'The defeat of the Regia Aeronautica sprang directly from incoherent air-war doctrine, the air industry's inability to adopt mass production techniques, and Italian technological backwardness.... But the fundamental reasons for the downfall of the Regia Aeronautica lay in Mussolini's disastrous strategic leadership and the incompetent, corrupt, and feckless Fascist regime he had created to rule Italy.'

Chapter 2

1 Anderson, J. D., *The Airplane: A History of its Technology* (Reston, Virginia, USA: American Institute of Aeronautics and Astronautics, 2002), pp. 81-130.
2 Minniti, F., *La rivoluzione verticale, Una storia culturale del volo nel primo Novecento* (Rome: Donzelli, 2018), pp. 74-78.
3 *Ibid.*
4 Fradeani, V., *Storia di un primato. Dalla Coppa Schneider all'impresa di Agello* (Milan: Mursia, 1976), p. 17.
5 *Ibid.*
6 *Ibid.*, p. 23.
7 *Ibid.*, p. 28.
8 *Ibid.*, p. 29.
9 See Pegram, R., *Schneider Trophy Seaplanes and Flying Boats, Victors, Vanquished and Visions* (Stroud: Fonthill, 2017), pp. 98-105.
10 *Ibid.*, pp. 142-159.
11 'The new aircraft, called M 39, was a monoplane sporting lowered wings fastened by tie rods, a fuselage and double floats. This solution would later become the standard for all racing seaplanes, both in Italy and abroad. The training together with the testing of the model inside the wind tunnel and the decision concerning the best shape of the floats after the trials in the tank took about a month. By the end of March the construction of the fuselages

was already under way, and in early April it was the turn of the metal parts. The project was going on and the design sketches were immediately turned into real work as soon as the definitive sketches were ready.' Castoldi, M., 'L'idrovolante da corsa nel decennio fascista', *L'Ala d'Italia*, vol. XI, p. 16 (Milan: La Cisalpina, 1933).

12 *Ibid.*

13 See Palanca, A., *Reparto Alta Velocità, Coppa Schneider e primati mondiali di velocità 1928/1934* (Rome: Stato Maggiore Aeronautica, Ufficio Storico, 1996), pp. 14-33.

14 *Ibid.*, pp. 34-49.

15 An interesting document is: Technical Memorandums National Advisory Committee for Aeronautics, No. 944, Italian High-Speed Airplane Engines by C. F. Bona (accessed 29 August 2018), ntrs.nasa.gov/archive/nasa/casi.ntrs.nasa.gov/19930094473.pdf.

16 *Ibid.*, pp. 227-228. The trophy is now on display at the Science Museum in London (accessed 30 August 2018), collection.sciencemuseum.org.uk/objects/co29807/the-schneider-trophy-1913-awards-aviation-marine-environments.

17 Fradeani, *op. cit.*, p. 96.

18 Segrè, C. G., *Italo Balbo: A Fascist Life* (Berkeley: University of California Press, 1992), pp. 225-227.

19 *Ibid*, p. 96.

20 *Ibid.*, p. 122.

21 *Ibid.*, p. 228.

22 'One of the major obstacles facing Italian aircraft designers in the years immediately before W.W. II, was the lack of a suitable liquid-cooled, in-line engine of sufficient power to satisfy the growing aerodynamic needs of fighter aircraft. A strange situation when one considers the brilliant successes gained by the Italian Schneiders Trophy racers powered with FIAT and Isotta Fraschini in-line engines.' Cattaneo, G., *The Macchi C. 202* (Leatherhead, Surrey: Profile Publications, 1965), p. 3.

23 Malizia, N., *Aermacchi, Bagliori di guerra. Flashes of War (Macchi MC2 200 – MC2 202 – MC2 205/V)* (Rome: IBN, 2006), pp. 90-91.

24 Segrè, *op. cit.*, p. 229.

25 Kershaw, I., 'Working Towards the Führer. Reflections on the Nature of the Hitler Dictatorship', *Contemporary European History*, vol. 2, no. 2, pp. 103-118 (Cambridge: Cambridge University Press, 1993).

26 Caldara, S., 'Come è nato l'Aer. Macchi C. 202, nostra intervista a Mario Castoldi', *L'Ala d'Italia*, vol. XX, no. 7, pp. 9-12 (Milan: La Cisalpina, 1942).

Chapter 3

1 Castoldi's student record is documented in the archive of the *Politecnico di Milano*, both in the annual register logs and in the student personal file. Historical archives of the *Politecnico di Milano*, Secretariat, Students' series—Title XIII, Class of 1913, 'Castoldi Mario.' The results of the individual exams

can be found in 'Repertori, Segreteria, serie Registri studenti', vol. 083; 084; 085; 090; 091; 092; 093.

2 Cardani, C., and Curami, A., 'Gli inizi dell'insegnamento dell'Aeronautica nella realtà milanese', *Annali di Storia delle Università italiane*, vol. 12, p. 207 (Bologna: Clueb, 2008).

3 *Ibid.*, p. 210: 'Del Fabbro entered the *Accademia Militare di Torino* in 1888, then went on to the *Scuola di applicazione di artiglieria e genio*, after which he was deployed with the *Brigata specialisti* in Rome'.

4 *Ibid.*, p. 214.

5 *Ibid.*, p. 215: 'With the end of the war, it can be said that the national aviation industry was practically concentrated, except for the Turin-based Aeritalia and the Pisa Saicm (*Società anonima italiana costruzioni meccaniche*), in the triangle between Como (Varese was still part of the province of Como), Milan and Bergamo. In fact, Nieuport-Macchi and the *Società Idrovolanti alta Italia* had based their operations in the region of Varese, while Milan and its province had Filotecnica Salmoiraghi, which produced tools for air navigation, Isotta Fraschini, building aviation engines under a French licence, Caproni Taliedo and that of Vizzola Ticino, in addition to Breda, which had converted to aircraft production during the war, while Airone, soon to be the Caproni *aeronautica bergamasca*, had its headquarters in Ponte San Pietro'.

6 This whole paragraph is a summary of the above-mentioned article by Cardani and Curami.

7 See Chapter One, pp. 13-26.

8 Castoldi, 'L'idrovolante da corsa nel decennio fascista', p. 12.

9 *Ibid.*

10 Rebora, E., 'Mario Castoldi: una vita per la velocità', *Rivista Aeronautica*, vol. 4, p. 612 (Rome: Libreria dello Stato, 1972).

11 The effectiveness of the contribution to the development of the aviation sector of the participation in the Schneider Trophy remains a subject of debate. A memorandum by De Pinedo addressed to Mussolini reported on the shortcomings of the plan drawn up by Balbo. Particularly, in the passage concerning the efforts made to support the promotion of the new armed force he wrote as follows: 'With a great deal of effort it is possible to put together a formation of seaplanes, for a cruise, an air force exercise, about fifteen squadrons, and increase the fame of the Air Force; but its effectiveness in war is quite another matter.... The Air Force is a military entity that is primarily of a technical nature; to be effective, it must be run by a military mind that is extremely competent in the technical field ... it is necessary for the managers ... first and foremost to ensure the true effectiveness of the air force, if neccessary by sacrificing their personality. In the meantime the aircraft needed for the immediate future are still not there, because the best intellectual and industrial energies of aeronautical technology have been engaged in the preparations for the Schneider Trophy; and, while the air force is going on without the funding and the aircraft it needs, an order for 500 light aircrafts—which will weigh heavily on our insufficient budget, not only for the purchasing costs but also for the maintenance costs—has been placed; in Germany they have ordered two huge Do Xs, which represent an overall cost

of 20 millions, and there are no plans for their war use; and while the airlines are multiplying, almost all the aircraft they use are foreign, Dornier, Fokker, Junkers, and the Italian models to replace them still do not exist. The sector is far from being ready for deployment'. Rochat, *Italo Balbo aviatore e ministro dell'aeronautica*, pp. 189, 191-193.

12 Rebora, *op. cit.*, p. 643.

13 Engineer Ermanno Bazzocchi, who replaced Castoldi as Macchi's technical direction, in a report on the Schneider Trophy said about his predecessor: 'They say he only flew once in his life'.

Chapter 4

1 Malizia, *Aermacchi, Bagliori di guerra, Flashes of War*, pp. 15-16.

2 Di Terlizzi, M., *Macchi MC202 Folgore, I* (Rome: IBN Editore, 1999), p. 7.

3 Cull, B., and Galea, F., *Hurricanes over Malta, June 1940–April 1942* (London: Grub Street, 2001), p. 8.

4 Lazzati, G., *I soliti quattro gatti* (Milan: Mursia, 2008), p. 21.

5 *Ibid.*

6 *Ibid.*, p. 22.

7 *Ibid.*, p. 37.

8 See the unit's diary logs on the aircraft under repair—with the same numbers, the G.50 always suffered more breakdowns than the Saetta.

9 Rebora, 'Mario Castoldi: una vita per la velocità', pp. 650-652.

10 *Ibid.*

Chapter 5

1 Mantelli, M. C., *et al.*, *Macchi M.C. 200 Macchi M.C. 202 Macchi M.C. 205* (Le-Grau-du-Roi: Edizioni REI France, 2017), p. 72.

2 Macchi's seaplanes, being built in wood, needed an extremely solid structure with a substantially higher number of ribs and longerons as compared to metallic structure planes. This tendency to over-engineer was then inherited by all the fighters designed by Castoldi.

3 'The essentially craft-based character of the Italian construction process is attested by the manufacturers themselves, who on the one hand mention how often the parts of an aircraft could not be fitted to others of the same model, on the other hand how, when occasionally examining captured enemy aircraft, our machines turned out to be finished individually, for example with an attention paid to the installation of wiring that had no equal on enemy planes. It is also well known that quality control could vary significantly from one company to another: Macchi fighters produced under licence from Breda systematically weighed 50–60 kg more than those produced by the parent company'. Alegi, G., 'Qualità del materiale bellico e dottrina d'impiego italiana nella seconda guerra mondiale: il caso della Regia Aeronautica', *Storia contemporanea*, vol. 6, p. 1202 (Bologna: Il Mulino, 1987).

4 Curami, A., 'Piani e progetti dell'aeronautica italiana 1939–1943: Stato Maggiore e industrie', *Italia contemporanea*, vol. 187 (Rome: Istituto Parri, 1992), p. 256.
5 Ciampaglia, G., 'Le benzine ad altissimo numero di ottani vero segreto delle aviazioni alleate nella II Guerra mondiale', *Rivista Italiana Difesa*, vol. 10 (Chiavari: Giornalistica Riviera, 2009), pp. 82-88.
6 On the availability of aviation fuel gas for the *Regia Aeronautica* until 1943, see Pedriali, F., *L'Italia nella guerra aerea. Da El Alamein alle spiagge della Sicilia (4 novembre 1942–9 luglio 1943)* (Rome: Aeronautica Militare, Ufficio Storico, 2010), p. 253.
7 Curami, *op. cit.*, p. 247.
8 'Undoubtedly, the model with the in-line engine is to be preferred.' Caldara, 'Come è nato l'Aer. Macchi C. 202', pp. 9-12.
9 In 1940, both planes were perhaps a match for the Hurricane in favourable conditions, definitely inferior to early mark Spitfires, to the French Dewotine D.520 and Arsenal VV.G33. Sullivan, *Downfall of the Regia Aeronautica, 1933–1943*, p. 142.
10 In the long run, relying constantly on licenced foreign design greatly reduced Italian planning capacities and ambitions in the field of aero engines. Alegi, *op. cit.*, p. 1203.
11 See also Cernuschi, E., 'Il motore impossibile', *Storia Militare*, vol. 120 (Parma: Albertelli, 2003), pp. 36-43.
12 The only Italian fighter with respectable performance was the Reggiane Re.2000. First flown in 1938, the Re.2000, powered by a Piaggo P.XI RC.40 radial engine rated at 870 hp, attained a maximum speed of 320 mph. Unfortunately, the Piaggio P.XI, which was a licence-built version of the Gnome et Rhône 14K Mistral Major, appeared to suffer from reliability problems and failed to qualify for the 1938 competition.
13 Sullivan, *op. cit.*, p. 140.
14 'In Italy, attempts were made to encourage the engine industry by launching competitions, but in 1938 both the tender for a 1,100 hp engine and the one for 1,500–1,600 hp, in which Alfa Romeo, Piaggio Isotta Fraschini and FIAT were invited to participate, had no major effect and it is significant that the same designers participating in the contemporaneous fighter combat competition had to fall back on the Daimler-Benz DB600 and 601 to meet the requirement of over 600 km/h, with an operating range of 2,000 km at 6,000 m and a weaponry of at least 2 cannons and 5 machine guns'. See Curami, *op. cit.*, p. 248. The task of producing a home-grown liquid-cooled engine was entrusted to Fiat in 1939, with the AS38 (initially an upright V-16 engine closely based on the FIAT AS8, which was originally designed to set speed records, and subsequently, under the inspiration of the DB600 series, an inverted V-12), but it turned out to be a lengthy and inconclusive enterprise.
15 Mantelli, *et al.*, *op. cit.*, p. 56.
16 *Daimler-Benz DB.601A - Alfa Romeo RA.1000 R.C.41*, available at www.alieuomini.it/pagine/dettaglio/uomini,5/daimler_benz_db_a_-_alfa_romeo_ra_r_c,154.html (Accessed on 1 July 2019).

17 Curami, *op. cit.*, p. 248.
18 Caldara, *op. cit.*, pp. 9-12.
19 Curami, *op. cit.*, p. 256.
20 *Daimler-Benz DB.601A - Alfa Romeo RA.1000 R.C.41*, *op. cit.*
21 Sgarlato, N., ed., *Folgore Storia e Tecnica* (Parma: Delta, 2017), p. 14.
22 *Daimler-Benz DB.601A - Alfa Romeo RA.1000 R.C.41*, *op. cit.*
23 Mantelli, *et al.*, *op. cit.*, p. 69.
24 'A beautiful, unarmed plane.'
25 Società Ernesto Breda, *Istruzioni e norme per il montaggio, la regolazione, l'impiego e la manutenzione del velivolo da caccia AER. MACCHI C. 202 con motore R.A. 1000 R.C. 41 I, I Serie BREDA, II Serie MACCHI, III Serie MACCHI* (Rome: Ministero dell'Aeronautica, Direzione Generale delle Costruzioni e degli Approvvigionamenti, 1942), pp. 66-75.
26 *Ibid.*
27 Gueli, M., 'L'Aermacchi C. 202 "Folgore"', *Storia militare*, vol. XXII, no. 244 (Parma: Albertelli, 2014), p. 62.
28 'The limited and badly arranged armament constituted a serious limitation for Italian aircraft. Fighters for a long time provided with only two 12.7 mm machine guns had to wait two years for a pair of 7.7 mm guns to be fitted. Even in 1943, the first series of the so-called 'series 5' aircraft left the factory without the intended 20 mm Mauser wing cannons. Also the effectiveness of 12.7 mm, theoretically better than that of 7.7, was seriously reduced by the unfortunate arrangement in the fuselage which, to allow shooting through the propeller disk, imposed a firing rate of only 300 rounds per minute. Consequently, the overall lethality index for a late production Macchi C.202 (two 12.7 and two 7.7) is around a value of 9.8 compared to 38.6 for the Spitfire Vb (two 20 mm and four 7.7) and 38.4 (six 12.7) for the American P-51 Mustang'. Alegi, *op. cit.*, p. 1201.
29 As attested by allied pilots, such as for example Spitfire pilot McGregor Peart in North Africa: 'I was on patrol one morning when I sighted two enemy aircraft, which turned out to be Macchi 202 fighters. Rather precipitately, without seeing his number two, I attacked the leader and was just going to fire my cannons and machine guns at him, when I noticed a lot of tracer passing close to my cockpit. I immediately broke hard to port, and saw my assailant, his number two, diving for the sea with his leader. Both escaped unscathed. It was the number two which nearly shot me down. He did actually hit me in the oil coiler. I was most surprised at the small calibre of his machine guns. The holes were the equivalent of our 22 calibre but of course were of a much higher power'. McGregor Peart, A., *From the North Africa to the Arakan, The Engrossing Memoir of a WWII Spitfire Ace* (London: Grub Street, 2008), pp. 77-78.
30 'One lesson of early fighting was that the RAF fighters' battery of RCMGs was less effective than expected. Firing at a redundant Bristol Blenheim from 180m to the rear with various British and German guns and ammunition, revealed that the .303 incendiary B MKVI bullets would set light to a Blenheim wing tank with only one hit in five; during the Battle only one or two of the eight

guns were normally loaded with this ammunition. Other .303 and 7.92-mm incendiaries were only half as effective. Similarly, while both German and British steel-cored armour-piercing (AP) rounds could penetrate up to 12 mm of armour plate if fired directly at it from 180 m, most of the bullets were deflected or tumbled by first passing through the fuselage skin or structure. In consequence, only a quarter to a third of the bullets reached the Blenheim's 4 mm-thick armour plate at all, and very few penetrated it'. Williams, A. G., 'Cannon or Machine Gun?', *Aeroplane Monthly*, vol. 377 (Stamford: Key Publishing, 2004), p. 58.

31 Pedriali, *op. cit.*, p. 242.

32 Recollections of *Sergente* Arnaldo Mauri, M.C.202 pilot of the 86ª *Squadriglia*, 7° *Gruppo* of 54° *Stormo*, Mauri, *Un pilota racconta*, available at www.alieuomini.it/AJAX/catalogo/dettaglio2_catalogo/16/ (Accessed on 1 July 2019).

33 'The true fighter, sound, safe, reliable.'

34 Sgarlato, ed., *op. cit.*, p. 66.

35 *Ibid.*, p. 3.

36 Di Napoli, C., and Mancini, R., *Macchi C.200/202/205, Aero Detail 15* (Tokyo: Art box, 1995), p. 78. In the M.C.202 manual, it mentions the fact that the steel tubing was present on some planes of series II and III only. See Società Ernesto Breda, *op. cit.*, p. 59bis.

37 'The construction solutions adopted often show great refinement in design combined with poor industrial qualities, as confirmed by the method chosen to compensate for the propeller torque … the left wing differed from the right one to compensate for the propeller torque. Given that the difference was not limited, as is often claimed, to a difference in the wing span but that the left wing was the same as the right one reproduced in scale, thus increasing not only the wing span, but also the cord, the thickness and the surface, it follows that this means of compensation was particularly ineffective because, being fixed, it was suitable for only one flying condition: it was enough to vary the speed or the power or some other condition for another means of compensation to be needed'. Alegi, *op. cit.*, p. 1200.

38 Enemy Aircraft Report No. 48/1, referring to Macchi M.C.202 MM7779 (Serie III) of 96ª *Squadriglia*, 9° *Gruppo*, 4° *Stormo*, captured intact in Libya in 1943, in Nijboer, D., *Spitfire V vs C.202 Folgore, Malta 1942* (Oxford: Osprey Publishing, 2014), p. 34.

39 Apostolo, G., *Aer.Macchi C.202. Ali D'Italia 2* (Turin: La Bancarella Aeronautica, 1996), p. 8.

40 Pacini, G., *Il volo cieco e quello notturno*, available at sites.google.com/site/gianaereo2/continuazione-di-gianaereo/il-volo-cieco (Accessed on 1 July 2019). Apparently, the initial models were not provided with the direction finder, therefore making the Macchi an *intercettore diurno* (daylight interceptor) as it was not capable of relying on instrument navigation. AerMacchi *storia militare*, p. 61. The 'B 30' (HF band) specially designed for standard use on M.C.202 was produced by both the Unda Radio of Como and Allocchio & Bacchini of Milan, and consisted of the TB 30 transmitter, the RB 30 receiver, the MB 30 modulator, of the QL 30 control panel, and of

the ALB 30 power supply, for a total weight of approximately 15 kg. The working frequency of the system was between 2.9 and 5.5 MHz controlled by quartz oscillators and the transmission power was about 27 W with a range in excess of 200 km. Automatic control to keep stable the frequency of the oscillators (a régime) occurred through the use of capacitors with a negative coefficient dielectric ceramic, that is, as the temperature increased, the capacity decreased, eliminating the 'drift' phenomenon. On the Macchi C.202, the B 30 system was housed inside the fuselage in the rear area practically behind the pilot and access to the ground was only possible through a service panel. In order to limit harmful mechanical vibrations during the flight, the devices were fitted during installation of special hinges equipped with dampers capable of 'absorbing' most of the vibrations. The only element installed in the cockpit was the QL 30 control panel, on which were the controls for the operation of the complex, such as the start-up of the booster using the main switch, the manual tuning, etc. The pilot, once on board, connected to the QL 30 control panel of the system thanks to a special radiotelephonic helmet. The radiotelephonic helmet most used in the RA was the SAFAR-model APR 8120, which was equipped with a headset and laryngophone for radio communications and an electric canvased cable of about 1.3 metres, with which the helmet was connected to the system. The decision to use laryngophones instead of microphones was due to the fact that in a noisy environment such as a piston-engine plane, it was necessary to improve the signal-to-noise ratio in order to obtain a better quality of vocal communication. The laryngophones had the characteristic of being shielded from the air but at the same time being sensitive to the mechanical movements of the larynx that was placed in contact with it. The operating frequency of the B 30 was regulated on the ground by the technicians and no tuning was possible for the pilot, who could only perform fine tuning adjustments. On the other hand, the MB 30 scanner was the one that collected the laryngophone signals to amplify and send them to the TB 30 transmitter input. From an operational point of view, the B 30 system, in addition to the in-flight communication between aircraft, could communicate with the ground via an RT 1000 vehicle-mounted station. Although the Italian B 30 system on paper appeared to be well thought-out, it turned out in reality to be unreliable due to the poor quality of some of the material components mainly attributable to the laryngophones, electrical cables and connectors with which it was set up. It should be emphasized that the B 30 was made up from five principal apparatuses as against the two of the British; this fact entailed the installation of more than double the quantity of electrical interconnections and wiring that consequently doubled the percentage of cases of breakdowns in flight of the B 30 compared with the British equivalent TR 1133B mounted on Spitfires from mid-1942. The final result was that in operational terms the B 30 was inferior to the TR 1133B. The total weights of the components of the system B 30 and TR 1133B were equivalent as well as the operational performances, the difference was in quality. The technical choice of using two different frequency ranges, HF for the Italian B30 and VHF for the British TR 1133B, did not penalise the B 30. However, the British one certainly was more compact and more modern than the latter, available at www.aireroma-lazio.it/wp-content/uploads/2016/05/sistemi-radio-a-confronto-WW2.pdf (Accessed on 5 July 2019).

41 On the manual for the M.C.202 of II *Serie*, by Macchi, the presence of the direction finder was not indicated; see Aeronautica Macchi, *Istruzioni e norme per il montaggio, la regolazione, l'impiego e la manutenzione del velivolo da caccia Aer.Macchi C. 202 con motore D. B. 601 II Serie* (Rome: Ministero dell'Aeronautica Direzione Generale delle Costruzioni e degli Approvvigionamenti, 1941), p. 131. It is presumable therefore that the first M.C.202s were deprived of the system, limiting them to the role of daylight, good-weather interceptors.

42 The direction finder was mentioned in the Società Ernesto Breda, *op. cit.*, p. 84.

43 See also Aeronautica Macchi, *Istruzioni e norme per il montaggio, la regolazione, l'impiego e la manutenzione del velivolo da caccia Aer.Macchi C. 202 con motore R. A. 1000 R. C. 41 I dalla IX alla XI Serie* (Rome: Ministero dell'Aeronautica Direzione Generale delle Costruzioni e degli Approvvigionamenti, 1942), p. 38.

44 After numerous accidents caused by the Italian oxygen masks, in order to operate in Malta the M.C.202s were hurriedly equipped with masks produced by the German company Drager; the *Draeger Auer* II oxygen masks were mentioned as being present on the M.C.202 of the IX to XII *Serie* (and presumably on those service afterwards); see Aeronautica Macchi, *Istruzioni e norme per il montaggio, la regolazione, l'impiego e la manutenzione del velivolo da caccia Aer.Macchi C. 202 con motore R. A. 1000 R. C. 41 I dalla IX alla XI Serie*, p.131.

45 Sgarlato, ed., *op. cit.*, p. 16.

46 Alegi, *op. cit.*, p. 1202.

47 MM91952 not completed.

48 Apparently some of the XII *Serie* planes were completed after the armistice.

49 Only forty-one completed.

50 Not produced.

51 *Ibid.*

52 Molteni, M., *L'aviazione italiana 1940–1945. Azioni belliche e scelte operative* (Bologna: Odoya, 2012), p.122.

53 *Ibid.*

54 Sgarlato, ed., *op. cit.*, p. 12.

55 Compare it to the detailed project of the Spitfire, being drawn up in November 1934, and the prototype flying for the first time in March 1936.

56 Apostolo, G., Cattaneo, G., and Massimello, G., *Aer.Macchi C.202, Ali D'Italia* (Turin: La Bancarella Aeronautica, 2006), p. 55.

57 Società Ernesto Breda, *op. cit.*, p. 59 bis.

58 Formed as the *Sezione Sperimentale* under the 23° *Gruppo* in Comiso in August 1941, the unit was armed with the first Re.2000 to test the model under combat conditions. The unit was heavily involved in operations against Malta, operating from bases in Sicily and Sardinia. After the 23° *Gruppo* was sent to Libya in December 1941, the *Squadriglia* became independent and

remained in Sicily. During 1942, it was re-equipped with Re.2000 III series, and remained stationed in Sicily until the spring of 1943. In the meantime, it received several CR.42NC for night fighting. By the end of 1942, the *Squadriglia* received a dozen M.C.200s and finally, in February 1943, it was supplied with three M.C.202s. In May 1943, the unit was disbanded and its pilots and machines reassigned to the 53° *Stormo*. See Apostolo, G. and Massimello, G., *Italian Aces of World War 2* (Oxford: Osprey Publishing, 2000), p. 43.

59 'Regarding the efficiency of sand filters, the British carried out a test on a C-202 captured in Malta: the subsequent report stated that although there was a substantial similarity in construction between the filter elements of the two aircraft, at full speed things changed significantly. In fact, it was found that in both aircraft at maximum speed, since these had a different fluid-dynamic behaviour, the material forming the filter of the Macchi C. 202 collapsed, decreasing the filtering area fully available to the engine, and generating an important pressure drop (the pressure drop at the end of the Macchi filter was, according to the report, 16 times greater than the pressure drop of the BF109 filter). Therefore it was evident that in full-flow conditions, the German engine was fed more efficiently than the Italian aircraft in terms of air and its carburation was better', in Jabes, D. F., 'Macchi C-202 Folgore, il caccia italiano di maggior successo durante la seconda guerra mondiale: un punto di vista anglossassone', *Ricerche Storiche*, vol. XLII, no. 1, pp. 150-151.

60 Massimello, G., 'CIAK! Per la Regia Aeronautica', *Storia militare*, vol. 128 (Parma: Albertelli, 2004), p. 18.

61 *Ibid.*

62 *Ibid.*

63 Gueli, *op. cit.*, p. 62.

64 *Ibid.*

65 *Ibid.*

66 Molteni, *op. cit.*, p. 415.

67 *Aeronautica Lombarda Assalto Radioguidato, immagini, scheda e storia*, available at www.alieuomini.it/catalogo/dettaglio_catalogo/aeronautica_lombarda_assalto_radioguidato,66.html (Accessed on 5 July 2019).

Chapter 6

1 The song mentioned at the beginning of the chapter, 'And if death does not want to go away, circle around it and do acrobatics', *E gira gira l'elica*, is a military song of the *Regia Aeronautica*, composed anonymously (maybe by Ezio Carabella) in 1942.

2 'The historian Giovanni de Lorenzo, evaluated the state of the *Regia Aeronautica* at the beginning of the war thus: "the apparently brilliant, casual, sporty, efficient and multi-faceted aspect credited by many to the Italian Air Force, did not necessarily live up to the reality, due to its lack of operational vision, professional qualifications, appropriate and clearly formulated philosophy suited to the times, modest preparation for the rationally organized

and harmoniously coordinated use of personnel on the technical, combat and training levels". Ceva adds: "In the years 1936–40, the *Aeronautica* maintained its habit of being an individualistic, heroic arm rather than a technical, collective one". On the shoulders of the undersecretary fell the problems not solved by his predecessors. The most serious were the incapacity of the aeronautical industry to design and produce an engine, the failed attempt to create a torpedo-bomber speciality, the tonnage of the bombs, the absolute technical inadequacy of the instrumentation that became clear during night flights and flights towards northern countries, all of which was complicated by "the inability to elaborate a fully fledged doctrine, capable of giving meaning to the request for total autonomy". Yet the Arma could boast a glorious list of records, including that of the inverted flight lasting three hours achieved by a Ca 113'. Bonaiti, E., *La Regia Aeronautica del Generale Francesco Pricolo*, available at www.icsm.it/articoli/ri/rapricolo.html (Accessed on 1 July 2019).

3 See also Ceva, 'L'aeronautica nella guerra civile spagnola', pp. 344-347.

4 'The *Aeronautica* could not fail to be affected by the orientations of the upper echelons and of the General Chief of Staff, who planned for an essentially terrestrial war ... therefore, a war at sea was not planned for ... in relation to this conception of war, the aerial strategy envisaged: an offensive with bombers against enemy territory to reduce the opponent's war capacity and hinder the use of its air and surface forces, and air defence of the Italian territory with fighters ... the aerial weapon was consequently almost exclusively made up of medium bombers and interceptor fighters, or fighters ... with little autonomy and therefore unsuitable for escorting bombers.' Licheri, S., *L'arma aerea italiana nella seconda guerra mondiale: 10 giugno 1940–8 maggio 1945* (Milan: Mursia, 1983), p. 17.

5 Most of the *Accademia Aeronautica* pilots fighting in the Second World War came from the courses *Rex*, *Sparviero*, *Turbine*, the *Urano*, and *Vulcano*, not completing their training at the *scuola di specialità* before the armistice.

6 11 *Scuole di Volo di 1° Periodo* and 21 *Scuole di Volo di 2° Periodo* by 1942. On the training of the *Regia Aeronautica* pilots, see Alegi, G., 'L'addestramento della Regia Aeronautica', *Storia Militare*, vol. 141, (Parma: Albertelli, 2005), p. 4.

7 Later a Macchi M.C.202 pilot in 51° *Stormo*.

8 Paravicini, P. P., *Pilota da caccia* (Milan: Mursia, 2011), p.18.

9 In the mid-1930s, the basic training aircraft was often the Caproni Ca.100. See Pagani, F., *Ali d'aquila. Duelli aerei nei cieli d'Europa 1936–1943* (Milan: Mursia, 2007), p. 41.

10 Dunning, C., *Courage Alone: The Italian Air Force, 1940–1943* (Manchester: Hikoki Publications, 1999), p. 210.

11 Nijboer, *Spitfire V vs C.202 Folgore, Malta 1942*, p. 46.

12 In Paravicini's case, it only consisted of a Ba.25, see Paravicini, *op. cit.*, p. 18.

13 In Giancarlo Galbusera's case (then in the 4°*Stormo*), at Pistoia's flying school in January 1942, the plane was a Saiman 202. See Brancaccio, G., 'Giancarlo Galbusera il cacciatore centenario', *Rivista Aeronautica*, vol. 3 (Rome: Libreria dello Stato, 2017), p. 104. It is therefore likely that the choice depended on the avaibility of planes at each flying school.

14 Paravicini, *op. cit.*, p. 18.

15 Garello, G., 'Piloti e personale di volo, simboli di un'età nuova (1923–1943)', in M. Ferrari, ed., *Le ali del ventennio. L'aviazione italiana dal 1923 al 1945* (Milan: Angeli, 2005), p. 172.
16 *Ibid.*
17 Paravicini, *op. cit.*, pp. 19-20.
18 G.50s and M.C.200s were added as they were retired from operational units, i.e. when they were war-weary machines and not combat-ready.
19 Paravicini, *op. cit.*, pp. 19-24.
20 Pagani, *op. cit.*, p. 47.
21 'For any newly arrived pilots [those of the 360ª *Squadriglia*, just before their tour of duty in Malta], this is where the third and last stage of their fighter training would take place. Replacement pilots would soon learn about the squadron's tactics and fighting discipline as taught at squadron level by individual commanders. The level of tuition would vary from squadron to squadron depending on the time available and the skill and patience of each individual squadron commander. The CO of the 360ª *Squadriglia*, Capitano Carlo Miani, taught his charges well since the unit did not suffer a single fatality during the Malta campaign in 1942.' Giorgio Apostolo, quoted in Nijboer, *op. cit.*, p. 63.
22 Bertozzi, G., *L'addestramento nella Regia Aeronautica*, available at www.facebook.com/groups/822772004588105/permalink/1107050059493630/ (Accessed on 5 July 2019).
23 Paravicini, *op. cit.*, pp. 28-30.
24 Bertozzi, *op. cit.*
25 Ghergo, G. F., 'La Caccia Italiana 1940–1943', *Storia militare*, vol. 149 (Parma: Albertelli, 2006), p. 11.
26 Pagani, *op. cit.*, p. 147.
27 *Ibid.*, p. 53.
28 Massimello, G., 'La caccia italiana nella seconda guerra mondiale', in Ferrari, ed., *Le ali del ventennio*, p. 189.
29 Pagani, *op. cit.*, p. 56.
30 *Ibid.*
31 *Ibid.*
32 Nijboer, *op. cit.*, p. 47.
33 The report of *Colonnello* Silvestri after an inspection (probably in 1936) of the 1° and 4° *Stormo*, the elite of the Italian fighter arm, is rather damning: "RT Connections. Lack of training also in relation to the delicateness and complexity of the on-board equipment and the difficulty of using the radio while flying means that this form of training cannot be adequate given the importance of the RT connection in air combat. Fighter pilots trained today for the RT connection are a minority' Arena, N., *I caccia a motore radiale* (Modena: Mucchi, 1980), pp. 29-30.
34 Pagani, *op. cit.*, p. 147.
35 *Ibid.*, p. 148.
36 The same report by *Colonnello* Silvestri observed: 'it is the type of training that creates the greatest difficulty, since the departments are not able to give the many pilots the large number of flying hours for training that navigation requires.' Arena, *op. cit.*, pp. 29-30.

37 Dunning, *op. cit.*, p. 210.
38 Paravicini, *op. cit.*, p. 21.
39 Massimello, *op. cit.*, p. 188.
40 Ernst Düllberg, *Staffelkapitän* of II *Gruppe* of JG27, observed that the Italian pilots were not keen on flying over the sea: 'I know from experience that they refused to fly over the sea although they possessed air-sea rescue organisations in Sicily. The flying ability of their pilots was excellent, however'. See Shores, C., *et al.*, *A History of the Mediterranean Air War, 1940–1945, II. North African Desert, February 1942–March 1943* (London: Grub Street, 2012), p. 17.
41 This was also confirmed by Fiorenzo Macchi: 'We Italians did not know air navigation, we were in jeopardy.... Sometimes due to the lack of preparation we did not know how to manage the plane that had been entrusted to us, we had to keep it to a minimum and exploit it only during the fight which could have been very long, otherwise in one way or another we lost control of the plane and it ended in tragedy. We had no suitable equipment, blue above, blue below, many landed in Tunisia, others on the Aegadian Islands without knowing where they were'. See Azzalin, *Quando il Sergente Pilota Fiorenzo Macchi, conobbe il Comandante Carestiato al Campo di Volo di Campoformido*, available at www.isses.it/fiorenzoMacchi.htm (Accessed on 5 July 2019).
42 Data were not collected for that year. See Garello, *op. cit.*, p. 171.
43 *Ibid.*, pp. 176-178.
44 Cadet Giuseppe Coccolini of the *Zodiaco* course remembered how the environment of the *Accademia Aeronautica* influenced morale: 'Admittedly we trainees, given our youth, accustomed to following a rigid daily routine to develop our sense of duty and without any share of responsiblity, we had no clear idea of the political and social reality of the time; we lived in isolation in the almost artificial atmosphere of a general consensus about the most important issues in the midst of the daily rhetoric of the official propaganda of the period. The complicity of the Italian intellectual classes in the creation of this atmosphere that had always accompanied us from school onwards was general; the war, albeit distant, also had a positive effect on the ideal of heroism for the motherland, for which everything had to be sacrificed. The example of the outstanding heroism of so many pilots was for us stimulating and positive. The total lack of information about the rest of the world together with the daily manipulation of the truth about Italy as well as an irrational obedience—almost an uncritical submission without any conscious consent—provided the foundation for a total absence of clear opinions and for an absolute ignorance of the direction in which our country was moving. However, the fall of Mussolini, decided by the *Gran Consiglio del Fascismo* on 25 July 1943 was greeted with spontaneous joy even if the invasion-liberation of Sicily was for many of us an unacceptable blow; too many had been complicit in this surrender'. Available at libro.corsozodiaco.it/02_il_nido_delle_aquile.pdf, p. 79.
45 Recollection of Ronaldo Scaroni, 151ª *Squadriglia*, in Nijboer, *op. cit.*, p. 62.

46 Garello, *op. cit.*, p. 176.

47 'During the first phase of the war, commanders usually attributed victories collectively to all those pilots who had taken part in a particular action. This situation subsequently changed during the course of the conflict following the instruction to unit commanders to keep a more detailed, and accurate, record of all aerial combats, indicating precisely by name the pilot, or pilots, to whom the victory had been awarded. However, there was still no uniform procedure in place at this time for the confirmation of aerial kills. Sometimes a third witness was deemed necessary for a victory to be credited to a pilot, whilst on other occasions only the post-sortie report from the individual directly involved in the engagement was required [usually, if an officer]'. Apostolo, and Massimello, *Italian Aces of World War 2*, pp. 44-46.

48 Fighter ace Luigi Gorrini, who was an NCO, complained that 'The non-commissioned officers were discriminated against in the awarding of medals: for them there had to be at least two in-flight witnesses. The officers on the other hand returned, reported and ... were believed on their word of honour. An officer returned to base, claimed to have shot down an aeroplane and was awarded a silver medal'. See Benzi, A., 'Intervista a Luigi Gorrini', *Storia del XX secolo*, no. 33, February 1999.

49 Fiorenzo Macchi, observed that no proper track was kept of individual victories: 'I remember that after the shooting down of enemy aircraft, our officers sometimes weren't too interested in reporting our victories for any future medals or awards: perhaps some of us wouldn't even come back. What use would it be? We tried to save the thing that was most important to us: our skins, perhaps without any medal to pin to the uniform, but alive!' See Azzalin, *op. cit.*

50 Ceva, *op. cit.*, p. 351.

51 'Looking at the different schools in detail, we can see that the "Cucaracha" kept the Squadron (8 planes) as a working unit, deploying it in a column with a front of two aircraft and a depth of four. The squadron commander led the first pair, while the others followed "with a negative step of six to seven metres, a distance between each pair of five to six metres, and a zero interval". If the Squadron operates in complete ranks the ninth aircraft is flanked by the leading pair. When the entire Group (24) flew together, the second and third Squadron, also listed as described, lined up to the right of the first, slightly behind it and each at an altitude of 500–1,000 metres higher than that of Squadron next to it. The "Asso di Bastoni" Group, on the other hand, abolished the Squadron as a combat unit, deploying the Group (24) in two echelons (12), each divided into two sections (6) composed of three pairs (2) or a triad and a couple. The whole group flew in line, with the second group a thousand metres above the first. The distance between the pairs was six metres and the distance between the sections was ten metres. The group commander flew over the first section of the first group. The "Gamba di Ferro" maintained the Squadrons as a compromise, deploying them at increasing heights like the "Cucaracha", but each Squadron formed a line of pairs and triads borrowed from the "Asso di Bastoni"', In Alegi, *op. cit.*, pp. 1210-1211.

52 The *Pattuglia* was defined by the *Addestramento dell'Aviazione da Caccia* manual of 1936 as the 'basic elementary unit of all higher-order formations' '. See Ufficio di Stato Maggiore della Regia Aeronautica, 1° Reparto—Divisione Addestramento, *Addestramento dell'aviazione da caccia* (Rome: Ministero dell'Aeronautica Laboratorio Fotomeccanico, 1936), p. 42.
53 Alegi, *op. cit.*, p. 1211.
54 Ghergo, *op. cit.*, p. 11.
55 Alegi, *op. cit.*, p. 1213.
56 An 'acrobatic mentality', as it was aptly called by Ghergo. See Ghergo, *op. cit.*, p. 12.
57 See Ceva, *op. cit.*, pp. 348-350.
58 Neville Duke undertook two tours of duty in North Africa, the first flying Tomahawks and then Kittyhawks with 112 Squadron, and then with 92 Squadron on Spitfires. Shores, *et al.*, *op. cit.*, p. 17.
59 Beurling, G., and Roberts, L., *Malta Spitfire: The Buzz Beurling Story* (London: Penguin Books, 2002), pp. 168-169.
60 *Ibid.*, p. 240.
61 Azzalin, *op. cit.*
62 Shores, *et al.*, *op. cit.*, p. 28.
63 *Ibid.*, p. 20.
64 The lack of mutual understanding of tactics between the Axis partners was evident also on the Italian side. *Sergente* Mauri commented on German pilots: 'To us, it looked as if they weren't giving it all they had, that is, they were not acrobatic enough'. Recollections of *Sergente* Arnaldo Mauri, *op. cit.*
65 Nijboer, *op. cit.*, p. 60.
66 Bianchi, G., *Il IV Stormo degli Assi—Lucchini Ferrulli Reiner e Teresio Martinoli* (Massa: Sarasota, 2018), p. 58.
67 Recollections of *Sergente* Arnaldo Mauri, *op. cit.*
68 *Ibid.*
69 'Until 1942 early warning was delegated to the DICAT (*Difesa Contraerea Territoriale*, Territorial Air Defence) based on the sighting service, organized since the peace on the whole national territory. This service consisted of look-out posts (*posti vedetta*, p.v.) suitably located throughout the national territory for an aircraft discovery service; from news collection centres (*centri raccolta notizie*, CRN) with the task of collecting news from a certain number of look-out posts and coordinate their transmission to the anti-aircraft defence commands (DICAT) existing in the localities in which the defence itself was organized. The set of a certain number of look-out posts of CRN and of one or more DICAT commands bore the name of Sighting Mesh and the total of all the meshes that of Sighting Network. A locality in which the anti-aircraft defence was also provided with artillery was called a *località di 1° grado* (1st degree location); those of *2° grado* (2nd degree) were provided only with machine guns; those of 3° *grado* (3rd degree) had no anti-aircraft defence, but only the PAA (*protezione anti aerea*, anti-air protection).
For each *località di 1° grado*, a command post was organized with a gunnery office with its own command observers from which to direct the action of the

anti-aircraft using a special telephone network, a radio station and signalling posts in charge of communicating by radio and optical means with possible national aeroplanes in flight ... during the course of the conflict an attempt was made to coordinate and integrate the various components of the territorial anti-aircraft defence through centralized commands, common radio and telephone links. The intervention of the *Luftwaffe* and the Flak put an end to the autonomous management by each armed force of the national anti-aircraft organization, which was integrated with the German radar sighting centres. Taking their cue from the organization of the Germans, the various chiefs of staff agreed on a plan for the unification of the various centres and commands in charge of aerial surveillance, creating the *servizio scoperta e segnalazione* (discovery and warning service) for sighting and aerial defence with extensive and complete functions. Benefiting from the organization of the Germans, early warning for aerial raids rose to thirty and even to forty-five minutes'. See Bertozzi, *Sistemi di difesa aerea dell'Asse nel Mediterraneo*, available at www.facebook.com/groups/822772004588105/permalink/1072556139609689/ (Accessed on 5 July 2019).

70 Artioli, G., *Comandante Costantino Petrosellini, Asso dell'Aeronautica Italiana*, available at www.anpaninfo.it/public/uploads/petrosellini_2017.pdf (Accessed on 1 July 2019).

71 It was a guided night-hunting procedure in which ground radars were used to guide night-fighter aircraft. In the stationary *Himmelbettstellungen* also anti-aircraft headlights and anti-aircraft batteries were used to support the anti-aircraft defence.

72 Molteni, *L'aviazione italiana 1940–1945*, p. 284.

73 'The national production of "radiolocalizers", as radar systems were called in Italy, was late and on a modest scale. Many apparatuses of German origin were installed during 1943. On 1 July in Calabria there were: a "Freya" and a "Wassermann" at Capo Spartivento, managed by the Luftwaffe; a "Freya" at Capo Vaticano, managed by the Lufwaffe; one "Freya" in Crotone and another in Isola Capo Rizzuto, both managed by the *Regia Aeronautica*. On 5 August, the German Command placed a "Freya" type radiolocalizer at Monte Scuro, in the Sila Grande, and on 16 August the "Wurzburg" of Capo S. Gallo (Palermo) was transferred to Vibo Valentia. This last type, unlike the "Freya" used for the sighting, was a fire-direction apparatus for the anti-aircraft artillery'. Pesce, G., *Guerra attraverso l'etere nel teatro mediterraneo* (Modena: STEM Mucchi, 1978), p. 359.

The first radars in Italy were installed in Sicily by the Luftwaffe, at the beginning of 1941, more precisely in Portopalo di Capo Passero, Pantelleria and Lampedusa to keep the Sicilian Channel and Maltese air activity under control. The apparatuses were of the Freya type. In January 1942 additional Freya radars arrived, a Wassermann radar (range 200 Km) to strengthen the long-range network, and several Würzbug-Riese, Loewe 40L and Wurzburg 62D radar needed to build *cellule guida-caccia* (day and night) for the X *Fliegerkorps* aircraft deployed on the airports of Catania, Comiso, Palermo and Trapani. These devices were installed in Agrigento, Cefalù, Palermo, Messina, Marsala,

Capo Passero, Catania and Pantelleria. Some *cellule guida-caccia* began to be managed by technical and operational personnel of the *Regia Aeronautica*, trained in Germany. The stations were connected by radiotelephony to the DICAT stations equipped with tactical tables, whose staff, having assessed the situation, gave instructions to the fighters and to the anti-aircraft artillery positions. Information was also sent to the DICAT stations by the optical sighting centres and by the aerophones scattered throughout the territory.

74 'The rest of Italian territory was not subjected to a heavy campaign of air raids so the deployment of new apparatus was slow and instead the decision was taken to deploy the apparatus in North Africa. In January 1942 the first Freya was installed in Tripoli and in June 1942 in Africa there were three Freya in Tripoli, Benghazi, Derna and two Würzburg radars in Benghazi and in the gulf of Bomba and the Italian fighter pilots usually operated under radar control, in July 42 the Benghazi Freya passed under the control of the *Regia Aeronautica*.... In January 1942 an Italian commission composed of Gen. Attilio Biseo and Col. Buffa and Moscatelli went to Germany to the 12th *Flieger Korps*. The result was a report which encouraged the adoption of the German apparatuses; the programme launched for Italy envisaged the adoption of 5 Freya apparatuses and 10 of the 40L type (40 Km range for *guida caccia*, comparable to the Wurzburg) by April 1942 and of 20 *guida caccia* cells composed of 1 Freya and 2 "Würzburg" by October 1942 in peninsular Italy up to Campania and of 13 cells in Sicily, Sardinia, Calabria and Puglia on the basis of the structure already established by the Germans, which was expected to be transfered to the Italians as and when trained personnel became available. To this was added a long-range warning network based on long-range Wassermann radars (200/300 km range).

'Overall, the programme envisaged the installation in Italy of 8 early warning cells with 1 Wassermann and 33 *guida caccia* cells with 109 radiotelemeters (33 Freya, 66 Würzburg and 10 Riese "Renna") as well as several hundred fire-direction radars for a total of 510 apparatuses.... At the time of the landing in Sicily an integrated interforce sighting system had been set up which had absorbed the previous sighting organizations of each individual branch of the armed forces, which were left only with the management of the units for the conduct of the fire.

As for the management of the electronic component, 8 battalions had been set up, of which 5 were operational and 3 under way, each battalion was of 4 or more companies called cells with detection tasks and fighter direction with radar equipment and 1 operations centre with a data processing station, with a fighter command, with a tactical table to trace routes for raiders and fighters.... On the whole, in July 1943 in continental Italy there were 27 apparatuses (24 managed by the *Regia Aeronautica* and 3 by the *Regio Esercito* of which two were of Italian construction, 1 Folaga with a 210 km and 1 Argo with a 300 km range) while the discovery nets and *guida caccia* in Sicily, Sardinia, Calabria and Puglia included a total of 34 devices (all German), 29 of which were managed by the *Luftwaffe*, 2 by the *Regia Aeronautica*, 2 by the *Regia Marina* and 1 by the *Regio Esercito* for a total of 61 devices of which 29 were managed by the *Luftwaffe* and 32 by Italians, which increased by the time of the armistice to 73 apparatuses (36 managed by German 37 by the Italians; 8 Wassermann, 44 Freya, 13 Würzburg, 6 Lorenz L40, 1 Argo, 1 Folaga) plus another 12 apparatuses managed by the Germans in other sectors under Italian control, 1 Wassermann in Crete and 11 Freya (7 in Greece 2 in Corsica and 2 in Rhodes)'. Bertozzi, *Sistemi di difesa aerea dell'Asse nel Mediterraneo*.

75 See also Pedriali, *L'Italia nella guerra aerea*, pp. 255; 345.

76 See also Poddigghe, G. C., *Un mito da sfatare il radar (italiano) nella 2^ gm. Una guerra tecnologica ed un'occasione perduta*, available at www.academia.edu/35904742/Un_mito_da_sfatare_IL_RADAR_italiano_NELLA_2_GM_UNA_GUERRA_TECNOLOGICA_ED_UN_OCCASIONE_PERDUTA (Accessed on 1 July 2019).

77 Recollections of *Sergente* Arnaldo Mauri, *op. cit.*

Chapter 7

1 Malizia, *Aermacchi. Bagliori di guerra, Flashes of War (Macchi MC2 200 – MC2 202 – MC2 205/V)*, pp. 100-101.

2 Gueli, 'L'Aermacchi C. 202 "Folgore"', p. 59.

3 *Ibid.*

4 Apostolo, *Aer.Macchi C.202. Ali D'Italia 2*, p. 11.

5 Molteni, *L'aviazione italiana 1940–1945*, p. 123.

6 This was actually a very dangerous manoeuvre, as specifically indicated by the M.C.202's manual: 'It is absolutely forbidden to perform inverted flight. It is allowed to pass momentarily into the upside-down position, during manouvres, but one shouldn't remain in that position even for a short period of time. Since the suction pipe in the fuel tank drains in the lower part, reversing the plane makes it suck up only petrol vapours and therefore causes the fuel pump to disengage'. Aeronautica Macchi, *Istruzioni e norme per il montaggio, la regolazione, l'impiego e la manutenzione del velivolo da caccia Aer.Macchi C. 202 con motore R. A. 1000 R. C. 41 I dalla IX alla XI Serie*, p. 204.

7 Mattioli, M., 'L'esordio del Macchi C.202', *Storia militare*, vol. 80, pp. 53-56 (Parma: Albertelli, 2000), p. 53.

8 On Frigerio, see Gustavsson, H., *Biplane fighter aces, Italy, Capitano Jacopo Frigerio, 29 October 1913–3 October 1955*, available at surfcity.kund.dalnet.se/italy_frigerio.htm (Accessed on 1 July 2019).

9 Mattioli, *op. cit.*, p. 53.

10 Malizia, N., *La Regia Aeronautica nella 2ª Guerra Mondiale. Dai Diari di Guerra 1940–1942* (Rome: IBN, 2016), p. 394.

11 Massimello, G., 'Il Capitano Pilota Giuseppe Pesola', *Storia militare*, vol. 251, pp. 58-65 (Parma: Albertelli, 2014), p.60.

12 Sgarlato, *Folgore Storia e Tecnica*, p. 42.

13 Malizia, *La Regia Aeronautica nella 2ª Guerra Mondiale*, pp. 395-396.

14 Gustavsson, H., *Biplane fighter aces, Italy, Capitano Ezio Viglione Borghese*, available at surfcity.kund.dalnet.se/italy_borghese.htm (Accessed on 1 July 2019).

15 King removed the overcoat from a dead Italian soldier, boarded an abandoned tank and drove it all through the night to reach Tobruk, successfully reaching British lines.
16 Recollections of *Sergente* Arnaldo Mauri, *op. cit.*
17 One of the 96ª *Squadriglia* aircraft returned early because of engine trouble.
18 Gustavsson, *Biplane fighter aces, Italy, Capitano Jacopo Frigerio, 29 October 1913–3 October 1955.*
19 *Ibid.*
20 He returned the same night to base, claiming one Hurricane and another as probable with the use of 630 rounds of ammunition.
21 One of the 80ª *Squadriglia* returning to base early because it developed engine trouble.
22 Malizia, *La Regia Aeronautica nella 2ª Guerra Mondiale*, p. 402.
23 *Ibid.*
24 Thomas Albert Meek made his way back to the unit on foot the day after.
25 Gustavsson, H., *Biplane fighter aces, Italy, Colonnello Pio Tomaselli*, available at surfcity.kund.dalnet.se/italy_tomaselli.htm.
26 Gustavsson, H., *Biplane fighter aces, Commonwealth, Squadron Leader Derrick Fitzgerald 'Gerald' 'Jerry' Westenra DFC and Bar, RAF no. 89782, 29 April 1918–17 August 1999*, available at surfcity.kund.dalnet.se/commonwealth_westenra.htm.
27 *Ibid.*
28 *Ibid.*
29 Malizia, *La Regia Aeronautica nella 2ª Guerra Mondiale*, p. 406.
30 Gustavsson, *Biplane fighter aces, Italy, Capitano Jacopo Frigerio, 29 October 1913–3 October 1955.*
31 *Ibid.*
32 Malizia, *La Regia Aeronautica nella 2ª Guerra Mondiale*, p. 409.
33 *Ibid.*
34 See also Gustavsson, H., *Biplane fighter aces, Italy, Capitano Clizio Nioi*, available at surfcity.kund.dalnet.se/italy_nioi.htm.
35 Malizia, *La Regia Aeronautica nella 2ª Guerra Mondiale*, p. 413.
36. The bombing was executed by the B-17Cs of No. 90 Squadron, and a M.C.202 was destroyed on the ground, along with a Ca.133 and with several casualties.
37 Known by the British as Marble Arch.
38 Massimello, 'Il *Capitano* Pilota Giuseppe Pesola', p. 62.
39 This is one of the reasons why in the 1930s the *Ministero dell'Aeronautica* virtually stopped all production of national in-line engines.
40 Malizia, *La Regia Aeronautica nella 2ª Guerra Mondiale*, p. 222.
41 On 3 April, both *Gruppi* of the 1° *Stormo* scrambled to intercept a formation of bombers escorted by fighters heading for Derna. The M.C.202s engaged the escort, made up of Tomahawks of No. 2 SAAF and 4 SAAF Squadrons, of No. 94 Squadron, and of Kittyhawks of No. 260 Squadron, the encounter later involving also some Kittyhawks of No. 450 Squadron and Hurricane IIbs of No. 274 Squadron. *Capitano* Clizio Nioi claimed one enemy fighter and

qualified as an ace, as the first pilot of the *Stormo* to achieve this status during the conflict. Sergeant William Marsh of No. 274 Squadron who was flying Hurricane IIb BD820/D recollected: 'Pukka dog-fight for ten minutes, 202 looping and rolling, got in snap shots at bottom of loops'. Gustavsson, *Biplane fighter aces, Italy, Capitano Clizio Nioi.*

42 'On the evening of this day the 54 MC202s of the 4° Stormo CT, which had been operating over Malta, arrived at Martuba, led by *T Col* Armando François. They joined the 1° *Stormo*, forming a force of more than 100 MC202s, the largest concentration of these fighters ever to be achieved in Libya.... Next day a *Comando Caccia* (Fighter Command) would be established at Martuba under the 1° *Stormo* commander, Col Alfredo Reglieri, to co-ordinate the activities of the four MC202-equipped units: 6° *Gruppo* (1° *Stormo*) *Magg* Mario Larcher; 17° *Gruppo* (1° *Stormo*) *Magg* Domenico Sciaudone; 9° *Gruppo* (4° *Stormo*) *Magg* Antonio Larsimont-Pergameni; 10° *Gruppo* (4° *Stormo*) *Magg* Paolo Maddalena. The three *squadriglie* of newly arrived 9° *Gruppo* were led by *S.Ten* Alvaro Querci (73ª), *Cap* Ezio Viglione-Borghese (96ª) and S.Ten Jacopo Frigerio (97ª), who would be replaced by Ten Fernando Malvezzi on 1 June. The commanders of the three *squadriglie* of the 10° *Gruppo* were Cap Franco Lucchini (84ª), *Cap* Ranieri Piccolomini (90ª) and *Ten* Orlando Mandolini (91ª)'. Shores, *et al.*, *A History of the Mediterranean Air War, 1940–1945, II. North African Desert, February 1942–March 1943*, Sunday, 24 May 1942.

43 Molteni, *op. cit.*, p. 224.

44 Gustavsson, H., *Biplane fighter aces, Italy, Sergente Maggiore Teresio Vittorio Martinoli Medaglia d'oro al valor militare*, available at surfcity.kund.dalnet.se/italy_martinoli.htm.

45 For a day-by-day description of air operations on the African front see Shores, *et al.*, *A History of the Mediterranean Air War, 1940–1945*, voll. I-III.

46 Malizia, *La Regia Aeronautica nella 2° Guerra Mondiale.*

47 The HALPRO unit, or Halverson Provisional was a specially trained bomber outfit, commanded by Colonel Harry A. Halverson, with 23 early B24Ds. This detachment was made up of members of the 98th Bombardment Group (Heavy) and was heading east with the intention of being used by the 10th Air Force in China for bombing raids on Tokyo. After they reached Fayid in Egypt however, it became apparent that they were needed to combat German forces in the immediate vicinity. And so they were kept in theatre. To HALPRO fell the honour of making the first USAAF bombing mission against the German forces in Europe. On the night of 11–12 June 1942 thirteen Liberators struck the oil refineries at Ploesti in Romania (a place that much later in the war would be the target for other American bombers, but with dreadful losses). The next 'HALPRO' mission was on 15 June. On 14 June a British supply convoy was headed for Malta—Operation Vigorous—with an Italian fleet on its way to intercept it. The morning after (15 June) seven U.S B24Ds joined RAF Liberators of No.160 Sqdn. to attack the Italian fleet with 500-lbs bombs. 'The force found the Italian fleet and damaged the BB Littorio but caused no other damage. The threat of air attack and the minor damage already suffered

drove the Italian fleet back to port. In the end, the HALPRO Detachment remained in the Mediterranean to form the 376th Bombardment Group, the first USAAF heavy bomber group in that theatre. National Museum of the US Air Forces, Early Operations. *Ninth/Twelfth Air Force in the Mediterranean*, 2018, available at www.nationalmuseum.af.mil/Visit/Museum-Exhibits/Fact-Sheets/Display/Article/1513334/early-operations-ninthtwelfth-air-force-in-the-mediterranean/ (Accessed on 1 July 2019).

48 Bianchi, *Il IV Stormo degli Assi*, p. 48.

49 Fuka was attacked by SAS commandos on the night of 7–8 July, with one M.C.202 of the 88th *Squadriglia* of the 6° *Gruppo* and a S.81T of the 4° *Stormo* destroyed, and heavily bombed and strafed by eighteen bombers and nearly seventy fighters on 20 July, with some losses by the 73ª *Squadriglia* both in terms of fighters and personnel, including the commanding officer, *Capitano* Luigi Mariotti, who was then replaced by *Tenente* Giulio Reiner.

50 The 75ª *Squadriglia* moved south picking up new M.C.202s at Ciampino and Capodichino along the way. They then flew to Derna, via Tamet and Benghazi K3. On 11 July and 14 July, the 74ª and 70ª *Squadriglie* followed a similar route. The 74ª *Squadriglia* joined the 75ª *Squadriglia* at Derna on 13 July, then both went to Abu Haggag on the 16th. Those M.C.202s had been rushed to the front line before sand filters could be installed, and a sandstorm at Derna on 31 August forced ten down. This had to be remedied under operational conditions, despite the heavy involvement in operations. Dunning, *Courage Alone*, p. 43.

51 It is possible that while based in Benghazi, the M.C.202s might have scrambled to intercept the B-24Ds of HALPRO, which bombed the harbour on several occasions. Massimello, G., 'Antonio Vizzotto, pilota e Comandante', *Storia militare*, vol. 190, pp. 13-24 (Parma: Albertelli, 2009), p. 20.

52 The section of M.C.202s was used for day protection cruises, while at night a night section of CR.42s was employed. See Dunning, *op. cit.*, p. 43.

53 Molteni, *op. cit.*, p. 256.

54 See also Shores, *et al.*, *A History of the Mediterranean Air War, 1940–1945, II. North African Desert, February 1942–March 1943*.

55 Benzi, 'Intervista a Luigi Gorrini'.

56 Malizia, *La Regia Aeronautica nella 2ª Guerra Mondiale*, p. 471. The twelve Martin Baltimores of No. 4 SAAF Squadron bombed the parking area of the 84ª *Squadriglia*, 10° *Gruppo*, 4° *Stormo*, destroying one M.C.202 on the ground and damaging other nine.

57 *Ibid.*, p. 473.

58 German radar arrived in Africa at the following dates:
01.42: the first Freya (Gerät F-Lafette [Z] 32) in the Mediterranean was set up to direct the Flak defences at Tripoli that were responsible for protecting the supply hub and dumps located there.
04.42: the first Würzburg-D-Gerät was set up on Bomba Bay near Tmimi airfield to the east of Derna and operated by 7.(Flum.)/Ln-Rgt. Afrika.
10.42: by October there were a total of 3 Freya (at Tripoli, Benghazi and Derna/Martuba) and 2 Würzburg-D (Benghazi and Gulf of Bomba) in North Africa.

03.43: Ln.-Abt. 62 was operating Freya in the Kairouan-Sousse area in Tunisia while Ln.-Abt. 63 was doing the same in northern Tunisia.
04.43: 15.(l.Flum.)/200 operated fighter-control radar site 'Jupiter' at Menzel Djemil near Bizerte/Tunisia. This was a night-fighter radar site.
04.43: 16.(l.Flum.)/200 operated fighter-control radar site 'Venus' at Kobra near Tunis. There was also a Freya site 'Tulpe' on Cap Kamart just to the north-east of Tunis. This was operated by 18./Ln.-Rgt. 200. (H-215-16). See Hoffmann, K. O., *Die Geschichte der Luftnachrichtentruppe. Band II—Der Weltkrieg. Teil I: Der Flugmelde- und Jägerleitdienst 1939–1945*, (Neckargemünd: Kurt Vowinckel Verlag, 1969).

59 Dunning, *op. cit.*, pp. 36; 56.
60 Bianchi, *op. cit.*, p. 59.
61 Malizia, *La Regia Aeronautica nella 2ª Guerra Mondiale*, p. 485.
62 *Ibid.*
63 Gustavsson, H., *Biplane fighter aces, Italy, Capitano Franco Lucchini Medaglia d'oro al valor militare*, available at surfcity.kund.dalnet.se/italy_lucchini.htm.
64 Malizia, *La Regia Aeronautica nella 2ª Guerra Mondiale*, p. 487.
65 Gustavsson, *Biplane fighter aces, Italy, Capitano Franco Lucchini Medaglia d'oro al valor militare.*
66 Dunning, *op. cit.*, p. 56.
67 *Ibid.*, p. 37.
68 About Italian fighters, Whittaker commented: 'Italian fighters had a very good performing aircraft in the Macchi 202. It lacked proper armament but exceeded the manoeuvrability of the BF109. The Italian pilots were more playful than the Germans—often performing a series of loops or doing acrobatics as if putting on an air show. I did not consider them to be as shrewd or deadly as the Germans, but certainly equally dangerous'. Shores, C., *et al.*, *A History of the Mediterranean Air War, 1940–1945, III: Tunisia and the End in Africa, November 1942–1943* (London: Grub Street, 2016), p. 616.
69 *Ibid.*, p. 45.
70 Malizia, *La Regia Aeronautica nella 2° Guerra Mondiale*, p. 500.
71 Shores, *et al.*, *A History of the Mediterranean Air War, 1940–1945, III: Tunisia and the End in Africa, November 1942–1943*, p. 259.
72 Gustavsson, H., *Biplane fighter aces, Italy, Capitano Giorgio Solaroli di Briona 17 July 1918–1996*, available at surfcity.kund.dalnet.se/italy_solaroli.htm.
73 The British did not achieve complete control of the air, in traditional terms, until very late in 1942, since the RAF remained equipped with few fighters that could match the Luftwaffe's Messerschmitt Bf 109 and the Folgore—RAF aircraft losses far outstripped those suffered by the Axis for most of the campaign—but had succeeded in deploying airpower by the second half of 1942 effectively, focussing on the use of fighters as multirole fighter-bombers in the interdiction and close air support roles. See Bronk, J., 'The Rise of the Fighter-Bomber in the Western Desert', *The RUSI Journal*, vol. 162, no. 4, pp. 50-59 (Taylor & Francis, 2017), pp. 50-59.
74 Shores, *et al.*, *A History of the Mediterranean Air War, 1940–1945, III: Tunisia and the End in Africa, November 1942–1943*, p. 96.

75 *Ibid.*, p. 101.

76 The SRAM (Squadra Riparazioni Aerei e Motori/Aircraft and Engine Repair Team) was the fulcrum of all maintenance, overhaul and repair activities of the *Regia Aeronautica's* aircraft with both fixed workshops at the airports and in the field. Many SRAMs operated as Gruppi Autonomi Officine Autocarrate (Autonomous Truck Workshop Groups) proving invaluable for salvaging aircraft many times in very difficult situations close to the front line. See Di Martino, B., 'L'organizzazione manutentiva della Regia Aeronautica', *Rivista Aeronautica*, vol. 5, pp. 96-103 (Rome: Libreria dello Stato, 2014), p. 101-103.

77 Shores et al., *A History of the Mediterranean Air War, 1940–1945, III: Tunisia and the End in Africa, November 1942–May 1943*, p. 118.

78 On 21 November, with its strength down to twenty-two M.C.202s, the 153° *Gruppo* moved back to Sciacca. Mattioli, M., and Caruana, R., *53° Stormo* (Oxford: Osprey Publishing, 2010).

79 Malizia, *La Regia Aeronautica nella 2ª Guerra Mondiale*, p. 520.

80 Shores, *et al.*, *A History of the Mediterranean Air War, 1940–1945, III: Tunisia and the End in Africa, November 1942–May 1943*, pp. 45.

81 *Ibid.*, p. 110.

82 Malizia, *La Regia Aeronautica nella 2ª Guerra Mondiale*, p. 520.

83 See also Dunning, *op. cit.*, p. 120.

84 Shores, *et al.*, *A History of the Mediterranean Air War, 1940–1945, III: Tunisia and the End in Africa, November 1942–May 1943*, p. 120.

85 *Ibid.*, p. 16.

86 *Ibid.*, p. 248.

87 Dunning, *op. cit.*, p. 31.

88 Shores, *et al.*, *A History of the Mediterranean Air War, 1940–1945, III: Tunisia and the End in Africa, November 1942–May 1943*, pp. 267-268.

89 Dunning, *op. cit.*, pp. 45; 55.

90 Shores, *et al.*, *A History of the Mediterranean Air War, 1940–1945, III: Tunisia and the End in Africa, November 1942–May 1943*, pp. 283; 290; 295.

91 *Ibid.*, p. 287.

92 'If I had to make a comparison between the 202 and all the other propeller fighters I piloted before, after and during the conflict, I would say that the Folgore was equivalent to the Spit V, apart from the armament, but it could not compete in general performance with the Spit IX, the Mustang and the Thunderbolt. These were decidedly machines of another generation, for instrumentation, on-board equipment, engine, etc. Perhaps the Spit V allowed a better handling than our Macchi, at least for a pilot who knew it well'. Recollections of *Sergente* Arnaldo Mauri, *op. cit.*

93 Frank Hill, CO of the 309th Squadron, 31st Fighter Group, felt that Spitfire Mk IX could 'outclimb, outdive and outturn anything the Germans and Italians could put up against us' and that Italian pilots 'had a reputation for doing great aerobatics, but if you stayed right in there you could sit on their tails through anything they tried'. Shores, *et al.*, *A History of the Mediterranean Air War, 1940–1945, III: Tunisia and the End in Africa, November 1942–May 1943*, pp. 608-610.

94 deZeng, H. L., *Luftwaffe Airfields 1935–45, Tunisia*, available at www.ww2.dk/Airfields%20-%20Tunisia.pdf (Accessed on 3 July 2019).

95 The latter *Gruppo* flew their first operation on 25 February 1943. They escorted German aircraft to attack Ben Gardane, then carried out strafing sweeps. Dunning, *op. cit.*, p. 44.

96 *Ibid.*, p. 31.

97 Shores, *et al.*, *A History of the Mediterranean Air War, 1940–1945, III: Tunisia and the End in Africa, November 1942–May 1943*, pp. 283; 290; 318; 347.

98 *Ibid.*, p. 352.

99 The 151° *Gruppo* had transferred from the Aegean to Pantelleria in November 1942, and with the Torch landings, to Sicily, at Chinisia. On 12 February 1943, the 151° *Gruppo* received its first four M.C.202s, these being followed by the end of the month by a few more. By late March, it would have nine M.C.202s and fifteen G.50s on strength. Mattioli, and Caruana, *op. cit.*, p. 89.

100 Shores, *et al.*, *A History of the Mediterranean Air War, 1940–1945, III: Tunisia and the End in Africa, November 1942–May 1943*, p. 397.

101 *Ibid.*, p. 383.

102 Dunning, *op. cit.*, p. 44.

103 It began to receive Macchi M.C.202s in September 1942, when based at Crotone, transitioning entirely to this plane from the beginning of 1943 at Torino-Caselle.

104 The *Stormo* was under the command of *Tenente Colonnello* Giovanni Zappetta, while the 7° *Gruppo* were under *Maggiore* Edoardo Molinari, and the 76ª, 86ª, and 98ª *Squadriglie* respectively under *Capitani* Adriano Visconti, Bruno Politi and Sergio Maurer.

105 Shores, *et al.*, *A History of the Mediterranean Air War, 1940–1945, III: Tunisia and the End in Africa, November 1942–May 1943*, p. 437.

106 *Ibid.*, p. 482. *Capitano* Tito Valtancoli of the 7° *Gruppo* claimed a Spitfire off the Tunisian coast on 14 April in the course of such a mission.

107 *Ibid.*, p. 449.

108 See also Molteni, *op. cit.*, p. 334.

109 *Ibid.*, p. 335.

110 Shores, *et al.*, *A History of the Mediterranean Air War, 1940–1945, III: Tunisia and the End in Africa, November 1942–May 1943*, p. 457.

111 *Ibid.*, p. 458.

112 *Ibid.*, pp. 417-418.

113 *Ibid.*, pp. 417; 483.

114 *Ibid.*, p. 504.

115 Nijboer, *Spitfire V vs C.202 Folgore, Malta 1942*, p. 67.

116 Mattioli, 'L'esordio del Macchi C.202', p. 53.

117 On Frigerio: Gustavsson, *Biplane fighter aces, Italy, Capitano Jacopo Frigerio, 29 October 1913–3 October 1955.*

118 Cull, B., and Galea, F., *Fighters Over Malta: Gladiators and Hurricanes 1940-1942* (Stroud: Fonthill, 2018), p. 142.

119 Molteni, *op. cit.*, p. 125.

120 Cull, B., and Galea, F., *Fighters Over Malta.*

121 Molteni, *op. cit.*, p. 125.
122 Nijboer, *op. cit.*, p. 67.
123 See also Cull, and Galea, *Hurricanes Over Malta*, p. 146.
124 Other sources claim that Leotta succumbed to a malfunction of the oxygen distribution system. In fact, during the mission that saw the loss of Leotta, several other pilots of the 9° and 10° *Gruppo*, felt intensely sick, while flying at 7,000 metres, and eleven pilots in all aborted the mission. Bianchi, *op. cit.*, p. 35.
125 *Ibid.*, p. 70.
126 Those interception stations, called CRIRA (*Centro Radio Intercettazioni Regia Aeronautica*), were positioned in Pantelleria and Bengasi, the one in Pantelleria aimed at tapping the communications in Malta, and with its secondary listening post in Erice worked as a primitive triangulation system for enemy aircraft. Intercepted information was sent to *Aeronautica della Sicilia*, and from there to the fighter units and eventually to the individual aircraft. A similar service, based in Sicily, was the *Servizio Alfa*. See Malizia, N., *Il 51° Stormo Caccia, storia di un reparto glorioso, 1939–2017* (Rome: IBN, 2017), p. 116.
127 See also Mattesini, F., *L'ultima offensiva aerea dell'Asse contro Malta e la crisi dei convogli libici (10-30 ottobre 1942)*, p. 31, available at www.academia.edu/36623345/LULTIMA_OFFENSIVA_AEREA_DELLASSE_CONTRO_MALTA_E_LA_CRISI_DEI_CONVOGLI_LIBICI_10_30_OTTOBRE_1942_FRANCESCO_MATTESINI (Accessed on 1 July 2019).
128 Dunning, *op. cit.*, p. 36.
129 For instance on 20 December, see Cull, and Galea, *Hurricanes Over Malta*, p. 167.
130 *Ibid.*
131 *Ibid.*, p. 261.
132 Molteni, *op. cit.*, p. 180.
133 Gustavsson, *Biplane fighter aces, Italy, Sergente Maggiore Teresio Vittorio Martinoli Medaglia d'oro al valor militare.*
134 Cull, and Galea, *Hurricanes Over Malta*, p. 271.
135 Bianchi, *op. cit.*, p. 41.
136 Noppen, R. K., *Malta 1940–42. The Axis' air battle for Mediterranean supremacy* (Oxford: Osprey Publishing, 2018), p. 83.
137 The *Stormo* was re-established on 1 January 1942. Dunning, *op. cit.*, pp. 47; 121.
138 Ward, J., *Hitler's Stuka Squadrons: The JU 87 at War 1936–1945* (Eastbourne: Gardners Books, 2004), p. 161.
139 Beurling, and Roberts, *Malta Spitfire*, Chapter IV, par. 3.
140 Nijboer, *op. cit.*, p. 63.
141 Molteni, *op. cit.*, p. 190.
142 Galea, F. R., 'Fighters Over Malta', *Malta Flypast*, vol. 7, pp. 90-96 (Malta: Aviation Museum Foundation, 2006), p. 96.
143 *Ibid.*
144 Nijboer, *op. cit.*, p. 65.

145 Dunning, *op. cit.*, p. 191.

146 The operational order was 'Successive waves of all the S.84 and CR.42 aircraft and torpedo bombers with maximum escort. Bombers and dive bombers with 5 minutes advance on torpedo bombers. Ammunition: *FF motobombe* for S.84 aircraft, 100 kg bombs for CR.42 aircraft. S.84s will launch frontal attack in the opposite direction to that of the convoy, launching *motobombe* at a distance of about 100 metres in front of the head unit. CR.42 aircraft will attack by dive bombing and strafing the naval units closer to the convoy to disrupt anti-aircraft defence. The S.84 and CR.42 aircraft will be provided with direct escort by MC202. After the action. MC202 will lower to counter enemy reaction against torpedo bombers, escorting them in the return flight'. See Mattesini, F., *La battaglia di mezzo agosto (operazione 'Pedestal'), il fallimento degli attacchi a massa degli aerosiluranti italiani*, p. 10, available at www.academia.edu/37658920/LA_BATTAGLIA_DI_MEZZO_AGOSTO_OPERAZIONE_PEDESTAL_IL_FALLIMENTO_DEGLI_ATTACCHI_A_MASSA_DEGLI_AEROSILURANTI_ITALIANI (Accessed on 7 July 2019).

147 *Capitano* Riccardo Spagnolini (351ª *Squadriglia*), *Tenente* Giovanni Franchini (351ª *Squadriglia*), *Tenente* Aristide Sarti (in '351-7' MM8342), *Tenente* Vittorio Bastogi (returned back home after a few minutes because of engine troubles), *Sottotenente* Giuseppe Bonfiglio (351ª *Squadriglia*), *Sergente Maggiore* Luigi Caroli (351ª *Squadriglia*), *Tenente* Giambattista Caracciolo (360ª *Squadriglia*), *Sottotenente* Romano Biasiol (360ª *Squadriglia*), *Sottotenente* Francesco Fagiolo (360ª *Squadriglia*), Maresciallo Remo Zedda (360ª *Squadriglia*), *Sergente Maggiore* Mario Varacca (360ª *Squadriglia*), *Sergente* Willy Malagola (360ª *Squadriglia*), *Tenente* Manlio Biccolini (378ª *Squadriglia*), *Tenente* Mario Mazzoleni (378ª *Squadriglia*), *Sergente Maggiore* Roberto Gaucci (378ª *Squadriglia*), and *Sergente Maggiore* Giovanni Gambari (378ª *Squadriglia*). See Gustavsson, H., *Biplane fighter aces, Italy. Capitano Duilio Sergio Fanali Medaglia d'oro al valor militare 21 June 1911–27 August 1987*, available at surfcity.kund.dalnet.se/italy_fanali.htm.

148 Mattioli, and Caruana, *op. cit.*, pp. 84-85.

149 Mattesini, *L'ultima offensiva aerea dell'asse contro Malta*, pp. 11-14.

150 See also Mattesini, F., *La guerra nel Mediterraneo dopo la rinuncia all'esigenza 'C.3', Luglio–Dicembre 1942. Gli studi e la realizzazione degli sbarchi in Corsica e Tunisia. Esigenze 'C.2' e 'C.4' (10–30 ottobre 1942)*, 2019, p. 86, available at www.academia.edu/38307960/LA_GUERRA_NEL_MEDITERRANEO_DOPO_LA_RINUNCIA_ALL_ESIGENZA_C.3_Luglio_Dicembre_1942_Gli_studi_e_la_realizzazione_degli_sbarchi_in_Corsica_e_Tunisia (Accessed on 7 July 2019).

151 Santoro, G., *L'Aeronautica Italiana nella Seconda Guerra Mondiale* (Milan-Rome: Esse, 1966), vol. II, p. 287.

152 Gustavsson, *Biplane fighter aces, Italy, Capitano Duilio Sergio Fanali Medaglia d'oro al valor militare 21 June 1911–27 August 1987.*

153 *Ibid.*

154 On 6 January, four Mk V Spirfires from No. 185 Squadron, led by Sqn Ldr Blair Whire, attacked two Folgores escorting a pair of E-boars north of Lampedusa Island. Flt Off. H. F. Wirhy (in EP791) fired at one of them, which was seen to lose height rapidly. It was probably the M.C.202 of *Sottotenente* Mario Proserpio of the 374ª *Squadriglia* that crashed between Giarre and Riposto.

155 Sgarlato, ed., *op. cit.*, p. 53.

156 Molteni, *op. cit.*, p. 244.

157 Malizia, *La Regia Aeronautica nella 2ª Guerra Mondiale*, p. 562.

158 Carter, K. C., Mueller, R., *The Army Air Forces in World War II: Combat Chronology, 1941–1945* (Washington, DC: Center for Air Force History, 1991), p. 75, 4 December 1942, available at archive.org/details/AFD-100525-035/page/n75 (Accessed on 3 July 2019).

159 Shores, C., *et al.*, *A History of the Mediterranean Air War, 1940–1945, IV: Sicily and Italy to the Fall of Rome 14 May, 1943–5 June, 1944* (London: Grub Street, 2018), p. 287.

160 The unit was based at Boccadifalco and by February 1943 was re-equipped with six M.C.202s. After several scrambles against USAAF bombers, the unit was depleted and was disbanded, passing its Macchis to the 53° *Stormo*. See Shores, *et al.*, *A History of the Mediterranean Air War, 1940–1945, III: Tunisia and the End in Africa, November 1942–May 1943*, p. 298.

161 Dunning, *op. cit.*, p. 158.

162 The aircraft were piloted by *Capitano* Riccardo Monaco, *Tenenti* Orazio Ferlin and Orfeo Mazzitelli, *Maresciallo* Antonio Lo Schiavo, *Sergenti Maggiori* Aldo Pipistrello, Gastone Fattoretto, Fausto Fornaci and Franco Sarasino. See Pedriali, *L'Italia nella guerra aerea*, p. 192.

163 armyaircorps-376bg.com, *Mission 91 on January 11, 1943*, available at www.armyaircorps-376bg.com/1943_11_jan_walker.html (Accessed on 7 July 2019).

164 armyaircorps-376bg.com, *Written recollection by Sergeant Theodore Drazkowski* [tail gunner of B-24D 41-11593 *Black Maria II* (code 50) piloted by Col. John H. Payne], available at www.armyaircorps-376bg.com/drazkowski_ted_430111.html.

165 Mattesini, F., and Cermelli, M., ed., *Le direttive tecnico-operative di Superaereo*, Vol. 2, Tomo II, Gennaio 1942–Settembre 1943 (Rome: SMA, 2012), p. 590.

166 Saggiomo, C., *I Cacciatori del Vesuvio* (Naples: Controcorrente, 2007), p. 79.

167 Lo Schiavo claimed the plane, but it seems that the only B-24 lost that day was shot down by flak. See Shores, *et al.*, *A History of the Mediterranean Air War, 1940–1945, II. North African Desert, February 1942–March 1943*.

168 Shores, *et al.*, *A History of the Mediterranean Air War, 1940–1945, III: Tunisia and the End in Africa, November 1942–1943*, p. 374. The first of the heavies to fall into Italian hands was the Consolidated B-24D 1-CO Liberator s/n 41-23659, nicknamed the *Blonde Bomber II*, based at Benghazi airfield (Libya). This B-24 was used by the 'Pyramiders' squadron, the 98th Bomber Group of the 47th Bomber Wing, a formation of 12th Air Force. On

20 February 1943, after a bombing mission on Naples, the *Blonde Bomber II* landed by mistake at Pachino airfield, being immediately captured by the Italians. In March, it was flown to the *Centro Sperimentale* at Guidonia, where it was studied in detail.

169 Bianchi, *op. cit.*, p. 81.

170 Recollections of *Sergente* Arnaldo Mauri, *op. cit.*

171 Molteni, *op. cit.*, p. 356.

172 Shores *et al.*, *A History of the Mediterranean Air War, 1940–1945, II. North African Desert, February 1942–March 1943*, Monday, 11 January 1943.

173 Saggiomo, *op. cit.*, p. 100.

174 Pedriali, *op. cit.*, p 200.

175 Paravicini, *Pilota da caccia*, p. 33.

176 Each fighter usually carried eight bomblets, of which four were ideally fused to blow up within the bombers box, and the other two couples, one 100 metres above and one 100 metres below it. In fact, the pilots of the 22° *Gruppo* evaluated the bomblets as less efficient than MGs and cannons, not least because of the difficulty of taking aim without any dedicated bombsight. Pedriali, *op. cit.*, pp. 207-208.

177 Shores, *et al.*, *A History of the Mediterranean Air War, 1940–1945, III: Tunisia and the End in Africa, November 1942–1943*, p. 470.

178 Paravicini, *op. cit.*, p. 34.

179 Shores, *et al.*, *A History of the Mediterranean Air War, 1940–1945, III: Tunisia and the End in Africa, November 1942–1943*, p. 514.

180 Pedriali, *op. cit.*, p 304.

181 The *Gruppo* moved one *Squadriglia* to Alghero from May to August, then to Foligno. Dewoitine D.520s fighters were received from the 2° *Stormo* when that unit disbanded on 13 August. By the date of the armistice (8 September 1943), it was based at Arena Metato with the 354ª (two M.C.202s), 355ª (three Dewoitine D.520s), and 370ª *Squadriglie* (three D.520s). Dunning, *op. cit.*, p. 57.

182 Shores, *et al.*, *A History of the Mediterranean Air War, 1940–1945, IV: Sicily and Italy to the Fall of Rome 14 May, 1943–5 June 1944*, p. 32.

183 *Ibid.*, pp. 34-38.

184 *Ibid.*, p. 40.

185 *Ibid.*, p. 49.

186 The 161° *Gruppo Autonomo* was composed of the 162ª, 163ª, and 164ª *Squadriglie,* but the 371ª *Squadriglia* joined the *Gruppo* from May until July 1943. The 163ª *Squadriglia* joined the 157° *Gruppo* between June and July. Dunning, *op. cit.*, p. 124.

187 *Ibid.*, p. 119.

188 Shores, *et al.*, *A History of the Mediterranean Air War, 1940–1945, IV: Sicily and Italy to the Fall of Rome 14 May, 1943–5 June 1944*, p. 58.

189 The *Gruppo*, on 359ª, 362ª, and 369ª *Squadriglia* arrived at Capodichino from Elmas on 26 December 1942 to refit with M.C.202s, but the availability for the plane was such that they never fully re-equipped. On 15 January 1943, 371ª *Squadriglia* temporarily joined the *Gruppo*. For bomber intercepts,

the *Gruppo* received in February some D.520s, and in April also the new FC.20bis for the same purpose, to no great success. From 10 May to 24 June, the *Gruppo* joined the 42° *Stormo*. The 362ª *Squadriglia* received the first prototype and ten pre-production models of the RE.2005, which were used for the defence of Rome and Naples, operating from Metato and Guidonia in June. On 10 July, eight RE.2005s from the 362ª *Squadriglia* went to Catania-Sigonella. By 14 July, the two survivors were passed to the 371ª *Squadriglia* when the 362ª *Squadriglia* returned to Italy. Ten more RE.2005s were received at Capua on 31 July. The unit spent until September 1943 defending the homeland. From mid-July, the 359ª and 369ª *Squadriglie* were at Capodichino, while the 150ª *Squadriglia*, detached from the 2° *Gruppo* had joined the 22° *Gruppo* in May and the 362ª *Squadriglia* were at Capua. On the eve of the armistice, the only aircraft still flying were nine M.C.202s.

190 Pedriali, *op. cit.*, p. 213.

191 Shores, *et al.*, *A History of the Mediterranean Air War, 1940–1945, IV: Sicily and Italy to the Fall of Rome 14 May, 1943–5 June 1944*, p. 81.

192 Gustavsson, H., *Biplane fighter aces, Italy, Capitano Domenico Bevilacqua 4 August 1912–10 June 1943*, available at surfcity.kund.dalnet.se/italy_bevilacqua.htm.

193 Paravicini, *op. cit.*, p. 45.

194 Pedriali, *op. cit.*, p. 469.

195 Gustavsson, *Biplane fighter aces, Italy, Capitano Franco Lucchini Medaglia d'oro al valor militare.*

196 Gustavsson, H., *Biplane fighter aces, Italy, Sottotenente Leonardo Ferrulli Medaglia d'oro al valor militare*, available at surfcity.kund.dalnet.se/italy_ferrulli.htm.

197 Shores, *et al.*, *A History of the Mediterranean Air War, 1940–1945, IV: Sicily and Italy to the Fall of Rome 14 May, 1943–5 June 1944*, p. 182.

198 Bianchi, *op. cit.*, p. 92.

199 *Ibid.*, p. 216.

200 *Ibid.*, p. 227.

201 *Ibid.*, pp. 248-249.

202 *Ibid.*, p. 326.

203 *Ibid.*, p. 333.

204 Stocchetti, R., *Aer. Macchi C.202 Folgore, immagini, scheda e storia*, available at www.alieuomini.it/AJAX/catalogo/dettaglio2_catalogo/16/.

205 See also Volta, F., ed., 'Dimensione cielo: aerei italiani nella Seconda Guerra Mondiale', *Caccia Assalto*, vol. II (Rome: Bizzarri, 1973), p. 49.

206 The 356ª *Squadriglia*, based at the Gioia del Colle airport, moved its fighters to Brindisi as the Germans approached the base, managing also to transfer some of its ground personnel via SM.82. The rest of the staff returned to the units as the British liberated the airfield a few days later, on 14 September. See Archivio Ufficio Storico (AUSAM), Fondo Diari Storici, II Guerra Mondiale, Diario Storico 1123, *Diario storico 356ª Squadriglia caccia terrestre. 1943*, 1943 set. 8-dic. 31.

207 Pier Ugo Gobbato, a pilot of the 4° *Stormo* and son of the director-general of Alfa Romeo, was tasked with salvaging what was possible in the factory at

Pomigliano: 'the Germans, while evacuating the area, occupied the Pomigliano d'Arco plant of Alfa Romeo, where the AR 1000 engines were built under the Daimler-Benz Licence (the DB601 with 1000 hp) with the parts arriving from Milan or from Germany. Before leaving, the Germans razed the plant to the ground by blowing up all the machines one by one and causing the whole shed to collapse on the wreckage. Despite this, they commissioned me, as the son of the director general of Alfa Romeo and moreover an engineer, to go and try to salvage spare parts for the engines of our aircraft among the rubble. On October 13, 1943, I was posted to Naples. In Pomigliano I found a friendly environment as a person, but an absolutely discouraging one for my task of salvage. We also set about the task in the rubble and managed to take something away, but above all (and this was the most important thing) to form, on the recommendation of *Colonnello* François, two teams of workers who voluntarily made themselves available to the *Aeronautica Militare*: one for the engines and the other for on-board equipment. With the help of these two groups and the salvaged material, the *Aeronautica* went on until its resources were exhausted'. See Gobbato, P. U., and Gobbato, U., *Due vite per l'automobile* (Milan: AISA, 2009), p. 8.

208 The *Regia Aeronautica* General Staff.

209 D'Amico, F., and Valentini, G., *Regia Aeronautica, II* (Carrollton, TX: Squadron Signal, 1986), p. 30.

210 *Ibid.*, p. 50.

211 *Ibid.*, p. 53.

212 Sgarlato, ed., *op. cit.*, p. 66.

213 The Luftwaffe, 1933–45, *Jagdlehrer-Überprüfungsgruppe*, available at www.ww2.dk/air/jagd/jagdlehrer.html (Accessed on 7 July 2019).

214 Those were M.C.202s MM91888, 91899 (XII *Serie*); 81891 (?); 91896, 91906, 91895, 91899, and 91901 (XII *Serie*). See Neulen, H. W., *Il Ricco Bottino, The Rich Booty, Italian Aircraft in Luftwaffe Service* (Milan: GAE, 2000), pp. 70-75.

215 M.C.202s MM7644 (?), 9731 (XII *Serie*), 7970 (V *Serie*), 91961 (XIII *Serie*), 6589 (XI *Serie*), 9541 (X *Serie*), 7747(III *Serie*, sources discordant, maybe lost in Africa?); 91887, 91879 (XII *Serie*), and 7428 (IV *Serie*). *Ibid.*, pp. 70-75.

216 M.C.202 MM91902. *Ibid.*

217 Test pilot Hans-Werner Lerche had similar experiences in 1943–44: 'On such still unmodified planes, therefore, heavy losses occurred. Thus it happened, for instance, apart from an aborted take-off, that some pilots taxiing in front of a hangar instead of throttling down gave full throttle and crashed into parked planes or into a hangar overcrowded with planes. Soon afterwards, to avoid such mistakes, which usually had serious consequences, German crews were forbidden to fly unmodified machines'. *Ibid.*, p. 33.

218 *Ibid.*, p. 35.

219 *Ibid.*, pp. 35-46.

220 MM91906–91918. See Sgarlato, ed., *op. cit.*, p. 66.

221 Ciglic, B., and Savic, D., *Croatian Aces of World War 2* (Oxford: Osprey Publishing, 2002), p. 62.

222 *Ibid.*, pp. 65-66.

223 *Ibid.*
224 *Ibid.*, p. 67.
225 Reconditioning implied the replacement of the engine, the propeller, the spinner cone, the cowling, the oil radiator, the empennages, and the radio apparatus. See Sgarlato, ed., *op. cit.*, p. 27.

Bibliography

Primary Sources

Archivio Centrale dello Stato (ACS), Roma, Ministero dell'Aeronautica, Gabinetto 1941, Busta 155.

Archivio Centrale dello Stato (ACS), Roma, Ministero dell'Aeronautica, Gabinetto 1942, Busta 108.

Ministero Degli Affari Esteri (MAE), Affari Politici 1931–1945, Busta 30.

Archivio Storico Aeronautica Militare (AUSAM), Roma, Libretti aerei, Busta. 5, fasc. 25—'Aer. Macchi C. 202'.

AUSAM, Fondo De Bernardi.

AUSAM, Emeroteca, Cart. 17.

AUSAM, Fondo Cometti, B. 27, F. 44.

AUSAM, Fondo Cometti, B. 27, F. 51.

AUSAM, Fondo Diari Storici II Guerra Mondiale, Diario 53 Gruppo CT 1942.

Aeronautica Macchi, *Istruzioni e norme per il montaggio, la regolazione, l'impiego e la manutenzione del velivolo da caccia Aer.Macchi C. 202 con motore D. B. 601 II Serie* (Rome: Ministero dell'Aeronautica Direzione Generale delle Costruzioni e degli Approvvigionamenti, 1941).

Aeronautica Macchi, *Istruzioni e norme per il montaggio, la regolazione, l'impiego e la manutenzione del velivolo da caccia Aer.Macchi C. 202 con motore R. A. 1000 R. C. 41 I dalla IX alla XI Serie* (Rome: Ministero dell'Aeronautica Direzione Generale delle Costruzioni e degli Approvvigionamenti, 1942).

Ufficio di Stato Maggiore della Regia Aeronautica, 1° Reparto - Divisione Addestramento, *Addestramento dell'aviazione da caccia* (Rome: Ministero dell'Aeronautica Laboratorio Fotomeccanico, 1936).

Ufficio di Stato Maggiore della Regia Aeronautica, 1° Reparto - Divisione Addestramento, *Formazioni di volo* (Rome: Ministero dell'Aeronautica Laboratorio Fotomeccanico, 1936).

Secondary Sources

Aga Rossi, E., *Una nazione allo sbando. L'armistizio italiano dell'8 settembre* (Bologna: Il Mulino, 2003).

Alegi, G., 'Qualità del materiale bellico e dottrina d'impiego italiana nella seconda guerra mondiale: il caso della Regia Aeronautica', *Storia contemporanea*, vol. 6, pp. 1197-1219 (Bologna: Il Mulino, 1987); 'L'arma fascistissima: il falso mito dell'aeronautica come la preferita del Regime', in M. Ferrari, ed., *Le ali del ventennio. L'aviazione italiana dal 1923 al 1945*, pp. 111-154 (Milan: Angeli, 2005); 'L'addestramento della Regia Aeronautica', *Storia Militare*, vol. 141 (Parma: Albertelli, 2005).

Alegi, G., and Catalanotto, B., *Nei Cieli di Guerra. La Regia Aeronautica a colori 1940-45* (Milan: Giorgio Apostolo, 1966).

Anderson, J. D., *The Airplane: A History of its Technology*, pp. 81-130 (Reston, Virginia, USA: American Institute of Aeronautics and Astronautics, 2002).

Apostolo, G., *Aer.Macchi C.202. Ali D'Italia 2* (Turin: La Bancarella Aeronautica, 1996).

Apostolo, G., and Massimello, G., *Italian Aces of World War 2* (Oxford: Osprey Publishing, 2000).

Apostolo, G., Cattaneo, G., and Massimello, G., *Aer.Macchi C.202, Ali D'Italia* (Turin: La Bancarella Aeronautica, 2006).

Arena, N., *I caccia a motore radiale* (Modena: Mucchi, 1980).

Artioli, G., *Comandante Costantino Petrosellini, Asso dell'Aeronautica Italiana*, available at www.anpaninfo.it/public/uploads/petrosellini_2017.pdf (Accessed on 1 July 2019).

Azzalin, R., *Quando il Sergente Pilota Fiorenzo Macchi, conobbe il Comandante Carestiato al Campo di Volo di Campoformido*, available at www.isses.it/fiorenzoMacchi.htm (Accessed on 1 July 2019).

Badoglio, P., *L'Italia nella Seconda Guerra Mondiale* (Milan: Mondadori, 1946).

Belpane, P., 'Le radio della Regia Aeronautica', *Ali Antiche*, vol. 105, pp. 2-9 (Rome: GAVS, 2012).

Benzi, A., 'Intervista a Luigi Gorrini', *Storia del XX secolo*, no. 33, February 1999.

Bertozzi, G., *L'addestramento nella Regia Aeronautica*, available at www.facebook.com/groups/822772004588105/permalink/1107050059493630/ (Accessed on 2 July 2019); *Sistemi di difesa aerea dell'Asse nel Mediterraneo,* available at www.facebook.com/groups/822772004588105/permalink/1072556139609689/ (Accessed on 2 July 2019).

Beurling, G., and Roberts, L., *Malta Spitfire: The Buzz Beurling Story* (London: Penguin Books, 2002); *Malta Spitfire: The Diary of an Ace Fighter Pilot* (London: Grub Street, 2012).

Bianchi, G., *Il IV Stormo degli Assi - Lucchini Ferrulli Reiner e Teresio Martinoli* (Massa: Sarasota, 2018).

Bonaiti, E., *La Regia Aeronautica del Generale Francesco Pricolo,* available at www.icsm.it/articoli/ri/rapricolo.html (Accessed on 1 July 2019).

Brancaccio, G., 'Giancarlo Galbusera il cacciatore centenario', *Rivista Aeronautica*, vol. 3, pp. 100-111 (Rome: Libreria dello Stato, 2017).

Bronk, J., 'The Rise of the Fighter-Bomber in the Western Desert', *The RUSI Journal*, vol. 162, no. 4, pp. 50-59 (Taylor & Francis, 2017).

Caldara, S., 'Come è nato l'Aer. Macchi C. 202, nostra intervista a Mario Castoldi', *L'Ala d'Italia*, vol. XX, no. 7, pp. 9-12 (Milan: La Cisalpina, 1942).

Cardani, C., and Curami, A., 'Gli inizi dell'insegnamento dell'aeronautica nella realtà milanese', *Annali di Storia delle università italiane*, vol. 12, pp. 207-223 (Bologna: Clueb, 2008).

Carter, K. C., and Mueller, R., *The Army Air Forces in World War II: Combat Chronology, 1941–1945* (Washington, DC: Center for Air Force History, 1991).

Caso, E., Garello, M., and Brotzu, G., *Dimensione Cielo: Aerei Italiani nella Seconda Guerra Mondiale, Scuola Collegamento* (Rome: Bizzarri, 1977).

Castoldi, M., 'L'idrovolante da corsa nel decennio fascista', *L'Ala d'Italia*, vol. XI, pp. 12-20 (Milan: La Cisalpina, 1933).

Cattaneo, G., *The Macchi C. 202* (Leatherhead, Surrey: Profile Pubblications, 1965).

Cernuschi, E., 'Il motore impossibile', *Storia Militare*, vol. 120, pp. 36-43 (Parma: Albertelli, 2003).

Ceva L., and Curami A., *Industria bellica anni trenta* (Milan: Angeli, 1992)

Ceva, L., *La condotta italiana della guerra: Cavallero e il Comando Supremo 1941–1942* (Milan: Feltrinelli, 1975).

Ceva, L., *Le forze armate* (Turin: UTET, 1981); *Africa Settentrionale 1940–1943* (Rome: Bonacci, 1982); 'Italy', in I.C.B. Dear e M.R.D. Foot, ed., *The Oxford Companion to the Second World War* (Oxford: Oxford University Press, 1995); *Guerra Mondiale, Strategie e industria bellica 1939–1945* (Milan: Angeli, 2000); 'L'aeronautica nella guerra civile spagnola', in M. Ferrari, ed., *L'aeronautica italiana. Una storia del Novecento*, pp. 337-374 (Milan: Angeli, 2004).

Ciampaglia, G., 'Le benzine ad altissimo numero di ottani vero segreto delle aviazioni alleate nella II Guerra mondiale', *Rivista Italiana Difesa*, vol. 10, pp. 82-88 (Chiavari: Giornalistica Riviera, 2009).

Ciglic, B., and Savic, D., *Croatian Aces of World War 2* (Oxford: Osprey Publishing, 2002).

Commissione italiana di storia militare, *L'Italia in guerra. Il 2° anno. 1941* (Gaeta: Stabilimento Grafico Militare, 1992).

Cull, B., and Galea, F., *Hurricanes over Malta, June 1940–April 1942* (London: Grub Street, 2001); *Fighters Over Malta: Gladiators and Hurricanes 1940–1942* (Stroud: Fonthill, 2018).

Curami, A., 'Piani e progetti dell'aeronautica italiana 1939–1943: Stato Maggiore e industrie', *Italia contemporanea: rassegna dell'Istituto nazionale per la storia del movimento di liberazione in Italia*, vol. 187, pp. 243-262 (Rome: Istituto Parri, 1992).

D'Amico, F., and Valentini, G., *Regia Aeronautica*, vol. 2 (Carrollton, TX: Squadron Signal, 1986).

De Angelis, I., 'Amedeo Mecozzi: de l'aviation d'assaut', *Penser les Ailes Françaises*, vol. 17, pp. 16-22 (Paris: Cesa, 2008).

De Felice, R., *Mussolini l'alleato*, 1. *L'Italia in guerra 1940–1943, I., Dalla guerra 'breve' alla guerra lunga* (Turin: Einaudi, 1996); *Mussolini l'alleato*, 1. *L'Italia in guerra 1940–1943, II., Crisi e agonia del regime* (Turin: Einaudi, 1996).

deZeng, H. L., *LuftwaffeAirfields 1935–45, Tunisia*, available at www.ww2.dk/Airfields%20-%20Tunisia.pdf (Accessed on 3 July 2019).

Di Martino, B., 'L'organizzazione manutentiva della Regia Aeronautica', *Rivista Aeronautica*, vol. 5, pp. 96-103 (Rome: Libreria dello Stato, 2014).

Di Napoli, C., and Mancini, R., *Macchi C.200/202/205, Aero Detail 15* (Tokyo: Art box, 1995).

Di Terlizzi, M., *Macchi MC202 Folgore, I* (Rome: IBN, 1999); *Macchi MC202 Folgore, II* (Rome: IBN, 2000).

Duma, A., *Quelli del cavallino rampante* (Rome: Edizioni dell'Ateneo, 1981).

Dunning, C., *Courage Alone: The Italian Air Force, 1940–1943* (Manchester: Hikoki Publications, 1999).

Evans, B., *The Decisive Campaigns of the Desert Air Force 1942–1945* (Barnsley: Pen and Sword, 2014).

Ferrari, M., ed., *Le ali del Ventennio. L'aviazione italiana dal 1923 al 1945. Bilanci storiografici e prospettive di giudizio* (Milan: Angeli, 2005).

Fradeani, V., *Storia di un primato. Dalla Coppa Schneider all'impresa di Agello* (Milan: Mursia, 1976).

Galea, F. R., 'Fighters Over Malta', *Malta Flypast*, vol. 7, pp. 90-96 (Malta: Aviation Museum Foundation, 2006).

Garello, G., 'Piloti e personale di volo, simboli di un'età nuova (1923–1943)', in M. Ferrari, ed., *Le ali del ventennio. L'aviazione italiana dal 1923 al 1945. Bilanci storiografici e prospettive di giudizio*, pp. 155-184 (Milan: Angeli, 2005).

Gentile, E., *Fascismo. Storia e interpretazione* (Rome-Bari: Laterza, 2008); *Il fascismo in tre capitoli* (Rome-Bari: Laterza, 2004).

Ghergo, G. F., 'La Caccia Italiana 1940–1943', *Storia militare*, vol. 149 (Parma: Albertelli, 2006).

Gobbato, P. U., and Gobbato, U., *Due vite per l'automobile* (Milan: AISA, 2009).

Gooch, J., *Mussolini and His Generals: The Armed Forces and Fascist Foreign Policy, 1922–1940* (Cambridge: Cambridge University Press, 2007).

Grassia, E., 'L'8 settembre 1943 e la Regia "fascistissima" Aeronautica', *Diacronie. Studi di Storia Contemporanea*, vol. 1, no. 25, 2016.

Grilletta, G., *KR 40-43. Cronache di guerra* (Cosenza: Pellegrini, 2003).

Gueli, M., 'L'Aermacchi C. 202 "Folgore"', *Storia militare*, vol. XXII, no. 244, pp. 56-67 (Parma: Albertelli, 2014).

Gustavsson, H., *Biplane Fighter Aces, Italy*, available at surfcity.kund.dalnet.se/italy.htm (Accessed on 3 July 2019).

Hoffmann, K. O., *Die Geschichte der Luftnachrichtentruppe. Band II—Der Weltkrieg. Teil I: Der Flugmelde- und Jägerleitdienst 1939–1945*, (Neckargemünd: Kurt Vowinckel Verlag, 1969).

Isnenghi, M., and Rochat, G., *La grande guerra, 1914–1918* (Bologna: Il Mulino, 2014).

Jabes, D. F., 'Macchi C-202 Folgore, il caccia italiano di maggior successo durante la seconda guerra mondiale: un punto di vista anglossassone', *Ricerche Storiche*, vol. XLII, no. 1, pp. 149-156 (Firenze: Polistampa 2012).

Keegan, J., *The Second World War* (London: Wetherby, 1989).

Kershaw, I., *Hitler 1936–1945: Nemesis* (London: Penguin Books, 2001); 'Working Towards the Führer. Reflections on the Nature of the Hitler Dictatorship', *Contemporary European History*, vol. 2, no. 2, pp. 103-118 (Cambridge: Cambridge University Press, 1993).

Knox, M. G., *Mussolini Unleashed 1939–1941. Politics and Strategy in Fascist Italy's Last War* (Cambridge: Cambridge University Press, 1982); *Common Destiny: Dictatorship, Foreign Policy, and War in Fascist Italy and Nazi Germany* **(Cambridge: Cambridge University Press, 2000)**; *Hitler's Italian Allies: Royal Armed Forces, Fascist Regime, and the War of 1940-1943* **(Cambridge: Cambridge University Press, 2000).**

Landers, D. S., *The Unbound Prometheus* (Cambridge: Cambridge University Press, 1972).

Lazzati, G., *I soliti quattro gatti* (Milan: Mursia, 1965).

Lehmann, E., *Le ali del potere. La propaganda aeronautica nell'Italia fascista* (Turin: UTET, 2010); *La guerra dell'aria. Giulio Douhet, stratega impolitico* (Bologna: Il Mulino, 2013).

Licheri, S., *L'arma aerea italiana nella seconda guerra mondiale: 10 giugno 1940–8 maggio 1945* (Milan: Mursia, 1983).

Mack Smith, D., *Le guerre del duce* (Bari: Laterza, 1976); *Mussolini* (London: Weidenfeld and Nicolson, 1981).

Maiolo, J., *Cry Havoc The Arm Race and the Second World War, 1931–41* (London: John Murray, 2010).

Malizia, N., *Aermacchi, Bagliori di guerra, Flashes of war (Macchi MC200 – MC2 202 – MC2 205/V* (Rome: IB, 2006); *Il 51° Stormo Caccia, storia di un reparto glorioso, 1939–2017* (Rome: IBN, 2017); *La Regia Aeronautica nella 2ª Guerra Mondiale. Dai Diari di Guerra 1940-1942* (Rome: IBN, 2016).

Mantelli, M. C., *et al.*, *Macchi M.C. 200 Macchi M.C. 202 Macchi M.C. 205* (Le-Grau-du-Roi: Edizioni REI France, 2017).

Massimello, G., 'Antonio Vizzotto, pilota e Comandante', *Storia militare*, vol. 190, pp. 13-24 (Parma: Albertelli, 2009); 'CIAK! Per la Regia Aeronautica', *Storia militare*, vol. 128 (Parma: Albertelli, 2004); 'Dal Folgore al Veltro', *Storia militare*, vol. 150, pp. 50-58 (Parma: Albertelli, 2006); 'Il Capitano Pilota Giuseppe Pesola', *Storia militare*, vol. 251, pp. 58-65 (Parma: Albertelli, 2014); 'La caccia italiana nella seconda guerra mondiale', in M. Ferrari, ed., *Le ali del ventennio. L'aviazione italiana dal 1923 al 1945. Bilanci storiografici e prospettive di giudizio*, pp. 183-190 (Milan: Angeli, 2005); 'Macchi C.204: il prototipo che non fu', *Ali Antiche*, vol. 104 (Rome: GAVS, 2009).

Mattesini, F., and Cermelli, M., ed., *Le direttive tecnico-operative di Superaereo* (Rome: SMA, 1991-1992); ed., *Le direttive tecnico-operative di Superaereo*, Vol. 2, Tomo II, Gennaio 1942–Settembre 1943 (Rome: SMA, 2012).

Mattesini, F., *La battaglia di mezzo agosto (operazione 'Pedestal'), il fallimento degli attacchi a massa degli aerosiluranti*, available at *italiani*, www.academia.edu/37658920/LA_BATTAGLIA_DI_MEZZO_AGOSTO_OPERAZIONE_PEDESTAL_IL_FALLIMENTO_DEGLI_ATTACCHI_A_MASSA_DEGLI_AEROSILURANTI_ITALIANI (Accessed on 5 July 2019); *La guerra nel Mediterraneo dopo la rinuncia all'esigenza 'C.3', Luglio-Dicembre 1942. Gli studi e la realizzazione degli sbarchi in Corsica e Tunisia Esigenze 'C.2' e 'C.4' (10-30 ottobre 1942)*, available at www.academia.edu/38307960/LA_GUERRA_NEL_MEDITERRANEO_DOPO_LA_RINUNCIA_ALL_ESIGENZA_C.3_Luglio_Dicembre_1942_Gli_studi_e_la_realizzazione_degli_sbarchi_in_Corsica_e_Tunisia (Accessed on 5 July 2019); *L'ultima offensiva aerea dell'Asse contro Malta e la crisi dei convogli libici (10-30 ottobre 1942)*, available at www.academia.edu/36623345/LULTIMA_OFFENSIVA_AEREA_DELLASSE_CONTRO_MALTA_E_LA_CRISI_DEI_CONVOGLI_LIBICI_10_30_OTTOBRE_1942_FRANCESCO_MATTESINI (Accessed on 5 July 2019).

Mattioli, M., 'L'esordio del Macchi C.202', *Storia militare*, vol. 80, pp. 53-56 (Parma: Albertelli, 2000).

Mattioli, M., and Caruana, R., *53° Stormo* (Oxford: Osprey Publishing, 2010).

Mauri, A., *Un pilota racconta*, available at www.alieuomini.it/AJAX/catalogo/dettaglio2_catalogo/16/ (Accessed on 5 July 2019).

McGregor Peart, A., *From the North Africa to the Arakan, The Engrossing Memoir of a WWII Spitfire Ace* (London: Grub Street, 2008).

Ministero dell'Aeronautica, Direzione Generale delle Costruzioni e degli Approvvigionamenti, Divisione Allestimento, *Collimatore a riflessione 'San Giorgio' tipo 'b' per velivoli da caccia e combattimento* (Rome: Ministero dell'Aeronautica Laboratorio Fotomeccanico, 1939).

Ministero dell'Aeronautica, Ufficio di Stato Maggiore della R. Aeronautica, *Norme provvisorie Per l'addestramento e l'impiego dell'aviazione da caccia* (Rome: Provveditorato Generale dello Stato, Libreria, 1925).

Minniti, F., 'Aspetti organizzativi del controllo sulla produzione bellica in Italia', *Clio*, vol. 6, pp. 305-340 (Rome: Elsinore, 1977); 'La politica industriale del Ministero dell'aeronautica. Mercato, pianificazione, sviluppo, 1935–1943', *Storia contemporanea*, vol. 12, no. 1-2, pp. 5-55 e 271-312 (Bologna: Il Mulino, 1981); 'Profilo dell'iniziativa strategica italiana dalla "non belligeranza" alla "guerra parallela"', *Storia contemporanea*, vol. 18, no. 6, pp. 1113-1195 (Bologna: Il Mulino, 1987); 'Gli obiettivi di guerra nella pianificazione operativa (1938–1940)', in *L'Italia in guerra – il primo anno – 1940* (Rome: Commissione italiana di storia militare, 1991); 'La realtà di un mito', in P. Ferrari, ed., *L'aeronautica italiana. Una storia del Novecento*, pp. 43-67 (Milan: Angeli, 2004); *La rivoluzione verticale, Una storia culturale del volo nel primo Novecento* (Rome: Donzelli, 2018).

Molteni, M., *L'aviazione italiana 1940–1945. Azioni belliche e scelte operative* (Bologna: Odoya, 2012).

Montanari, M., *Le operazioni in Africa Settentrionale, I. Sidi elBarrani (Giugno 1940–Febbraio 1941)* (II ed., Rome: Ufficio Storico SME, 2000); *Le operazioni in Africa Settentrionale, II. Tobruk (Marzo 1941–Gennaio 1942)* (II ed., Rome: Ufficio Storico SME, 1993); *Le operazioni in Africa Settentrionale, III. El Alamein (Gennaio–Novembre 1942)* (II ed., Rome: Ufficio Storico SME, 2006); *Le operazioni in Africa Settentrionale, IV. Enfidaville (Novembre 1942–Maggio 1943)* (Rome: Ufficio Storico SME, 2005); *La Campagna di Grecia, I* (Rome: Ufficio Storico SME, 1980); *L'Esercito italiano alla vigilia della 2ª guerra mondiale* (Rome: Ufficio Storico SME, 1982); *Politica e strategia in cento anni di guerre italiane. 3.1. Il periodo fascista. Le guerre degli anni Trenta* (Rome: Ufficio Storico SME, 2005).

Neulen, H. W., *Il Ricco Bottino, The Rich Booty. Italian Aircraft in Luftwaffe Service* (Milan: GAE, 2000); *In the Skies of Europe, Air forces allied to the Luftwaffe 1939–1945* (Ramsbury, UK: Crowood Press, 2005).
Nijboer, D., *Spitfire V vs C.202 Folgore, Malta 1942* (Oxford: Osprey Publishing, 2014).
Noppen, R. K., *Malta 1940–42. The Axis' air battle for Mediterranean supremacy* (Oxford: Osprey Publishing, 2018).
Overy, R., *The Air War 1939–1945* (Lincoln, Nebraska, USA: Potomac Books, 2004); *Why the Allies won* (London: Pimlico, 2006).
Pacini, G., *Il volo cieco e quello notturno*, available at sites.google.com/site/gianaereo2/continuazione-di-gianaereo/il-volo-cieco (Accessed on 5 July 2019).
Pagani, F., *Ali d'aquila. Duelli aerei nei cieli d'Europa 1936–1943* (Milan: Mursia, 2007).
Palanca, A., *Reparto Alta Velocità, Coppa Schneider e primati mondiali di velocità 1928/1934* (Rome: SMA, 1996).
Paravano, E., *Progettazione e produttività dell'industria aeronautica italiana dalle origini al 1943. Le relazioni della 'Direzione Costruzioni Aeronautiche' dell'Aeronautica Militare*, Tesi di Laurea Magistrale in Scienze Storiche, Dipartimento di Scienze Storiche, Geografiche e dell'Antichità, Università degli Studi di Padova, a. a. 2014/2015.
Paravicini, P. P., *Pilota da caccia* (Milan: Mursia, 2011).
Paxton, R., *The Anatomy of Fascism* (London: Penguin, 2005).
Pedriali, F., *L'Italia nella guerra aerea. Da El Alamein alle spiagge della Sicilia (4 novembre 1942–9 luglio 1943)* (Rome: Aeronautica Militare, Ufficio Storico, 2010); 'Jagdwaffe Sizilien', *Storia militare*, vol. 174, pp. 27-37 (Parma: Albertelli, 2008).
Pegram, R., *Schneider Trophy Seaplanes and Flying Boats, Victors, Vanquished and Visions* (Croydon: Fonthill, 2017).
Pesce, G., *Guerra attraverso l'etere nel teatro mediterraneo* (Modena: STEM Mucchi, 1978); 'La produzione bellica per la Regia Aeronautica', *Rivista Aeronautica*, vol. 3 (Rome: Libreria dello Stato, 1993).
Poddighe, G. C., *Un mito da sfatare: il radar (italiano) nella 2^ gm. Una guerra tecnologica ed un'occasione perduta*, available at www.academia.edu/35904742/Un_mito_da_sfatare_IL_RADAR_italiano_NELLA_2_GM_UNA_GUERRA_TECNOLOGICA_ED_UN_OCCASIONE_PERDUTA (Accessed on 5 July 2019).
Postiglioni, U., and Degl'Innocenti, A., *Colori e schemi mimetici della Regia Aeronautica: 1935–1943*, (Rome: GMT, CMPR-GAVS, 1997).
Pricolo, F., *La Regia Aeronautica nella seconda guerra mondiale, novembre 1939–novembre 1941* (Milan: Longanesi, 1971).
Rainero, R. H., and Biagini, A., ed., *L'Italia in guerra. Il 1° anno – 1940. Cinquant'anni dopo l'entrata dell'Italia nella 2ª guerra mondiale. Aspetti e problemi* (Rome: Commissione Italiana di Storia Militare, 1991).
Rebora, E., 'Mario Castoldi: una vita per la velocità', *Rivista Aeronautica*, vol. 4, pp. 611-664 (Rome: Libreria dello Stato, 1972).
Rocca, G., *I disperati. La tragedia dell'Aeronautica italiana nella Seconda Guerra Mondiale* (Milan: Mondadori, 1991).
Rochat, G., *Italo Balbo, aviatore e Ministro dell'aeronautica, 1926–1933* (Ferrara: Bovolenta, 1979); *Le guerre italiane 1935–1943. Dall'impero d'Etiopia alla disfatta* (Turin: Einaudi, 2005).

Saggiomo, C., *I Cacciatori del Vesuvio* (Naples: Controcorrente, 2007).
Santoni A., and Mattesini F., *La partecipazione tedesca alla guerra aeronavale nel Mediterraneo (1940–1945)* (Parma: Albertelli, 2005).
Santoro, G., *L'Aeronautica Italiana nella Seconda Guerra Mondiale* (Milan-Rome: Esse, 1966).
Segrè, C. G., *Italo Balbo. Una vita fascista* (Bologna: Il Mulino, 1988).
Sgarlato, N., ed., *Folgore Storia e Tecnica* (Parma: Delta, 2017).
Shores, C., Massimello, G., Guest, R., Olynyk, F. J., and Bock, W., *A History of the Mediterranean Air War, 1940–1945, II. North African Desert, February 1942–March 1943* (London: Grub Street, 2012); *A History of the Mediterranean Air War, 1940–1945, III: Tunisia and the End in Africa, November 1942–1943* (London: Grub Street, 2016).
Shores, C., Massimello, G., Guest, R., Olynyk, F. J., and Bock, W., Thomas, A., *A History of the Mediterranean Air War, 1940–1945, IV: Sicily and Italy to the Fall of Rome 14 May, 1943–5 June, 1944* (London: Grub Street, 2018).
Sica, E., 'Giulio Douhet and the Influence of Airpower education in Interwar Italy' in R. Wakelam, D. Varey and E. Sica, eds., *The Evolution of Air Force Education 1914–1995*, available at www.academia.edu/35605875/Giulio_Douhet_And_The_Influence_Of_Airpower_Education_In_Interwar_Italy_in_The_Evolution_of_Air_Force_Education_1914-1995_edited_by_Randall_Wakelam_David_Varey_and_Emanuele_Sica_Wilfrid_Laurier_University_Press_accepted_for_publication_Fall_2018_ (Accessed on 5 July 2019)
Simoncelli, M., 'L'industria militare italiana nella seconda guerra mondiale: lineamenti storici', *Sistema Informativo a Schede*, no. 1-2, pp. 1-10 (Rome: Archivio Disarmo, 1996).
Società Ernesto Breda, *Istruzioni e norme per il montaggio, la regolazione, l'impiego e la manutenzione del velivolo da caccia AER. MACCHI C. 202 con motore R.A. 1000 R.C. 41 I, I Serie BREDA, II Serie MACCHI, III Serie MACCHI* (Rome: Ministero dell'Aeronautica, Direzione Generale delle Costruzioni e degli Approvvigionamenti, 1942).
Stocchetti, R., *Aer. Macchi C.202 Folgore, immagini, scheda e storia*, available at www.alieuomini.it/AJAX/catalogo/dettaglio2_catalogo/16/ (Accessed on 5 July 2019).
Sullivan, B. R., 'Downfall of the Regia Aeronautica, 1933–1943', in R. Higham and S. J. Harris, ed., *Why Air Forces Fail: The Anatomy of Defeat*, pp. 135-176 (Lexington: University of Kentucky Press, 2006).
The Luftwaffe, 1933–45, *Jagdlehrer Überprüfungsgruppe*, available at www.ww2.dk/air/jagd/jagdlehrer.html (Accessed on 5 July 2019).
Volta, F., ed., 'Dimensione cielo: aerei italiani nella Seconda Guerra Mondiale', *Caccia Assalto*, vol. II (Rome: Bizzarri, 1973).
Ward, J., *Hitler's Stuka Squadrons: The JU 87 at War 1936–1945* (Eastbourne: Gardners Books, 2004).
Williams, A. G., 'Cannon or Machine Gun?', *Aeroplane Monthly*, vol. 377, (Stamford: Key Publishing, 2004).